Home Cooking

Over 100 Recipes
for Classic Comfort Food

ALAN ROSEN & BETH ALLEN

PHOTOGRAPHY BY MARK FERRI

The Taunton Press

The Taunton Press
Inspiration for hands-on living®

THE TAUNTON PRESS, INC.,
63 South Main Street, PO Box 5506,
Newtown, CT 06470-5506
e-mail: tp@taunton.com

Editor: Pam Hoenig
Copy editor: Nina Rynd Whitnah
Indexer: Heidi Blough
Jacket and Interior design: Carol Singer
Layout: Carol Singer
Photo editor: Erin Giunta
Cover and Interior photographer: Mark Ferri
Food stylist: A.J. Battifarano
Prop stylist: Francine Matalon-Degni

LIBRARY OF CONGRESS CATALOGING-IN-PUBLICATION DATA
Rosen, Alan, 1969-
  Junior's home cooking : over 100 recipes for classic comfort food / Alan Rosen & Beth Allen.
      pages cm
  Includes index.
  ISBN 978-1-60085-903-8
1. Comfort food. I. Allen, Beth (Elva Elizabeth) II. Title.
TX740.R5926 2013
641.3--dc23
                          2013026921

PRINTED IN THE UNITED STATES OF AMERICA
10 9 8 7 6 5 4 3 2 1

About the recipes in this book: The recipes in this book have been adapted in the Junior's style, in small quantities for preparation in the home kitchen using ingredients available in the retail market and/or online. Many of these desserts are baked regularly at Junior's and are available in Junior's restaurants, by mail order, and/or on the Internet at www. juniorscheesecake.com. Others have been created in the Junior's style especially for this book.

The following names/manufacturers appearing in Junior's Home Cooking are trademarks: Argo®, Better Than Bouillon®, Bob's Red Mill®, Cheez Whiz®, Eagle Brand®, Gold Medal Wondra®, Grand Marnier®, Hellmann's® Real Mayonnaise, Hershey's® Special Dark Chocolate, King Arthur®, Kitchen Bouquet®, Marshmallow fluff®, NABISCO® FAMOUS® Chocolate Wafers, NABISCO® Nilla® Wafers, Old Bay®, OREO®, PHILADELPHIA®, Quaker®, Skippy®, Splenda®, Tabasco®

Props: plates/platters (cover, butternut squash soup, cobb salad, baby back ribs, cheesecake), ceramic skillet (corned beef hash), cakestand (cheesecake), condiment bowl (mini pigs in the blanket, sliders, lobster roll), mug (pull aparts), glasses (Reuben, lobster roll, Jr's club, fruit summer salad, cheesecake), linens (crabcakes, cheesecake, roasted vegetables, blueberry cheesecake muffins), from Fishs Eddy, www.fishseddy.com, 889 Broadway, NYC 10003, 212-420-9020; Dogbone White Formica® Laminate (Texas bowl of red, doughnuts), Multifleck Formica® Laminate (little fellas, pumpkin cheesecake), Tangle Smoke Formica® Laminate (cheesesteak, pickled salads) from Formica Corporation, www.formica.com, 1-800-FORMICA

Acknowledgments

My special, delicious thanks to…

All my friends and family at Junior's—For being my home away from home over the years…for welcoming me into their kitchens and their restaurants . . . for serving *The Best* comfort food every day prepared just the way I like it . . . and for this chance to be the co-author of yet another cookbook for Junior's. This book is our fourth! Three, including this one, I have co-authored with Alan Rosen (the grandson of the Junior's founder, Harry Rosen), and the first one, *Welcome to Junior's!*, written with his father, Walter, and his uncle, Marvin. Indeed, it has been a delectable and wonderful journey!

Alan Rosen—To know Alan Rosen is to know Junior's. As the third-generation owner of Junior's and my co-author, Alan strives every day to be *The Best* in everything he does—*and that's what Junior's is to me.* Alan, and everyone around him, works toward keeping the Rosen traditions alive—by cooking and serving "all you want as you want it," often from recipes handed down over generations. Alan and Junior's stand for top quality . . . that is, every dinner served at their restaurants, every cheesecake shipped, every chicken fried or pie baked from a recipe in this book is simply *The Best* you have ever tasted.

For this fourth book, on great home cooking, Alan always found time (over a plate of their fantastic cheese blintzes!) to share more of the Junior's story with me, this time focusing on cooking for friends and family. How he grills a whole side of salmon fillet at his backyard barbecues…why Junior's Macaroni & Cheese is the creamiest ever… how every sandwich stacked, every soup pot simmered, every hamburger grilled, and every cheesecake baked always comes out *to perfection. That's the Alan Rosen Way . . . and that's The Junior's Way.*

The Rosen Family—Priceless family traditions and memories of Grandpa Harry have been shared with me during interviews with the Rosens over the years: Alan, his father, Walter, and his brother Kevin. Many of Grandpa's recipes are still served at Junior's today!

The many other professionals in the Junior's restaurant family, who have always been willing to help: skilled bakers, cake decorators, chefs, sous chefs, cooks, waiters, waitresses, counter servers, office staff, and on and on—without them, this fourth book would never have happened.

The Team at Junior's Flagship Restaurant in Brooklyn—general manager Allen Fleming, who showed me exactly how each salad is created, plated, and served; executive chef Adam Marks, who invited me into the kitchens many times to view first-hand the Junior's way of broiling a steak, frying crab cakes, or grilling a Reuben; restaurant manager Hastings Stainrod and waiter Eugene French (always smiling); Luis Mendez (expert bobka baker!); plus the outstanding office staff—manager Colette Swanston-Harris (fast fact-finder extraordinaire); Sharon Harris (greeter and expeditor); and financiers Richard Bradley and Louis Incatasciato.

The Team at Junior's on Broadway—general manager Miles Ellis and chef Darian Vito, invaluable sources of how Junior's makes everything, especially those Baked Individual Meat Loaves with Mushroom Gravy and delicious Bar-B-Q Baby Back Ribs (both in this book).

Bakery manager Jason Schwartz, who was quick to respond to my queries about a baking recipe or resolve a baking issue . . . and Amanda Fortier, research and development manager, who shared first-hand how Junior's mixes, bakes, stacks, and torches 360 Crème Brûlée Cheesecakes at a time.

And in my consumer test kitchen—Chef Donna Boland, who tested my family-sized recipes of Junior's specialties alongside me, often mixing, making, and baking them several times to get them perfect; plus my husband, John Allen, around to offer support and taste every recipe.

Nancy Weinberger, marketing whiz, who continues to help expand Junior's into more locations, QVC, mail order, Internet, and wholesale channels.

Pam Hoenig, my exceptional food editor, who once again on this fourth Junior's cookbook has been as close as my computer keys, perfecting every tip, technique, and recipe . . . checking and triple-checking every word . . . helping us choose the Junior's specialties for the book, both on or off the menu, then editing every recipe to ensure success time after time.

Carolyn Mandarano, senior managing editor at The Taunton Press, who helped me visualize and create *Junior's Home Cooking,* for you to read, cook from, and enjoy serving your family and friends. She was always there, along with the extraordinary creative staff at Taunton, planning, managing, supporting, and advising the creation of this book—from its original concept all the way to every beautiful page.

The Photography Team—The delicious photographs scattered among these pages required an exceptional team highly skilled in photographing food, from appetizers to desserts: photographer Mark Ferri, and his assistant James Slater, food stylist A.J. Battifarano, and her assistant Maryann Pomeranz, and prop stylist Francine Matalon-Degni.

And most of all, my heart-filled thanks to you, the readers—those who already love Junior's…who bake or buy Junior's famous cheesecakes for your family and friends . . . frequently dine at one of Junior's restaurants . . . as well as those just discovering Junior's for the very first time. Each of you makes the countless hours spent cooking alongside the Junior's chefs and cooks, interviewing the staff to scribe every fabulous technique, then creating, testing, and tasting each recipe well worth every delicious, delectable bite!

— Beth Allen

Contents

Introduction

Ever since Harry Rosen opened Junior's in 1950, this legendary Brooklyn restaurant has been known as *the place* to go for delicious comfort food cooked to perfection and served by a friendly welcoming staff—a home away from home for many—for three generations. Here, owner Alan Rosen shares this Brooklyn family's traditions, which now reach around the world.

Entertaining, the Junior's Way...

At Junior's, we serve only *The Best* . . . we serve all you want, as you want it . . . and whenever you want it. We want everyone to have a good time, whatever time of day you come. That's the way it was when my grandpa first opened the doors at Junior's on Election Day in 1950. That's the way it always has been, and still is today. We haven't changed. It's what keeps our customers coming back again and again.

We call it *The Junior's Way*. Walk into a Junior's—whether it's our flagship store in Brooklyn or any of our other Junior's restaurants—and you'll feel right at home, even if you've never been here before. "Welcome to Junior's," a well-dressed greeter will say, and you'll immediately be glad you came! You're handed a menu—it's seven pages long; there's something for everyone. It's classic comfort food—with so many of your favorites, it's hard to choose! Maybe fried chicken with a side of French fries? Crab cakes? Roast turkey with stuffing? Cobb salad? Or a bowl of steaming homemade soup and a half a sandwich? You decide!

Your meal comes as you would expect: well prepared, delicious, and plenty to share with your family and friends. Toward the end of your meal, your waiter reminds you to "Save room for dessert!" You take his advice, for you can't leave without having a slice of our famous cheesecake. One bite, and you're convinced: this is the creamiest, lightest yet richest cheesecake you've ever tasted—cheesecake made the real New York way. And that's *The Junior's Way*.

Supper at the Rosens...

When I entertain my friends and family, I entertain *The Junior's Way:*
- Serve well-prepared comfort foods that everyone knows and loves.

• Buy and cook an abundance of down-home foods, so folks have all they want, as they want it.
• Keep it casual, like inviting friends over for a Sunday backyard barbecue.
• Serve a variety of foods, so there's something for everybody (my favorite entertaining menu is salmon and steaks—not just one, but both, hot off the grill and still sizzling!—plus a simple tossed salad and Junior's Original New York Cheesecake for dessert).
• Buy the best ingredients I can find.
• Often serve buffet style, so folks can choose what they want, *when* they want it.
• Cook more food than we can eat, so guests end up taking food home—they leave happy!

I want my home to be the go-to place—for my kids, my kids' friends, the parents of my kids' friends, my friends. I like when they come to enjoy a great meal and have a good time. My wife is the great planner and handles the do-ahead prep, making everything come together at the same time. I take care of the main dish, such as grilling the steaks. This makes me feel like a hero—I love that!

A Go-to Plan…

To enjoy entertaining for 4 or even 24, and to feel comfortable doing it, you need a Go-to Plan of the right recipes:

• five favorite dishes—ones you are most proud of
• simple-to-make foods—simple is often *The Best*
• recipes that take little last-minute fuss and a minimum of do-ahead prep. And time it right! Have the ham out of the oven before guests arrive.
• foods that are easy to serve together: some served cold, others room temperature, a couple right out of the oven and still bubbling or hot off the grill
• dishes that you've made many, many times and that always come out the same way; when entertaining, you want to take out the guesswork, and put in the confidence and success
• foods that look great and taste great

In addition, it's good to:

• Cook foods in dishes that can go straight to the table whenever possible, so foods stay hotter longer.
• If you want to try something new, make it once or twice for your family first—and have a fallback recipe at the ready, in case something goes wrong.
• If serving a buffet, pick foods that have "staying power"—ones that can stand on the buffet at their best for at least half an hour, preferably longer, and are easy to replenish from the kitchen.

On the Menu…

Here's how *Junior's Home Cooking* came to be. Folks are always asking me how I grill salmon and lobster tails so they are juicy on the inside and crispy on the edges…what I put on my steaks to make them *The Best*…how I make Vidalia onions so rich, deep brown, and bursting with flavor. And at Junior's, everyone wants to know how we fry our potato pancakes so crispy…grill our Reubens so they are hot and perfectly melted…prepare our baby back ribs so they are lip-smacking yummy and moist with every bite. We even make macaroni and cheese extra-special at Junior's. It's so good, cheesy, and creamy, there won't be one piece of macaroni left. Like many of Junior's favorites, we've been making this dish the same way since the 1950s; it hasn't changed.

Folks want to know how to make and serve the same comfort foods *The Junior's Way*—and how to make their creations taste down-home delicious every time. So, we've brought together many of our signature recipes at Junior's: Caesar Salad, Cheese Blintzes, Club sandwich, BAR-B-Q Baby Back Ribs, and Our Famous Original New York Cheesecake. Plus we've developed others not on the menu, but created in *The Junior's Way*. They are simply *The Best!* It's our hope you'll find many that become your go-to recipes—bringing Junior's, and the foods we're known and loved for, into your home.

—*Alan Rosen*
Owner, Junior's,
Third Generation

Appetizers

As you might expect, Junior's appetizers come oversized, often overstuffed, and always over-delicious. Here, we've taken some of their signature favorites and turned them into great party foods. Junior's BAR-B-Q Sliders are a down-sized version of their famous pulled pork sandwiches, perfect for parties—or have two and call it dinner! Junior's Chopped Chicken Liver makes a perfect appetizer spread when served on slices of party rye and topped with cucumber for a bit of crunch. Their Buffalo shrimp come to the table hot and crispy, with two dipping sauces—one spiced up with Tabasco®, the other cool and creamy with the addition of blue cheese. They are guaranteed to disappear fast. Want to really impress your friends? Bring out a platter of Smoked Salmon Canapés, delicious mouthfuls of smoked salmon, flavored crème fraîche, cucumber, and a sprig of dill on top. Happy entertaining!

These deviled eggs, while not served at Junior's, have the same special touch as all their recipes—they look and taste The Best. First, boil the eggs gently, not vigorously, and watch the cooking time closely, so the yolks come out bright yellow instead of a light greenish color. Turn the eggs a few times during boiling so the yolks will be centered. Add fresh lemon juice, a little Dijon mustard, and some onion to spark up the deviled yolk mixture, and you're on your way to creating a tasty appetizer. Choose your favorite combination: black caviar, minced crisp bacon, smoked salmon topped with salmon caviar, or spicy jalapeño. If you're giving a party or going to one, make all four!

deviled eggs

MAKES 16 DEVILED EGG HALVES

8 extra-large eggs

¼ cup Hellmann's® Real Mayonnaise (don't use light or nonfat)

2 tablespoons minced white onion

2 teaspoons fresh lemon juice

1 teaspoon Dijon mustard

¼ teaspoon Tabasco, or to taste

Kosher salt and ground white pepper, to taste

GARNISHES (use the one you wish)

Red salmon roe caviar (less expensive), American black paddlefish caviar (moderately priced), or imported black Sturgeon caviar (expensive)

Paprika

1. Place the eggs in a single layer in a large saucepan and cover with 2 inches of water. Bring to a boil over medium heat and boil gently for 2 minutes, turning the eggs a couple of times during cooking to center the yolk. Cover, remove from the heat, and let the eggs sit in the pan for 15 minutes. Using a slotted spoon, transfer the eggs to a bowl of ice water and let set until cool enough to handle. Peel and cut the eggs into halves lengthwise. Scoop out the yolks into a bowl and refrigerate the whites.

2. To the yolks, add the mayonnaise, onion, lemon juice, mustard, and Tabasco. Mash with a fork until smooth. Season with salt and pepper to taste and add a drop or two more of Tabasco, if you like.

3. Pipe the yolk mixture into the whites or fill them using a small spoon, mounding each in the center. Garnish with red or black caviar or sprinkle with paprika. Refrigerate, tightly covered, until ready to serve. These are best when served the day they are made. Do not freeze.

continued

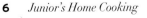

HICKORY-SMOKED BACON DEVILED EGGS

Fry ¾ pound thick-sliced hickory-smoked bacon in a medium skillet over medium heat until crisp. Drain on paper towels and mince into small bits. Add ½ cup of the minced bacon to the deviled yolk mixture. Garnish the finished deviled eggs with the remaining bacon bits instead of the caviar or paprika.

SMOKED SALMON DEVILED EGGS

Add ¼ cup minced smoked salmon to the deviled yolk mixture. Garnish with red salmon caviar (roe) instead of black caviar or paprika.

HOT & SPICY DEVILED EGGS

Add 3 tablespoons seeded and minced fresh jalapeño peppers and ¼ teaspoon ground cumin to the deviled yolk mixture. Taste, then add a little more Tabasco, if you like. Do not garnish with caviar, but sprinkle with plenty of paprika.

The Junior's Way

Piping the yolk mixture into the whites, instead of simply scooping it, is well worth the effort, especially if you're serving guests or taking the eggs to a party. Be sure to mince all of the ingredients well. Use a large open-star pastry tip so the yolk mixture flows through the tip easily and evenly.

Junior's is known for "wow-ing" its customers—and these canapés are guaranteed to impress! We've also included a variation for a smoked salmon party platter that Alan often prepares when he and his wife entertain.

smoked salmon canapés

MAKES ABOUT 32 CANAPÉS; RECIPE MAY BE DOUBLED

FOR THE SPREAD

One 8-ounce container crème fraîche (substitute full-fat sour cream if crème fraîche is unavailable)

1 tablespoon minced red onion

2 teaspoons Dijon mustard

1 teaspoon fresh lemon juice

3/4 teaspoon kosher salt, or to taste

1/8 teaspoon ground white pepper, or to taste

4 to 5 drops Tabasco, or to taste

FOR THE CANAPÉS

1 pound very thinly sliced smoked salmon (about 1/8 inch or thinner)

Eight 4-inch-square slices Danish pumpernickel or rye bread, 1/4 inch thick

1 large seedless cucumber

Kosher salt

Fresh dill sprigs

1. Measure all of the ingredients for the spread into a medium bowl. Mix gently with a rubber spatula until thoroughly combined. Cover with plastic wrap and refrigerate.

2. Cut the salmon into strips 3½ x 1 inch. You will need 32 pieces.

3. Cut the bread slices diagonally from corner to corner, two times, so that each slice yields 4 triangles, for a total of 32 triangles. As you work, cover the bread with a damp paper towel to keep it from drying out.

4. Slice 16 rounds of cucumber, each 1/8 inch thick, then cut each one in half, making 32 semicircles.

5. Assemble the canapés: Working in batches of 8 at a time, spread a heaping teaspoon of the spread on each triangle of bread. Place a semicircle of cucumber on each, on an angle, and sprinkle with a little salt. Fold (but do not crease) a piece of salmon in half and perch on top of the cucumber slice so the ends of the cucumber show. Garnish each with a small sprig of dill. As you work, place the completed canapés on a plate, cover with plastic wrap, and refrigerate while you prepare the rest. Refrigerate until ready to serve. These are best served the day they are made. Do not freeze.

continued

ALAN'S SALMON PLATTER

Arrange 1 pound of very thinly sliced (⅛ inch thick or thinner) smoked salmon (the best you can afford!) along the top and bottom of a serving platter, overlapping the slices as you go. In the center of the platter, mound 1 cup coarsely chopped red onion at one end, ⅓ cup drained capers in the center, and 1 cup diced (½-inch) ripe bright-red tomatoes at the other end. Garnish with 2 large lemons, sliced first into ⅛-inch-thick rounds, then into semicircles, tucking them between the slices of salmon. Add a few sprigs of fresh dill if you wish. Make two recipes of the spread (see the recipe on page 9) and spoon into your prettiest small serving bowl. Refrigerate until ready to serve. Serve with pumpernickel or rye party bread, as for the canapés, but this time, cut each slice of bread into 2, not 4, equal triangles. Makes about 12 light-brunch or light-lunch servings.

The Junior's Way

Buy the best smoked salmon (the kind commonly referred to as "lox") with the prettiest pinkish-red color you can find and afford—and buy it the day you plan to serve it: Norwegian smoked salmon is considered to be one of the best; others to look for are Atlantic salmon and those from the north Pacific, such as Chinook and Coho.

Although you will not find stuffed clams at Junior's, we wanted to give you this recipe that's made "their way"—with the very best ingredients. Start with cherrystone clams, which are large enough to hold plenty of the tasty stuffing. These are great for entertaining, as you can cook and stuff them a couple of hours ahead, then refrigerate until ready to bake and serve.

baked stuffed clams

MAKES 16 STUFFED CLAMS

2 dozen cherrystone clams

4 ounces thick-sliced hickory-smoked bacon, diced

⅓ cup minced red onion

⅓ cup diced (¼-inch) red bell pepper

2 teaspoons minced garlic

1 cup fresh breadcrumbs (see The Junior's Way on page 21) or plain dried breadcrumbs

½ cup minced fresh flat-leaf parsley

2 teaspoons dried oregano

Kosher salt and coarsely ground black pepper, to taste

6 tablespoons (¾ stick) unsalted butter, melted, plus more if needed

2 tablespoons fresh lemon juice

Olive oil, for drizzling

½ cup freshly grated Parmesan cheese, or to taste

Paprika

1. Clean and steam the clams just until they open (see The Junior's Way on page 12).

2. Remove the clams from their shells, discarding the clam foot. Break apart the clamshells. Choose 16 of the cleanest, nicest looking shells and rinse them; toss out the rest. Return one clam to each of the 16 shells. Mince the remaining 8 clams and set aside.

3. Fry the bacon in a large skillet over medium heat until cooked but not crisp. Remove the bacon with a slotted spoon to paper towels to drain. Pour off all but 3 tablespoons of the drippings. Add the onion, bell pepper, and garlic to the skillet and cook, stirring, over medium heat, until soft. Remove the skillet from the heat.

4. Return the bacon to the skillet along with the minced clams. Add the breadcrumbs, parsley, oregano, and salt and pepper to taste. Stir in the butter and lemon juice, adding a little more of each if needed to bring the mixture together. Return the skillet to medium heat and toss until the mixture is hot, 2 to 3 minutes.

continued

5. Spoon some of the stuffing over each of the 16 clams in their shells, mounding and packing the stuffing slightly with your hands. Lightly drizzle the stuffing with olive oil, top with the Parmesan, and sprinkle with paprika. At this point, you can bake the clams or cover with plastic wrap and refrigerate up to a couple of hours until company comes.

6. When you're getting ready to serve the clams, heat the oven to 425°F. Place the clams in a shallow pan and bake them until the stuffing is hot and the cheese is lightly browned, about 10 minutes. Serve immediately. Do not store or freeze.

The Junior's Way

Buy only clams that are closed—not ones that are opened, or ones with shells that are chipped, broken, or damaged. Refrigerate until it's time to clean and steam them.

To clean clams, scrub the shells under cold running water with a wire brush or a firm kitchen scrubbing brush. Fill a bowl halfway with cold water and stir in 1 tablespoon cornmeal (this helps to cleanse the clams of sand). Gently place the clams in the water and add a little more water if needed to cover them completely. Let the clams stand for about 20 minutes, giving them enough time to cleanse themselves of any sand or salt they may have collected. Lift the clams out of the water with your hands, leaving the sand on the bottom of the bowl.

Steam the clams in a large covered pot in 1 inch of boiling salted water until they open, 6 to 10 minutes. Discard any clams that do not open.

It was the 1990s in Brooklyn. Folks who had left our city started returning—and others came. Everybody began stopping into Junior's for all types of food and, of course, only the best was good enough. The food kept getting better, in a distinctive Brooklyn way. These Buffalo shrimp are Junior's take on Buffalo chicken wings, with the hot sauce served on the side as a tangy tomato dipping sauce. And, of course, they come with Junior's version of the traditional cooling blue cheese sauce. Be sure to buy enough shrimp . . . these disappear fast!

brooklyn-style buffalo shrimp

MAKES ABOUT 2½ DOZEN SHRIMP (8 TO 10 APPETIZER SERVINGS)

1½ pounds extra-large shrimp (24 to 30), peeled and deveined with tails left on

FOR THE BATTER
4 extra-large eggs
1½ cups all-purpose flour
1 tablespoon kosher salt
1 tablespoon baking powder
1 teaspoon ground white pepper
1½ cups whole milk

FOR THE BREADING
2 cups all-purpose flour
¼ cup yellow cornmeal
1½ tablespoons Old Bay® seasoning
1 tablespoon paprika
1 teaspoon Cajun seasoning, or to taste
2 teaspoons kosher salt

continued

1. Wash the shrimp and lay them out on paper towels to dry.

2. In a large bowl, whisk together all the batter ingredients and let stand for 15 minutes. Meanwhile, in a shallow baking dish, mix together all the breading ingredients.

3. Place a wire rack on a baking sheet. Working in small batches, dredge the shrimp first in the breading, shaking off any excess. Then coat the shrimp in the batter, one at a time, turning to coat it well. Let any excess batter drip off, then roll the shrimp in the breading again. Set the shrimp on the rack. When they are all coated, refrigerate for about 15 minutes to set the coating.

4. While the shrimp chill, make the Buffalo Sauce (ingredients on page 14): In a medium saucepan, whisk together the ketchup, vinegar, tomato juice, and Tabasco. Slowly whisk in the sugar, salt, and pepper until well blended. Heat over medium heat until hot; set aside and keep warm.

5. Make the Brooklyn Blue Cheese Dressing (see page 14) and chill.

6. Meanwhile, preheat the oven to 200°F (you need a warm oven to keep the fried shrimp hot while you're frying the rest). Fit a large shallow pan with a wire rack.

continued

2 cups ketchup

½ cup cider vinegar

⅓ cup tomato juice

2 teaspoons Tabasco, or as much as you like

⅓ cup sugar

1 teaspoon kosher salt, or to taste

1 teaspoon ground white pepper, or to taste

Canola or other vegetable cooking oil (not olive oil)

1 recipe Brooklyn Blue Cheese Dressing (recipe follows)

1½ cups sour cream

8 ounces blue cheese, such as Maytag Blue, a crumbly Gorgonzola, or a Roquefort (but not one of the creamy Danish blues), crumbled (about 1 cup)

1 tablespoon red-wine vinegar

A few drops of Worcestershire sauce

Kosher salt and ground white pepper, to taste

7. Heat ½ to ¾ inch of oil in a large frying pan (an iron skillet is great if you have one) over medium heat until hot but not smoking (360° to 365°F). Gently slide the shrimp into the hot oil. It's best to cook only 6 to 8 shrimp at a time, depending upon the size of your skillet; the shrimp shouldn't touch each other. Fry until puffy and golden brown, 3 to 4 minutes per side, turning the shrimp over only once. Transfer the shrimp with a slotted spatula or spider to the rack and keep warm in the oven while frying the rest of the shrimp. Add a little more oil if needed, pouring it down the side of the hot skillet to warm it.

8. Serve the shrimp piping hot with the warm Buffalo Sauce and chilled Blue Cheese Dressing in small bowls for dipping. Do not store or freeze these shrimp.

brooklyn blue cheese dressing

This sour cream offsets the heat of the Buffalo dipping sauce.

MAKES 1 PINT (2 CUPS)

Place the sour cream in a medium bowl and gently fold in the blue cheese. Blend in the vinegar, some Worcestershire, and as much salt and pepper as you like. Cover and chill until serving time. Refrigerate any extra dressing, tightly covered, and use within a week.

The Junior's Way

Don't skimp on the breading and don't rush the battering. Take time to roll each shrimp over and over in the breading, then turn each one in the batter to get as thick of a coating as possible. Let any excess batter drip away, then roll in the breading again, coating each shrimp well. Chill the shrimp for about 15 minutes to set the coating so it stays on during frying.

These little pigs are a popular item on Junior's party trays. They are exactly what you would expect: small sausages wrapped in pastry. But in true Junior's style, these are extra special: they are wrapped in delicate puff pastry blankets. These piggies are fast and easy to make, thanks to the frozen puff pastry you can buy in your local market. Before rolling them, we smear the pastry with a little Dijon. And the best part? They can be made ahead, placed in the freezer, then baked right before guests arrive.

mini pigs in the blanket

MAKES 30 PIGS; RECIPE CAN BE DOUBLED

½ cup (1 stick) unsalted butter, melted, plus more softened butter for the pan

1 sheet frozen puff pastry dough from a 14- to 16-ounce package (see The Junior's Way on page 17)

20 small cocktail sausages or ten 6-inch-long thin hot dogs

½ cup Dijon mustard

1. Butter two baking sheets with the softened butter. Set out the puff pastry sheet to thaw, according to the package instructions.

2. While the pastry thaws, heat 3 tablespoons of the melted butter in a non-stick grill pan or skillet over medium-high heat (do not let it brown or burn). Grill the cocktail sausages or hot dogs in the hot butter until golden brown, turning frequently. Remove to a cutting board until cool enough to handle. If using hot dogs, cut them into 2-inch-long pieces.

3. When the pastry has thawed enough so you can unfold it without tearing, lay out the sheet on a piece of aluminum foil or a lightly floured work surface. Cover with a sheet of plastic wrap to prevent the dough from sticking to the rolling pin. Roll out into a 15 x 12-inch rectangle, trimming off any rough edges. Using a pastry brush or your fingers, spread the mustard over the pastry and out to the edges. Cut crosswise into four equal strips 15 x 3 inches, then cut each strip into five 3-inch squares. You will have 20 pastry squares.

continued

4. To shape these little piggies, lay a sausage diagonally across the center of each mustard-coated pastry square, near one corner. Roll the sausage up in the square toward the opposite corner and seal (see The Junior's Way). The little sausage will peek out at both ends. Place on the prepared baking sheets, seam side up. (At this point, you can either bake the piggies or freeze them. When ready to bake, pick up with step 5—there's no need to defrost them.)

5. Preheat the oven to 400°F. Warm the remaining 5 tablespoons butter over low heat. Brush the pastry-wrapped pigs with the butter, then bake until they are puffed and golden and have light golden brown edges, about 9 minutes. Serve hot, right out of the oven.

The Junior's Way

Here are two tips from the pastry chefs at Junior's:

- Frozen puff pastry dough comes in sheets, one or two per package. Some are made with pure butter and others with vegetable shortening. We prefer the flavor of the all-butter ones, but both work well in this recipe. You choose!
- After rolling each pastry square diagonally around a sausage, stretch it a little if necessary to make a 1/2-inch overlap on top. Secure the pointed end with a dab of water, pressing it to the center of the pastry blanket to seal securely. Place each piggy on the baking sheet, pointed tip up.

"When my grandpa opened Junior's in the 1950s, chopped chicken liver was on the dinner menu under the Appetizer choices. It's still made the same way today," explains Alan. *"We use it to make our popular chopped chicken liver sandwiches, too, on our famous club rye bread."*

junior's chopped chicken liver

MAKES 2 CUPS CHOPPED LIVER (6 TO 8 APPETIZER SERVINGS)

2 extra-large eggs

2 extra-large white onions

¼ cup (½ stick) unsalted butter

1 pound fresh chicken livers, cleaned (see The Junior's Way)

1 to 2 teaspoons kosher salt, or to taste

½ teaspoon coarsely ground black pepper, or to taste

1 teaspoon minced garlic

Olive oil, for drizzling on livers

1 large cucumber, cut into ¼-inch-thick rounds

Slices of party rye bread

1. Place the eggs in a small saucepan and cover with 2 inches of water. Bring to a boil over medium heat and boil gently for 2 minutes, turning the eggs a couple of times during cooking to center the yolks. Cover, remove from the heat, and let the eggs sit in the pan for 15 minutes. Using a slotted spoon, transfer the eggs to a bowl of ice water and let set until cool enough to handle. Peel the eggs, breaking them up into fine pieces with your hands as they do at Junior's, and refrigerate.

2. Meanwhile, cut the onions crosswise into ⅛-inch-thick rounds. Melt the butter in a large skillet over medium heat. Add the onions and cook, stirring frequently, until golden brown, about 15 minutes (important!). Transfer to a plate to cool.

3. Meanwhile, heat the oven to 425°F. Arrange the cleaned livers in a single layer on a rimmed baking sheet, sprinkle with 1 teaspoon of the salt, the pepper, and garlic and drizzle with a little oil. Roast until browned, 10 to 15 minutes, turning the livers once. Transfer to a plate to cool.

4. Pulse the chicken livers in a food processor with the onions a few times until the liquid from the onions pulls the mixture together. The mixture should be a spread with some visible chunks—not a smooth paste. Transfer to a bowl, add the eggs, and mix gently. (At Junior's, they slip on food-service gloves and mix it with their hands.) Taste and add more salt and pepper if you like. Refrigerate for at least an hour to chill before serving.

5. Spoon the chopped liver into a serving bowl in the center of a serving platter. Surround with alternating cucumber slices and slices of rye bread. Serve immediately or keep chilled until serving time. Refrigerate any leftovers, tightly covered, and serve the next day. Do not freeze.

JUNIOR'S CHOPPED LIVER SANDWICH

Take 2 slices of rye bread and spread one side of both slices with a little mayonnaise or softened butter. Top one slice mayonnaise side up with a thick layer of chopped liver, top with a crisp lettuce leaf, and cover with the second slice, mayonnaise or butter side down. Cut in half and serve immediately with dill pickle spears.

The Junior's Way

Buy the best chicken livers you can find, then check for and discard any visible fat, green parts, or membranes before roasting (very important)!

These mini meatballs are a great appetizer to pass around to your guests. They also stand up well on a counter for friends to help themselves.

mini meatballs

MAKES ABOUT 3 DOZEN 1-INCH (MINI) MEATBALLS

FOR THE MEATBALLS
Unsalted butter, softened

Canola or other vegetable oil

1/2 cup finely chopped white onion

1 teaspoon minced garlic

1/2 cup fresh soft or plain dried breadcrumbs (see The Junior's Way)

3 tablespoons whole milk

1/2 pound ground beef chuck (80% to 82% lean)

1/2 pound ground pork

1 1/2 teaspoons kosher salt

1/2 teaspoon freshly ground black pepper

3/4 teaspoon ground cardamom, or to taste

3/4 teaspoon ground nutmeg, or to taste

1 extra-large egg yolk, slightly beaten with a fork

1/3 cup minced fresh curly-leaf parsley, plus extra for garnish

FOR THE SAUCE
1/2 cup bottled chili sauce

1/2 cup grape jelly

1 1/2 teaspoons fresh lemon juice

1/4 teaspoon kosher salt, or to taste

1/4 teaspoon coarse ground black pepper, or to taste

1. Heat 1 tablespoon each of the butter and oil in a large skillet over medium heat. Add the onion and garlic and cook, stirring, until the onion is soft (but not browned!), 7 to 8 minutes.

2. Meanwhile, mix the breadcrumbs with the milk and set aside to soften.

3. In a large bowl, mix the beef, pork, salt, pepper, cardamom, nutmeg, egg yolk, and parsley. Add the sautéed onion and soaked breadcrumb mixture. Toss thoroughly with your hands and shape into 1 1/4-inch balls; you will have about 36.

4. Add 2 tablespoons each of butter and oil to the skillet used for cooking the onion and return to medium heat. Brown the meatballs in batches (do not overcrowd them) until light golden brown on all sides, turning them continuously and adding a little more butter and oil if needed. (This will take 3 to 4 minutes, depending upon how many meatballs you are frying at a time.) Do not overcook them or the meatballs can become dry (remember, they continue to cook another minute or two after you remove them from the skillet). Transfer to paper towels to drain while you cook the remaining batches. Wipe out the skillet.

5. Combine all of the sauce ingredients in the skillet and stir over low heat until the jelly melts and the sauce is hot. Add the meatballs and stir for about 2 minutes to be sure they are heated through.

6. Transfer the meatballs to a serving plate using a slotted spoon and pour the sauce into a small dipping dish. Garnish with some chopped parsley and set out some decorative toothpicks. These meatballs can be prepared the morning you plan to serve them; refrigerate, tightly covered, and reheat in the sauce right before serving. Refrigerate any leftovers, tightly covered, and serve the next day. Do not freeze.

The Junior's Way

- To make fresh breadcrumbs, cut the crusts off white bread, tear into pieces, and pulse several times in a food processor to make coarse crumbs. Watch carefully to be sure the crumbs do not become too fine or dusty. You will need 1 thick slice (or 2 thin slices) of bread to make $1/2$ cup of crumbs. Be sure the bread is at least one day old and at room temperature so the bread processes into crumbs easily and doesn't clump together.
- When frying, it's best to use softened room-temperature butter, not cold butter that's directly from the refrigerator, because if you need to add more butter while cooking, the skillet will come back to temperature faster.

The regulars at Junior's know their sandwiches will arrive overstuffed, mile-high, and the best they've every tasted, especially the pulled pork sandwiches. And no wonder. This favorite begins with the long, slow roasting of a pork shoulder roast, also known as a pork butt, that's been rubbed with a brown-sugar mix spiced up with cumin, coriander, and cinnamon. Don't rush this step, as it's what makes the pulled pork juicy and tender. Top with a generous helping of Junior's chipotle sauce . . . make it as hot as you dare. Scoop a generous helping onto appetizer-sized slider buns or supper-sized hamburger buns. And get ready to sink your teeth into one of the best barbecue sandwiches ever!

junior's bar-b-q sliders

**MAKES 3 QUARTS PULLED PORK AND 1 QUART SAUCE
(ENOUGH FOR ABOUT 24 SLIDERS OR 8 MEAL-SIZED SANDWICHES)**

FOR THE BAR-B-Q PORK RUB

1 cup firmly packed dark brown sugar

1 tablespoon kosher salt

1 tablespoon coarsely ground black pepper

2 teaspoons ground cumin

1 teaspoon onion powder

1 teaspoon ground coriander

1 teaspoon ground cinnamon

FOR THE PULLED PORK

1 pork butt (shoulder roast), about 7 pounds, tied

2 to 3 tablespoons vegetable oil

continued

1. Heat the oven to 350°F. Mix all the ingredients for the rub together and generously massage all over the pork. Transfer to a large roasting pan. Add enough water to the pan to come two-thirds of the way up the sides of the roast. Cover the pan tightly or, if your pan doesn't have a cover, use a large piece of foil, pinching it tightly all around the edges. Roast until the meat is fork-tender—and we mean fork-tender! That is, you should be able to insert a dinner fork in the meat and easily rotate it around. This usually takes about 4 hours; be sure to check occasionally and add more water if needed to keep the liquid at least halfway up the sides of the roast.

2. Meanwhile, prepare the Junior's BAR-B-Q Sauce recipe (see page 24) in a large saucepan. Stir in the rest of the ingredients to make the Chipotle BAR-B-Q Sauce.

3. Heat the broiler. When the pork has cooled enough so you can handle it, use two forks to break it apart into coarse shreds. Transfer the shredded meat to a

continued

1 recipe Junior's BAR-B-Q Sauce
(recipe follows), prepared using
1½ tablespoons ground cumin

1 to 2 tablespoons puréed chipotle
peppers in adobo sauce, to taste

¼ cup fresh lime juice

½ teaspoon ground coriander

¼ cup minced fresh cilantro,
or to taste

FOR SERVING

Slider or meal-sized hamburger
buns, opened and lightly toasted

Creamy Coleslaw (optional;
recipe follows)

large bowl and toss several times with a generous amount of the chipotle sauce.
Spread the pulled pork out in a broiler-proof pan and broil about 6 inches
from the heat until the meat glistens and the sauce caramelizes and browns
around the edges. This will take just a few minutes; watch closely.

4. Serve the pulled pork on toasted slider buns as appetizers or toasted meal-
sized hamburger buns. If serving for dinner, scoop some coleslaw into the
sandwich, if desired. This pulled pork freezes great, since it already has been
tossed with some of the sauce. Extra sauce can also be frozen for up to 2 weeks
in a freezeproof container; leave about an inch at the top, as liquids expand as
they freeze.

junior's bar-b-q sauce

*This is one of those old-fashioned barbecue sauces with the zing of vinegar,
the sweetness of brown sugar, and plenty of spice—but not too much. The
heat comes from chili powder and Tabasco, so decrease or increase them as
you like. Try this sauce when you're grilling burgers—you'll be glad you did!
If you have any sauce left over, cover tightly, refrigerate, and use within a
week, or freeze for up to 4 weeks.*

1½ cups distilled white vinegar

1½ cups firmly packed dark
brown sugar

1 cup ketchup

½ cup bottled chili sauce

2 tablespoons chili powder

2 tablespoons Worcestershire
sauce

1 tablespoon onion powder

1 tablespoon ground cumin

4 to 6 large cloves garlic, minced

Kosher salt, to taste

Tabasco, to taste

MAKES 1 QUART OF SAUCE; RECIPE CAN BE DOUBLED

1. Combine all the ingredients except the Tabasco in a large saucepan. Bring to
a simmer over high heat.

2. Reduce the heat to maintain just a simmer and cook, uncovered, until the
flavors have blended, about 30 minutes. Stir occasionally to prevent sticking.
Season to your taste with Tabasco. Let cool completely before storing in the
refrigerator or freezer.

creamy coleslaw

For their dinner-sized pulled pork sandwiches, Junior's tops the pork with a scoop of this coleslaw.

MAKES 1½ QUARTS

6 cups shredded green cabbage

1 cup shredded carrots

1 cup Hellmann's Real Mayonnaise (don't use light or nonfat)

2 tablespoons cider vinegar

1 tablespoon sugar

1 large clove garlic, minced,

½ teaspoon kosher salt

½ teaspoon freshly ground black pepper

In a large bowl, combine the cabbage and carrots. In a small bowl, blend together the remaining ingredients. Toss with the cabbage mixture until coated and refrigerate, tightly covered, long enough for the slaw to thoroughly chill and the flavors to blend throughout, at least 2 hours or overnight.

The Junior's Way

The secret to these sliders happens under the broiler, right before serving. The direct heat caramelizes the sugar in the sauce that's on the slices of meat, making them glisten.

Signature Salads

Sit down at a table at Junior's around lunchtime or later, and their signature Roumanian coleslaw welcomes you, along with a bowl of pickled beets and yet another of pickled cucumbers. The regulars know these items will never appear on their bill . . . it's Junior's gift to you, just for coming. You'll fast discover that Junior's is known for the freshest salads around. And this collection is *The Best!* Their most popular is the Caesar Salad, which we've dressed up with fresh salmon that has been grilled on a cedar plank. We've included a couple of extra-pretty salads — an "arranged" salad, miniature red and yellow beets with goat cheese, as well as the company-pleasing Fresh Fruit Salad with Poppyseed Dressing. You'll also find salads that make the meal, such as Junior's Cobb Salad, served with their blue cheese dressing, and the lunchtime favorite, Grown-up Tuna Mac. We haven't forgotten the dressings, which you can whisk up for one of these salads or drizzle over one of your own favorites. At Junior's, any time is salad time!

These pickled cucumbers are like no other . . . they stay crisp and slightly crunchy even up to a week in the refrigerator. The secret is the sauce, the same one Junior's has also used to make their Roumanian Health Slaw and Pickled Beets and Onions ever since they opened their doors in the 1950s. These three salads still greet customers as they sit down at Junior's for a meal today. To make this recipe at home, you'll need a piece of cheesecloth.

pickled cucumbers
and onions

MAKES 2 QUARTS (8 CUPS)

FOR THE SAUCE

2 tablespoons pickling spices

3 large cloves garlic, peeled and halved

Cheesecloth

4 cups cider vinegar, divided, plus more after cooking, if you wish

2½ cups sugar

2 cups water

1 teaspoon kosher salt

FOR THE CUCUMBERS AND ONIONS

4 large cucumbers, ends trimmed and peeled (see The Junior's Way on page 30)

2 extra-large white onions

1 tablespoon snipped fresh dill

2 teaspoons kosher salt

1. To make the sauce, place the pickling spices and garlic in the center of a square of cheesecloth and tie into a bag with cotton string. Place in a large saucepan with 3 cups of the vinegar, the sugar, water, and 1 teaspoon of salt. Bring to a full boil over high heat. Boil, uncovered, for 10 minutes, making sure the sugar dissolves completely. Stir in the remaining 1 cup vinegar, remove from the heat, fish out the spice bag, and discard. Taste the sauce and add a little more vinegar if you wish.

2. While the sauce boils, cut the prepped cucumbers into ¼-inch-thick slices on the diagonal (you need about 8 cups). Use a sharp slicing knife with a smooth edge. Place in a large bowl.

3. Peel the onions and cut vertically in half. Place on a cutting board, flat side down, and slice into ¼-inch-thick half-moons (you need 3 cups). Blanch the onions in boiling water for 1 to 2 minutes, strain, rinse under cold water, and drain. Add to the cucumbers, sprinkle all with the dill and the 2 teaspoons of salt, and toss to coat.

continued

4. Pour the hot sauce over the cucumbers and onions, and let the salad stand for 1 hour at room temperature until wilted. Cover with plastic wrap and refrigerate until thoroughly chilled or overnight. Any leftovers keep well in the refrigerator, tightly covered, for up to 1 week.

ROUMANIAN HEALTH SLAW

Prepare the sauce as directed in Step 1 on page 28 for the cucumbers. Grate 2 to 3 large carrots into shreds about ¼ inch wide, using the medium grating disc of a food processor or the large holes of a box grater; you can also shred them into long strips using a carrot peeler (you need 1 cup). Toss with 1 cup coarsely chopped onion, 1 cup chopped red bell pepper, and 2 teaspoons kosher salt. Remove the core from a large cabbage (3 to 3½ pounds) and shred into strips about ¼ inch wide, using a medium grating disc of a food processor, the large holes of a box grater, or a chef's knife (you need 12 cups). Add to the carrot mixture, pour over the hot sauce, and toss. Let wilt for 1 hour and store as directed for the cucumbers. Makes 2 quarts (8 cups).

PICKLED BEETS AND ONIONS

Prepare the sauce as directed in Step 1 on page 28 for the cucumbers. Buy 6 pounds of beets with tops (you may use regular beets like Junior's or red and yellow miniatures). Trim the beets (you need 6 cups) and cook, with a few leaves, in boiling salted water to cover until tender. Drain, peel under cold running water, and slice ¼ inch thick. Cut and blanch the onions as for the cucumbers. Stir together the beets and onions, cover with the hot sauce, let wilt for 1 hour, and store as directed for the cucumbers. Makes 2 quarts (8 cups).

The Junior's Way

Using a peeler, remove a thin strip of peel from top to bottom of each cucumber. Leave a strip of green, then remove a second strip. Repeat, working around the cucumber until you have a green-and-white striped cucumber.

In Greece, this rustic country salad is typically known as a summer salad, for it showcases vegetables plentiful at markets during that time of year. But in America, it's a year-round standby in local restaurants and diners across the country. The authentic Greek salad has chunks of fresh tomatoes, cucumbers, and peppers, plus cubed fresh feta and Greek Kalamata olives. Small pickled peppers called peperoncini also often appear. Look for the golden Greek varieties, as they are sweeter than the Italian kinds.

greek salad

MAKES 4 TO 6 SIDE SALADS

1 recipe Mediterranean Dressing (page 47)

6 to 8 large ripe Roma tomatoes or 3 large heirloom tomatoes (yellow, red, purple; 1½ to 2 pounds)

1 extra-large or 2 medium cucumbers

1 large green bell pepper

1 large red bell pepper

1 medium red onion

1 cup pitted whole black Greek olives, preferably Kalamata

8 ounces feta cheese

Pickled peperoncini, for garnish (optional)

1. Make the dressing; set aside.

2. Prepare the vegetables and place in a large salad bowl: Cut the tomatoes into 1-inch chunks. Peel, seed, and cut the cucumbers into 1-inch chunks. Stem and seed both bell peppers and remove the white ribs. Cut into 1-inch triangles. Peel the onion and cut into a 1-inch dice. Add the olives (leave whole; do not cut!) and toss. Refrigerate until ready to serve.

3. Right before serving, whisk the dressing again and drizzle over the chilled salad. Cut the feta into ½-inch cubes (or leave in a large rectangle). Top the salad with the cheese. Garnish the salad bowl with hot peppers, if you wish.

The Junior's Way

Greek feta cheese is traditionally made from 100% sheep's milk. Its main characteristic? Feta goes through a brining or pickling process, giving the cheese its traditional salty, tangy flavor, plus a crumbly texture. Feta is often sold packed inside tightly sealed containers, floating in water or oil. A tip from Junior's chefs: Keep feta stored in the container and liquid you purchased it in. Before using, rinse the cheese under cold running water.

This salad has that true chef's touch. The good news is that roasting the beets can be done the day before. Let them cool, cover with plastic wrap, and refrigerate until it's time to assemble the salads.

roasted miniature beet salad with fresh goat cheese

MAKES 4 SIDE SALADS; MAY BE DOUBLED TO SERVE 8

4 pounds miniature beets (both red and golden yellow preferred), with tops removed but not peeled (14 to 16)

1/2 cup water

3 tablespoons extra-virgin olive oil

Kosher salt and coarsely ground black pepper

1 recipe Junior's Balsamic Dressing (page 51)

1/2 cup large walnut pieces

One 8-ounce log chèvre (fresh goat cheese), chilled, then cut into 4 thick slices

4 to 6 ounces baby arugula or baby spinach (about 4 cups lightly packed), washed and dried

1/2 small red onion, slivered

1. Preheat the oven to 400°F. Spread out the beets in a single layer in a shallow roasting pan lined with foil. Splash the beets with the water, drizzle them with the oil, and sprinkle generously with salt and pepper. Cover with a second piece of foil, close the packet tightly, and roast the beets until fork-tender, at least 1 hour. Open the packet carefully (see The Junior's Way).

2. Meanwhile, make the dressing.

3. Toast the walnuts in a nonstick skillet over medium-high heat for 3 to 5 minutes, tossing them frequently.

4. To plate the salads, cut the red beets in half, leave the golden beets whole, and divide among four salad plates. Place a slice of chèvre on each plate, standing it up against the beets. Mound a handful of arugula on top of the beets, cascading off to one side. Scatter over a few slivers of onion. Sprinkle some walnuts on each salad. Using a pointed spoon, such as a grapefruit spoon, swirl some of the dressing onto each plate. Chill the salads until ready to serve.

The Junior's Way

Roasting the beets inside a foil packet speeds up the roasting time and cooks the beets evenly. When opening the packet after the beets have roasted, use pot holders and stand back to avoid the scalding hot steam!

Leave it to Junior's to make even potato salad look and taste The Best *we've ever seen. First start with fresh-cooked red potatoes, no larger than 2 inches wide (be sure to leave their skins on). Add shreds of carrots, bites of hard-boiled eggs, some fresh dill, and a little red onion. Toss it all together in a mayonnaise and sour cream dressing spiced up with Dijon mustard. This is one of those potato salads that is delicious when first made but tastes just as good the next day—perhaps even better, because the flavors have had the chance to blend together. This salad is perfect to fix the day before a backyard barbecue.*

junior's red skin potato salad

FOR THE SOUR CREAM DRESSING

3/4 cup Hellmann's Real Mayonnaise (don't use light or nonfat)

1/3 cup full-fat sour cream (don't use light or nonfat)

2 tablespoons Dijon mustard

1 teaspoon kosher salt, or to taste

1 teaspoon sugar

1/4 teaspoon garlic powder

1/2 teaspoon ground white pepper, or to taste

1 teaspoon chopped fresh dill, or to taste (optional)

FOR THE SALAD

1 teaspoon kosher salt

3 pounds red skin potatoes (leave their skins on)

4 extra-large eggs

3/4 cup chopped fresh parsley

1/2 cup finely shredded carrots

1/2 cup finely chopped red onion

2 tablespoons chopped fresh dill

MAKES 8 TO 10 SERVINGS; 2 QUARTS (8 CUPS)

1. In a small bowl, mix the dressing ingredients. Taste the dressing, adding more salt, pepper, and dill, if you like. Cover with plastic wrap and refrigerate.

2. Half-fill a large saucepan with water and add the salt. Slice the unpeeled potatoes crosswise 1/4 inch thick and add to the pot. Bring to a boil over high heat, then reduce the heat to medium and simmer the potatoes, uncovered, until just tender, about 10 minutes (don't overcook!); then drain the potatoes well and place in a large bowl.

3. While the potatoes cook, place the eggs in a small saucepan and cover with cold water. Bring to a boil over medium heat and boil gently for 2 minutes. Remove the pan from the heat, cover, and let the eggs stand in the water for 15 minutes. Using a slotted spoon, transfer the eggs to a bowl of cold water and let stand until they are cool enough to handle. Peel, then coarsely chop the eggs and add to the potatoes in the bowl. Add the parsley, carrots, red onion, and dill and toss until mixed well.

4. Spoon the dressing over the potato mixture and gently turn over and over with a rubber spatula until all of the ingredients are well coated. Be careful not to break up the potatoes. Cover with plastic wrap and chill until it's time to serve. Refrigerate any leftovers and serve the next day.

You'll find a fresh fruit cup on the menu at Junior's, but it's not fancy like this one. Make this salad for a special dinner, or when the ladies are coming for lunch, or for a festive holiday buffet. The best part: You can prepare it an hour ahead and refrigerate. You might want to make a double recipe of the poppyseed dressing, as this one is so good, folks will want extra helpings.

fresh fruit salad with poppyseed dressing

MAKES 6 SIDE SALADS

1 recipe Poppyseed Dressing (page 49)

One 5-ounce package baby lettuce or baby romaine leaves

One quarter of a 5-pound seedless watermelon, or 1 Sugar Baby watermelon, cut in half

1 large ripe cantaloupe or honeydew, cut in half and seeded

3 cups bite-sized fresh pineapple chunks (from one 2-pound pineapple, peeled and cored, or buy the chunks already cut up, in your grocer's fruit department)

2 cups sliced fresh strawberries (about 1 quart)

1 cup fresh blueberries

1. Make and refrigerate the dressing. Wash and spin-dry the greens. Arrange a lettuce bed on a large serving platter or shallow bowl.

2. Using a melon baller, scoop large balls from the watermelon and cantaloupe. If you do not have a melon baller, cut into bite-sized pieces.

3. Scatter the melon balls on top of the greens, then the pineapple and strawberries, adding the blueberries last. Generously drizzle with the poppyseed dressing right before serving.

From 1926 until it closed in 1985, the Brown Derby restaurant in Los Angeles, located on the corner of Hollywood and Vine, was the place to "see and be seen" during the glamorous movie-making era. One night, the story goes, some famous late-night guests arrived, well after the kitchen had closed. Starting with "a little of this and a little of that," owner Robert Cobb created a chicken and egg salad that fast became a well-loved tradition. The original version was topped with Roquefort cheese and a red-wine vinaigrette. At Junior's, customers have their choice of dressings. Try their creamy rich Blue Cheese Dressing or Roasted Garlic Red-Wine Vinaigrette. Double this recipe for a summer supper for eight.

junior's cobb salad

1 recipe Junior's Blue Cheese Dressing (page 45) or Roasted Garlic Red-Wine Vinaigrette (page 50)

4 extra-large eggs

2 extra-large ripe tomatoes

1 large cucumber

4 ears fresh corn, grilled (see The Junior's Way on page 38), or 2 cups frozen corn kernels

Unsalted butter, softened

Kosher salt and ground white pepper

2 large red bell peppers, seeded and cut into ¾-inch dice

Olive oil, for sautéing and grilling

1 extra-large white onion, cut into ½-inch dice

1½ pounds boneless skinless chicken breasts

½ pound thick-sliced hickory-smoked bacon

One 5-ounce bag baby lettuces, washed and dried

8 ounces blue cheese, crumbled

MAKES 4 MAIN-DISH SERVINGS

1. Make the salad dressing and refrigerate.

2. Place the eggs in a single layer in a small saucepan and cover with 2 inches of water. Bring to a boil and cook for 2 minutes, turning the eggs a couple of times to center the yolks. Cover, remove from the heat, and let the eggs sit in the pan for 15 minutes. Using a slotted spoon, move to a bowl of ice water and let set until cool enough to handle. Peel the eggs and cut into 1-inch pieces.

3. Meanwhile, cut the tomatoes into ¾-inch cubes. Peel and seed the cucumber, then cut into ¾-inch cubes.

4. Shuck, butter, season, grill, and steam the corn, then cut the kernels off the cobs. If using frozen corn kernels, melt ¼ cup (½ stick) butter in a hot skillet over medium-high heat and toss the frozen kernels until deep golden brown. Transfer to a plate to cool.

5. In a medium skillet over medium-high heat, sauté the diced bell peppers in a little olive oil under tender. Remove with a slotted spoon and set aside. Add the onion and sauté in a little more oil until tender.

continued

6. Rub the chicken breasts with a little oil and sprinkle with 1 teaspoon salt and ½ teaspoon pepper. Grill the chicken outside on a medium-high grill or on the stovetop in a lightly oiled nonstick grill pan over medium-high heat. Cook until the juices are clear when cut at the thickest point, 10 to 12 minutes, turning once. Let stand for 5 minutes, then slice into 1½-inch pieces. Meanwhile, cook the bacon in a medium skillet over medium heat just until crisp, then drain and crumble into large pieces.

7. Line four pasta bowls or dinner plates with the lettuces. Arrange one-fourth of each of the ingredients in each bowl in sections in this order: bacon, eggs, tomatoes, corn, cucumbers, blue cheese, red bell peppers, and onion. Mound the chicken in the center. Serve the dressing on the side for diners to pour over as much as they like. This salad is best when served while the chicken is still warm or chilled. Store any leftovers in the refrigerator, tightly covered, and enjoy the next day.

The Junior's Way

Roasted corn is a signature ingredient in Junior's Cobb Salad—the whole ears are grilled, then the kernels cut off to serve in this salad. Here's how they do it. First, remove the husks, smear the kernels with softened unsalted butter, and season with salt and pepper to taste. Place the ears on a preheated grill over medium-hot coals or in a grill pan over medium-high heat. Grill, turning the ears frequently with tongs until they are deep golden brown all around and tender (watch carefully so they do not burn). Transfer the ears to a plate and cover with foil to steam. When cool enough to handle, cut the corn kernels off the cobs.

Leave it to Junior's to know how to make salads always look fresh and appetizing, even when you need them to wait for guests to arrive. This grilled chicken salad gets even more flavorful as it stands on a buffet table. It's tossed with grilled corn kernels, broccoli florets, shreds of carrots, bits of red pepper, and fresh lettuces. It "goes Asian" when finished with a rice vinegar, soy, and peanut dressing and a sprinkling of toasted sesame seeds. Then it's all topped off with crispy wonton wrappers.

asian chicken salad

MAKES 4 MAIN-DISH SALADS; DOUBLE THE RECIPE FOR 8

1 recipe Asian Dressing (page 47)

6 ounces wonton wrappers

Canola or peanut oil, for frying

4 cups broccoli florets

4 ears fresh corn, grilled (see The Junior's Way on page 38), or 2 cups frozen corn kernels

Unsalted butter, softened

Kosher salt and ground white pepper

1 bunch scallions (about 8)

4 large carrots

2 large red bell peppers

1½ pounds boneless skinless chicken breasts

2 tablespoons teriyaki sauce

8 cups salad greens (baby lettuces or romaine and iceberg), washed and dried

2 tablespoons sesame seeds, toasted (see The Junior's Way on page 40)

1. Make the dressing; set aside.

2. Cut the wonton wrappers into 3 x 1-inch strips. Heat ½ inch of oil in a large sauté pan or deep skillet over medium-high heat until moderately hot but not smoking (360° to 365°F). Add the wonton strips in batches, in a single layer, and fry until golden and crisp, about 30 seconds per side, turning once. Using a slotted spoon, transfer to a wire rack to drain.

3. Half-fill a large saucepan with salted water; bring to a boil over high heat. Add the broccoli florets and blanch until crisp-tender, 1 to 2 minutes. Using a slotted spoon, transfer to a bowl of ice water to stop the cooking, then drain.

4. Shuck, butter, season, grill, and steam the corn, then cut the kernels off the cobs. If using frozen corn kernels, melt ¼ cup (½ stick) butter in a hot skillet over medium-high heat and toss until deep golden brown. Transfer to a plate to cool.

5. Slice the green parts of the scallions ½ inch wide on the diagonal. Peel and shred the carrots. Stem and seed the bell peppers, then cut into ¾-inch dice.

continued

6. Lightly brush the chicken breasts all over with the teriyaki sauce and sprinkle with ½ teaspoon white pepper. Grill the chicken outside on a medium-high grill or on the stovetop in a lightly oiled nonstick grill pan over medium-high heat. Cook until the juices are clear when cut at the thickest point, 10 to 12 minutes, turning once. Let stand for 5 minutes, then slice into 1½-inch pieces.

7. Place the chicken in a large bowl. Drizzle with a few tablespoons of the dressing. Add the broccoli, corn, carrots, and red pepper, then the greens to the bowl. Add more dressing and toss to mix.

8. Top with the scallions and sprinkle the toasted sesame seeds over all. Scatter some of the wonton strips on top. Serve immediately or at room temperature with the extra dressing and the rest of the wontons. Store leftovers in the refrigerator, tightly covered, and serve the next day.

The Junior's Way

- Wonton wrappers, which you can find in Asian markets and some supermarkets, are the "noodles" in this salad. They come almost transparent or white and opaque. Simply fry them until they're crispy in a little oil and transfer them to a rack to drain. Consider buying more than needed for this salad as they make a great snack any time.

- Toasting sesame seeds is simple! Measure the seeds into a small, dry nonstick skillet and place over medium heat. Using a solid (not slotted) spatula, toss frequently for about 5 minutes, just until the seeds turn golden and fragrant. Watch closely and do not let them turn dark brown or burn. Remove from the heat and spread out on a heatproof plate to cool. You can also buy already toasted sesame seeds in the spice section of the supermarket.

This is not just any tuna and macaroni salad. As you might expect, this salad, made that special Junior's Way, is chock full of white meat tuna, packed in water, not oil. And there's much more! Cheddar cheese adds richness...fresh peppers and carrots contribute freshness and crunch...and pickle relish in the mayonnaise dressing sparks up the flavor. This is the perfect main-dish salad for an informal supper for friends and family.

grown-up tuna mac

MAKES 6 MAIN-COURSE SERVINGS; 2 QUARTS (8 CUPS)

2 cups elbow macaroni

1 teaspoon kosher salt

1 teaspoon vegetable oil

Three 5- to 6-ounce foil pouches albacore white tuna packed in water

8 ounces sharp yellow Cheddar cheese, cut into $1/2$-inch cubes

1 cup coarsely chopped red bell pepper

$3/4$ cup finely chopped white onion

$1/4$ cup chopped fresh parsley

1 recipe Fast Mayonnaise Dressing (page 46)

Bibb, Boston, or romaine lettuce leaves, washed and dried

1. Fill a large saucepan half full with water and bring to a full boil. Add the macaroni, salt, and oil; cook per the package directions until al dente. Transfer to a strainer and rinse under cold running water. Drain well and place in a large salad bowl.

2. Rinse the tuna in a strainer under cold running water. Transfer to paper towels, pat dry, and break into bite-sized pieces. Add to the bowl, along with the cheese, bell pepper, onion, and parsley, and toss gently.

3. Whip up the dressing and gently fold into the salad, coating all of the ingredients well. Refrigerate for at least an hour to allow the flavors to blend. Serve on lettuce leaves. Store any leftovers in the refrigerator, tightly covered, and serve the next day.

"What is Junior's most popular salad?" I asked Allen Fleming, general manager of Junior's flagship restaurant in Brooklyn, one day. He quickly answered: "That's an easy one—it's our Caesar salad. It's most often ordered topped with grilled breast of chicken; grilled salmon is a close second."

Here's a new fun twist on the Caesar, especially when you're entertaining. Grill the salmon fillets on cedar planks.

planked salmon caesar salad

MAKES 4 MAIN-DISH SALADS

Cedar plank (1 large or 4 smaller individual planks), plus extras for serving

FOR THE SALAD
1 recipe Caesar Dressing (page 46)

1 large clove garlic, halved

2 to 3 large hearts of romaine, washed and dried

1 cup shredded Parmesan cheese, plus extra for sprinkling (about 6 ounces)

1 recipe Country Croutons (page 44) or one 5-ounce package Caesar-flavored croutons

FOR THE SALMON
1/2 cup (1 stick) unsalted butter

Juice of 1 large lemon

4 boneless salmon fillets, 1 to 1 1/2 inches thick (6 to 8 ounces each)

Olive oil, for brushing

Kosher salt and coarsely ground black pepper, to taste

1. Soak the plank(s) (see The Junior's Way on page 44). Prepare the dressing and refrigerate. Rub the inside of a large salad bowl with the garlic halves, then discard them. Wash and dry the romaine, then cut crosswise into 1 1/2-inch-wide strips and place in the bowl. Refrigerate while you're grilling the salmon.

2. Preheat an outdoor grill to medium. Melt the butter and whisk in the lemon juice until thickened; set aside. Pull out any pin bones from the fillets (tweezers work well). Brush the salmon with the oil and season with the salt and pepper. Refrigerate until ready to grill.

3. Set the grill grate 5 inches directly above the heat/coals. Place the soaked plank(s) on the grate and heat for a few minutes, just until they begin to smoke. Place the salmon on the plank(s), skin side down. Close the top of the grill. Cook the salmon for 5 to 6 minutes per side, depending on the thickness and the way you like your salmon. Baste frequently with the lemon butter. Remove the fillets from the grill on the plank(s).

4. Toss 1/2 to 2/3 cup of the dressing with the romaine, 1 cup of cheese, and the croutons until coated, adding more dressing if needed. To serve, divide the salad among four serving plates. Using a spatula, separate the salmon from its skin. Top each serving with a fillet. Sprinkle with a little extra shredded Parmesan and serve immediately with some extra dressing, if you like.

continued

country croutons

8 slices day-old bread
¼ cup olive oil
2 tablespoons minced fresh parsley
1 teaspoon garlic salt, or to taste
Freshly ground black pepper, to taste

Here is a great way to use yesterday's bread. At Junior's, you'll find croutons only on their Caesar salad. At home, you'll want to try them in all kinds of meat and vegetable salads, using whatever kind of bread you choose: country white, whole wheat, rye, toasting white, even pumpernickel. Junior's croutons are larger than most (they're 1-inch cubes) and are lightly seasoned, with no cheese. Adding extra flavors is up to you—and the possibilities are endless. Try Parmesan cheese for Italian salads, fresh thyme or rosemary for chicken salads, fresh marjoram for roast beef salads. For topping bowls of soups, use slices of French baguette, about ¾ inch thick, instead of cutting them into squares (do not remove the crusts). Since baguettes are often thin, you will probably be able to fit two on the top of each bowl.

MAKES ABOUT 4 CUPS CROUTONS

1. Preheat the oven to 350°F. Trim the crusts from the bread and cut into 1-inch cubes.

2. Toss the bread cubes with the oil, parsley, garlic salt, and pepper in a medium bowl until evenly coated.

3. Spread in a single layer on a baking sheet and bake until golden and crispy, 18 to 20 minutes, tossing once or twice. Let cool. Store in a covered container or zip-top plastic bag at room temperature and use within a week.

The Junior's Way

- Buy individual untreated cedar planks or 1 large enough to hold 4 salmon fillets. Soak the planks in warm salted water for a couple of hours.

- If you prefer not to plank or even cook outside, you can cook the salmon stovetop. Leave the skin on the fillets and place on a preheated grill pan set over medium heat. Cook for about 4 minutes on the first side and 2 to 3 minutes on the second side for medium doneness, basting frequently with the lemon butter. Remove from the grill pan and peel off and discard the skin. Put together the salad as directed in step 4 on page 42.

"We want everyone who comes to Junior's to enjoy our food—their way,"
explained Allen. "So we don't choose their dressing . . . they do!" Here are
some of Junior's signature dressings.

dressings

junior's blue cheese dressing

Here's a rich, simple-to-make dressing that can hold its own on steak, sliced roasted chicken, a hearty spinach salad, or roasted fingerling potatoes. Choose a slightly creamy blue cheese that crumbles easily, such as Maytag Blue, Gorgonzola, Irish Cashel Blue, or a Roquefort.

MAKES 2 CUPS

3/4 cup Hellmann's Real Mayonnaise (don't use light or nonfat)

1 1/2 cups full-fat sour cream (don't use light or nonfat)

1 cup (4 ounces) crumbled blue cheese

3 tablespoons minced white onion

2 to 3 tablespoons fresh lemon juice

Kosher salt and ground white pepper, to taste

Blend the mayonnaise and sour cream together in a deep medium bowl. Gently stir in the blue cheese and onion. Add 2 or 3 tablespoons of lemon juice, depending upon how thick or thin you like your dressing. Season to your taste with salt and pepper. Store in the refrigerator, tightly covered, for up to 1 week.

lemon vinaigrette

This fresh-tasting vinaigrette is great drizzled over pasta salads, chicken salad, or fresh fruit. It's also nice on grain salads, slaw, and carrot salad.

MAKES ABOUT 1 CUP

1/3 cup fresh lemon juice

2 tablespoons balsamic vinegar (preferably white)

2 large cloves garlic, minced

2/3 cup extra-virgin olive oil

Kosher salt and coarsely ground black pepper

Whisk the lemon juice, vinegar, and garlic together in a small deep bowl. Slowly drizzle in the oil, whisking constantly, until the dressing thickens slightly and emulsifies. Season to your taste with salt and pepper. Store in the refrigerator, tightly covered, and use within 2 days. Whisk again before using.

caesar dressing

This is the real Caesar deal, raw egg, anchovies, and all. If you prefer not to use the raw egg, add 2 tablespoons mayonnaise instead. This also makes a tasty topping to grilled or broiled fish fillets.

MAKES ABOUT 1½ CUPS

1 extra-large egg yolk or
2 tablespoons Hellmann's Real Mayonnaise (don't use light or nonfat)

2 teaspoons Dijon mustard

2 large cloves garlic, minced

1 teaspoon sugar

½ teaspoon ground white pepper

½ teaspoon kosher salt

¼ teaspoon anchovy paste, or to taste

1¼ cups good olive oil

¾ cup freshly grated Parmesan cheese (about 3 ounces)

1. In a food processor or blender, place the egg yolk, mustard, garlic, sugar, pepper, salt, and anchovy paste and process until smooth.

2. With the motor running, slowly add the oil through the feed tube and process until creamy. Add the cheese and process for about 30 seconds. Use this dressing the day you make it; keep refrigerated, tightly covered, until ready to use.

fast mayonnaise dressing

When you need a dressing quick, this one whips up in an instant. True to the Junior's Way, it uses only "real" full-fat mayonnaise, as lower-fat or nonfat varieties can break and get watery. The other secrets are the pickle relish, which adds great tanginess, and fresh lemon juice, bringing out all of the flavors. Fold it into macaroni or other pasta salads, tuna salad, or shrimp salad or spoon it over sliced fresh tomatoes and cucumbers.

MAKES ABOUT 1¼ CUPS

1 cup Hellmann's Real Mayonnaise (don't use light or nonfat)

⅓ cup pickle relish, drained

1 tablespoon fresh lemon juice

Kosher salt and ground white pepper

Stir the mayonnaise, relish, and lemon juice together in a small deep bowl, then season to your taste with salt and pepper. Store in the refrigerator, tightly covered, and use within 2 days.

asian dressing

Whisk peanut oil into rice vinegar and soy sauce to make this Asian-inspired dressing. Drizzle over Asian salads, especially ones using cellophane or rice noodles.

MAKES ABOUT 1¼ CUPS

¼ cup fresh lime juice
¼ cup rice vinegar
3 tablespoons soy sauce
1 tablespoon sugar
1 tablespoon grated peeled fresh ginger
2 large cloves garlic, minced
⅔ cup peanut or vegetable oil
Kosher salt and crushed red pepper

1. Whisk the lime juice, vinegar, soy sauce, sugar, ginger, and garlic together in a small deep bowl.

2. Slowly drizzle in the oil, whisking constantly, until the dressing slightly thickens and emulsifies. Season to your taste with salt and red pepper. Store in the refrigerator, tightly covered, and use within 2 days. Whisk again before using.

mediterranean dressing

Typically a Mediterranean dressing starts with red-wine vinegar and an aromatic olive oil. Add a few herbs such as basil and oregano and, of course, some fresh garlic. Use it to dress a Greek salad or hearty pasta salads, drizzle it over broiled fish, or try it as a dressing for steamed vegetables, such as broccoli or fingerling potatoes.

MAKES ABOUT 1 CUP

¼ cup red-wine vinegar
1 tablespoon fresh lemon juice
1 teaspoon Dijon mustard
2 large cloves garlic, minced
1 teaspoon dried basil
1 teaspoon dried oregano
¾ cup extra-virgin olive oil
Kosher salt and coarsely ground black pepper

1. Whisk the vinegar, lemon juice, mustard, garlic, basil, and oregano together in a small deep bowl.

2. Slowly drizzle in the oil, whisking constantly, until the dressing thickens slightly and emulsifies. Season to your taste with salt and pepper. Store in the refrigerator, tightly covered, and use within 2 days. Whisk again before using.

everyday dressing

Whisk, don't shake, this salad dressing! That's one of Junior's secrets for making a dressing that is very slow to separate—and chances are good this one won't separate at all. Drizzle this over any fresh green salad. It's especially nice over tender butter lettuce, green curly-leaf lettuce, baby spinach, mesclun, and red and green baby romaine.

MAKES ABOUT 1¼ CUPS; DOUBLE THE RECIPE TO MAKE 1 PINT

¼ cup white-wine vinegar or champagne vinegar

2 tablespoons fresh lemon juice

2 tablespoons Dijon mustard

2 large cloves garlic, minced

1 cup extra-virgin olive oil

Kosher salt and coarsely ground black pepper, to taste

1. Whisk the vinegar, lemon juice, mustard, and garlic together in a small deep bowl.

2. Slowly drizzle in just enough of the oil, whisking constantly, until the dressing thickens slightly and emulsifies. Season to taste with salt and pepper. Store in the refrigerator, tightly covered, and use within 3 days. Whisk again before using.

The Junior's Way

The best ratio to remember when making a true French vinaigrette like this one is "1 to 3"—that's 1 part vinegar, or other acid such as lemon juice, to 3 parts oil. The addition of mustard, garlic, tomato paste, or cream—usually added along with the vinegar—helps to keep the droplets of oil suspended and the emulsion stabilized. Work in a small deep bowl. Slowly drizzle the oil into the vinegar while whisking vigorously. If the dressing does separate, a quick whisking brings it back.

poppyseed dressing

This is a must-make dressing for the fresh fruit salads of summer. It will keep in the refrigerator for a couple of days . . . just be sure not to put it on the coldest shelf.

MAKES 2 CUPS

½ cup cider vinegar

1 cup sugar

2 tablespoons grated or minced white onion

2 tablespoons poppy seeds

1 teaspoon dry mustard

1 teaspoon kosher salt

1 cup canola or vegetable oil (no olive oil, please!)

1. Place all ingredients, except the oil, in a food processor or blender and process until blended.

2. With the motor still running, slowly add the oil in a steady stream through the feed tube and process just until the dressing thickens slightly and emulsifies. Store in the refrigerator, tightly covered, and use within 2 days. Stir gently before using.

junior's russian dressing

This dressing is served on the side with Junior's Reuben sandwiches. It's so good that you'll find many other foods it matches up perfectly with, like sliced roasted turkey or chicken salad, a cold poached salmon salad, cold roast beef, or a fresh tomato salad.

MAKES ABOUT 1¾ CUPS

¾ cup ketchup

½ cup Hellmann's Real Mayonnaise (don't use light or nonfat)

⅓ cup bottled chili sauce

¼ cup drained pickle relish

Half of a large dill pickle, finely chopped

⅓ cup finely chopped green bell pepper

¼ cup finely chopped onion

1. Whisk the ketchup, mayonnaise, chili sauce, and relish together in a deep medium bowl.

2. Stir together the pickle, green pepper, and onion until mixed in a small bowl. Add to the ketchup-mayonnaise mixture and whisk until evenly distributed throughout. Store in the refrigerator, tightly covered, and use within 2 days. Serve cold.

roasted garlic red-wine vinaigrette

This vinaigrette is a Junior's favorite. The secret is to roast the garlic until it's soft and fragrant.

MAKES ABOUT 1 1/2 CUPS

1/3 cup red-wine vinegar

1 tablespoon Dijon mustard

3 cloves roasted garlic (see The Junior's Way), smashed

1 tablespoon honey

1 cup extra-virgin olive oil

Kosher salt and coarsely ground black pepper

1. Whisk the vinegar, mustard, garlic, and honey together in a small deep bowl.

2. Slowly drizzle in the oil, whisking constantly, until the dressing thickens slightly and emulsifies. Season to your taste with salt and pepper. Store in the refrigerator, tightly covered, and use within 2 days. Whisk again before using.

The Junior's Way

To roast garlic, start with a fresh head of garlic with white skin. Peel away the layers, leaving just the thin skin around the cloves. Slice off 1/2 inch of the pointed end of the garlic, exposing the cloves. Stand the bulb, top end up, on a piece of foil or in a garlic-cooker and drizzle with 1 to 2 teaspoons olive oil, allowing time for the oil to sink in between the cloves. Close tightly and bake at 375°F until soft and golden, about 1 hour. When cool enough to handle, squeeze or pull out the roasted cloves with your fingers. Smash the cloves with the side of a chef's knife and use in dressings or blended into softened butter to make a delicious garlic butter.

junior's balsamic dressing

Take a tip from Junior's: This is one of those dressings that is so versatile it's handy to keep a bottle in your refrigerator. It's a rich burgundy-colored, full-flavored vinaigrette, with more vinegar than the typical vinaigrette—plus a hint of mustard and spice. Toss it into grain salads, spoon it onto roasted beef and steak salads, drizzle it over watermelon and berry salads, or ladle it generously over ripe heirloom tomatoes. Whatever it dresses, it brings out great flavor, making dishes their very best.

¼ cup balsamic vinegar

1 tablespoon red-wine vinegar

1 tablespoon honey

1 tablespoon Dijon mustard

½ teaspoon soy sauce

1 large clove garlic, minced

⅔ cup extra-virgin olive oil

Kosher salt and coarsely ground black pepper

MAKES ABOUT 1 CUP

1. Whisk both of the vinegars, the honey, mustard, soy sauce, and garlic together in a small deep bowl.

2. Slowly drizzle in the oil, whisking constantly, until the dressing thickens slightly and emulsifies. Season to your taste with salt and pepper. Store in the refrigerator, tightly covered, and use within 2 days. Whisk again before using.

The Junior's Way

Balsamic vinegar comes in many colors, flavors, and prices. For only a few dollars, you can buy a decent balsamic vinegar in your local supermarket or gourmet store. These are ones that have been industrially produced in a matter of hours and labeled "balsamic vinegar of Modena." The authentic traditional "artisan" balsamic vinegars come from the Emilia-Romagna region in Italy and have been aged in wooden barrels for an average of 12 years. Expect to pay dearly for these. But the differences don't stop there. There are red balsamics and white ones . . . some with garlic or spice, and others infused with essence of fruits. Balsamic vinegars can vary greatly in acid, sweetness, viscosity, and flavor.

Super Soups

The regulars at Junior's know you can get a delicious bowl of soup every day, any time from late morning until closing. And what a bowl of soup! Whichever one you order, it's guaranteed to be freshly made, full of the best quality ingredients, and one of the best spoonsful of soup you've ever tasted. Home-made Matzoh Ball Soup is one of Junior's signature soups — it's always on the menu, arriving with a couple of oversized balls ($2\frac{1}{2}$ inches in diameter!) in every bowl. In our recipe, we offer you the option of making mini matzoh balls as well as the Junior's-sized ones. You can also always order Junior's French Onion Soup, topped with Swiss cheese that's been melted to a golden brown, or a steaming bowl of chili . . . both are hearty enough to turn into a light supper. And every Friday at Junior's flagship restaurant in Brooklyn, bowl after bowl of creamy New England Clam Chowder is ladled up, each chock full of juicy clams, Yukon Gold potatoes, and chunks of bacon. The soup of the day changes daily, of course, but now you can make seven of Junior's special soups any day you like . . . turn the page and pick your favorite!

All it takes is one spoonful to know that Junior's onion soup is something special. And they've been making it the same way since the 1940s, when Grandpa Harry was running the Enduro Steak House on the very spot where Junior's flagship restaurant stands today. The soup cooks begin by sautéing white onion slices in plenty of butter, slowly and gently, until they are soft and translucent. Then they add a rich stock . . . Junior's makes their own every day, but a good quality store-bought one works, too. Next comes a generous splash of sherry, followed with some slow simmering. Now the soup is ladled into individual crocks, topped off with one or two large croutons and a couple of slices of Swiss, then popped under the broiler, just until the cheese melts. It's brought to the table still bubbling hot.

french onion soup with swiss cheese

MAKES ABOUT 2 QUARTS (4 LIGHT-MEAL SERVINGS); RECIPE MAY BE DOUBLED

4 pounds Spanish onions

½ cup (1 stick) unsalted butter

1 tablespoon sugar

6 cups beef broth or stock, plus extra if you like (homemade or store-bought)

2 tablespoons dry sherry

2 to 3 tablespoons concentrated beef soup base (see The Junior's Way on page 56) or granulated bouillon

1 teaspoon kosher salt, plus more to taste

½ teaspoon ground white pepper, plus more to taste

continued

1. Peel the onions and cut into thin slices, ⅛ to ¼ inch thick, using the medium disk of a food processor or by hand. Separate the slices into rings.

2. Melt the butter in a large soup pot over medium-low heat. Add the onions and sugar and sauté slow and easy until the onions are soft, translucent, tender, a deep golden brown in color, and their edges have browned. This will take about 45 minutes. Do not rush this step by raising the level of heat.

3. Add the broth, increase the heat to high, and bring to a full boil. Add the sherry and 2 tablespoons of the beef soup base, the salt, and pepper. Reduce the heat to a slow simmer and cook, uncovered, for 30 minutes, adding more broth if you like your soup extra-soupy. Taste the soup and add more beef base, salt, and/or pepper if you like.

continued

FOR THE CROUTONS

½ cup (1 stick) unsalted butter

1 teaspoon garlic salt

Eight ¾-inch-thick slices French baguette or four ¾-inch-thick slices bread (country white or Club Rye Onion Loaf on page 196)

Eight 1-ounce slices deli-style Swiss cheese (see The Junior's Way)

4 scallions (green part only), cut ¼ inch thick on the diagonal (optional)

4. Make the croutons while the soup simmers: Preheat the oven to 350°F. Melt the butter, stir in the garlic salt, and use this to butter both sides of the bread. Arrange the slices in a single layer on a baking sheet and bake until golden and crispy, about 15 minutes, turning once. Keep warm.

Ladle about 2 cups of soup into each of 4 individual-serving heatproof crocks that can go under the broiler, making sure each one has a generous serving of onions as well as broth. Top each crock with 2 small French bread croutons or 1 large one and cover with 2 slices of cheese. Set the crocks on a baking sheet and broil until the cheese melts, bubbles, and turns golden brown, about 5 minutes. Don't worry if the cheese drips over the edges of the crocks, as that makes it even more like it's served at Junior's. Top each crock with a few sliced scallions if you like. Serve immediately. Do not refrigerate or freeze this soup.

The Junior's Way

- Flavor your onion soup the way they do at Junior's, with a concentrated beef soup base product like Better Than Bouillon®. Sold in jars, it's made from roasted beef and beef broth, and adds a deep, rich flavor to any broth. It's available in other flavors as well, including chicken, vegetable, mushroom, turkey, and ham. Look for it alongside the bouillon cubes in the supermarket. One teaspoon of soup base equals 1 teaspoon of granulated bouillon or one dehydrated bouillon cube. We recommend starting with 1 tablespoon of beef soup base per quart of soup, then taste it for flavor, particularly salt, before adding more. We have found you can add a little extra to the hot soup, if needed, during the last 5 minutes of cooking.
- Junior's tops each crock of their onion soup with two slices of deli-style Swiss cheese. Look for one that has been aged long enough to develop a slightly sweet, slightly nutty taste.

A good chicken stock is an essential ingredient in any kitchen—especially Junior's. "My grandfather knew how to take a pot of water, a chicken, and some vegetables and turn them into a good chicken stock. He called it 'making wine from water.' We still make it this same way today," says Alan. The stock is the starting point for Junior's signature matzoh ball soup; you can also turn it into your own homemade chicken soup (see the variation on page 58).

homemade chicken soup
with mini matzoh balls

MAKES ABOUT 3 QUARTS
(ABOUT 6 LIGHT-MEAL SERVINGS; ONE SERVING IS 2 CUPS STOCK AND 5 OR 6 MINI MATZOH BALLS)

One 5-pound chicken or bone-in chicken parts, white and dark meat

15 cups water, plus more if needed

1 tablespoon kosher salt

1 teaspoon ground white pepper

1 extra-large onion (8 to 10 ounces)

8 ounces carrots

1 large turnip (8 ounces)

1 large parsnip (6 ounces)

3 ribs celery with leaves

3 tablespoons concentrated chicken soup base or granulated chicken bouillon (see The Junior's Way on page 58)

1 recipe Mini Matzoh Balls (page 59)

1. Place the chicken in a large soup pot, pour the water over top, add the salt and pepper, and bring to a boil over high heat. Skin off any foam that rises to the surface.

2. Meanwhile, peel the onion and cut into 8 pieces. Peel the carrots, turnip, and parsnip, and cut into 1-inch chunks. Cut the celery into 1-inch chunks. Add the vegetables to the pot along with the chicken soup base. Bring the pot back to a boil. Reduce the heat to medium low and simmer, uncovered, for 2 hours, adding a little more water if needed to keep the ingredients covered at all times. Check the stock occasionally and skim off any fat that rises to the top.

3. While the stock simmers, make the Mini Matzoh Balls.

4. Strain the stock through a large sieve into a heatproof bowl. You should have about 12 cups; if not, add a little more boiling water to make 12 cups. Discard the chicken meat, bones, and vegetables, since all the flavors are now in the stock. Return the strained stock to the soup pot and bring back to a simmer. Add the cooked matzoh balls and heat through.

continued

5. To serve, place 5 or 6 mini matzoh balls in each soup bowl and ladle over the steaming stock. Let any leftover stock or soup cool to room temperature. Refrigerate, tightly covered, and use within 2 days. The stock (without the matzoh balls) may be frozen for up to 2 months. Defrost the stock, then prepare the matzoh balls and add to the hot stock as directed in step 4.

HOMEMADE CHICKEN SOUP

Follow steps 1 and 2 to make the stock and strain the stock as directed in step 4. Omit the Mini Matzoh Balls. Pour the strained stock back into the soup pot. Add 2 cups peeled white pearl onions, 1 pound carrots cut into 1-inch pieces, and 3 ribs celery cut into 1-inch pieces. Bring to a boil over high heat, reduce the heat to medium low, and simmer, uncovered, for 40 minutes. Now, stir in 2 pounds cooked boneless, skinless chicken meat (breast and thighs) cut into 1½-inch cubes, 2 cups cooked fine egg noodles, and 1 cup frozen peas. Simmer for 20 minutes more or until the soup is piping hot throughout. Makes 6 main-course servings.

The Junior's Way

- Junior's uses a concentrated chicken soup base to flavor their chicken stock as it simmers. We like Better Than Bouillon; look for it in the supermarket, near the bouillon cubes, or online. Sold in a jar, it's made from real chicken meat, natural chicken juices, and flavorings. As a rule of thumb, it's best to begin with 1 tablespoon per quart of stock, then taste it and stir in more if you wish. One teaspoon of this soup base equals 1 teaspoon granulated bouillon or one dehydrated bouillon cube.

- Take a tip from Junior's: Never, ever cover the stockpot while it simmers. Some liquid will boil away, leaving less soup in the pot but what's left will have a much more delicious, concentrated flavor.

mini matzoh balls

5 extra-large eggs
⅓ cup vegetable oil
⅓ cup boiling chicken stock
(recipe on page 57)
1¼ cups matzoh meal
1½ teaspoons kosher salt
½ teaspoon ground white pepper

Chicken soup with matzoh balls is a signature recipe at Junior's. If you want to make the traditional larger matzoh balls instead of these minis, scoop up a heaping tablespoon of the dough, not a teaspoon, and steam the matzoh balls for about 20 minutes.

MAKES ABOUT 3 DOZEN MINI MATZOH BALLS (ABOUT 1½ INCHES WHEN COOKED)

1. Using a wire whisk, beat the eggs in a medium bowl until frothy (this will take about 2 minutes). Add the oil and stock and whisk until combined. Using a wooden spoon, stir in the matzoh meal, salt, and pepper and continue to stir until the mixture pulls together into a thick batter. Cover and refrigerate for 30 minutes.

2. Meanwhile, fill a stockpot half-full with salted water (see The Junior's Way) and bring to a boil over high heat.

3. Use a heaping teaspoonful of dough and your hands to shape the matzoh batter into 1-inch balls. Drop the balls into the boiling salted water, cooking them in two or three batches, depending on the diameter of your pot.

4. Lower the heat, cover the pot, and simmer the mini matzoh balls for 15 minutes. Check one to see if it's cooked all the way through (see The Junior's Way). Remove the matzoh balls using a slotted spoon. Add the balls to the soup or store any extras in the refrigerator in zip-top plastic bags and use the next day.

The Junior's Way

- When cooking the matzoh balls, be sure to add 1 teaspoon salt to the water before sliding in the balls of dough.

- Do not overfill the pot with balls. Add only enough so the balls can cook and float in a single layer.

- Cover the pot tightly and don't peek while the matzoh balls are steaming. When the cooking time is over, remove one ball and check that it is cooked through before removing the rest.

Most of us grew up enjoying a lunch of tomato soup and a grilled cheese sandwich. This recipe takes old-fashioned cream of tomato soup to new heights. Fresh tomatoes are roasted with onions and herbs, then simmered with canned fire-roasted tomatoes for a double dose of tomato-y flavor. A fast whirl in the food processor plus a lacing of cream and it's ready. You'll be very glad you decided to make tomato soup this grown-up way!

roasted tomato soup

MAKES 2 QUARTS (6 FIRST-COURSE OR 4 LIGHT-MEAL SERVINGS)

4 pounds ripe beefsteak tomatoes

2 cups coarsely chopped Spanish onions

4 to 5 large cloves garlic, halved

1/4 cup olive oil

2 teaspoons kosher salt, plus more to taste

1 teaspoon freshly ground black pepper, plus more to taste

10 fresh thyme sprigs, plus more for garnish, if you wish

One 28-ounce can whole tomatoes, preferably fire-roasted

1 teaspoon sugar, or to taste

2 1/2 cups chicken broth or stock, plus more if needed

1/2 cup heavy whipping cream, or more to taste

Scallions (green parts only), cut 1/4 inch thick on the diagonal (optional)

1. Preheat the oven to 400°F. Peel the tomatoes (see The Junior's Way on page 62). Halve them and cut out the stems and any hard white cores. Place in a large roasting pan and scatter the onions and garlic over the top in a single layer. Drizzle with the oil and sprinkle with the salt and pepper. Scatter the thyme sprigs on top. Roast, uncovered, until the vegetables are soft and the tomatoes start to brown, 30 to 45 minutes. Remove the thyme sprigs, stripping off the leaves and letting them fall back into the pan.

2. Transfer the mixture to a large soup pot. Add the canned tomatoes with their juices and stir in the sugar. Break up the tomatoes with a spoon and stir in the broth. Bring to a boil over high heat, reduce the heat to medium, and simmer, uncovered, until the flavors have blended, 20 to 30 minutes, adding more broth as needed to reach the consistency you like.

3. Carefully transfer the hot soup to a food processor or blender and purée just until the mixture comes together (you may need to do this in batches). There should be bits of tomatoes throughout and that's good. Return the soup to the pot and blend in the cream, adding more, 1 tablespoon at a time, if you prefer it creamier. Taste the soup and add more salt and/or pepper if you wish.

continued

Ladle the soup into individual bowls and garnish with sliced scallion greens and a short sprig of fresh thyme if you like. Let any leftover soup cool to room temperature. Refrigerate, tightly covered, and enjoy within 2 days. Do not freeze this soup.

CREAM OF TOMATO SOUP

Prepare as directed, increasing the heavy cream in Step 3 to 1 to $1\frac{1}{2}$ cups, depending on how creamy you like your soup.

The Junior's Way

We recommend peeling the tomatoes before roasting them, as they will soak up more of the onion and roasting flavors. Cut an X in the bottom of each whole tomato. Blanch the tomatoes, a couple at a time, in boiling water for 1 to 2 minutes, just until the skins wrinkle and begin to peel off. With a slotted spoon, transfer the tomatoes to a bowl of ice water and slip off the skins. Cut the tomatoes in half before roasting.

This soup is a treat. It is full of tiny bites of true Idaho baking potatoes that have been slowly baked until tender, then whipped with a little cream. Fill the soup pot with chicken stock and milk and simmer with the potato skins a while to give even more potato flavor. Now whisk this into the mashed potatoes along with lots of cream to make the best-tasting soup ever. Be sure to use baking potatoes for this soup, not boiling potatoes. They are low in moisture, have a mealy texture, and whip up easily after baking.

baked potato soup

MAKES 2 QUARTS (4 LIGHT-MEAL SERVINGS)

2 pounds Idaho or russet baking potatoes (about 4 large)

FOR THE STOCK

Skins from the potatoes

2 cups whole milk

2 cups chicken broth or stock (homemade or store-bought)

1 tablespoon concentrated chicken soup base (see The Junior's Way on page 58) or granulated chicken bouillon

1 teaspoon kosher salt, plus more as needed

1 teaspoon ground white pepper, plus more as needed

FOR THE SOUP

3 cups heavy whipping cream (not light cream or half-and-half)

4 scallions (green part only), cut ⅛ inch thick on the diagonal

Full-fat sour cream (optional)

1. Preheat the oven to 425°F. Scrub the potatoes well and bake, turning them once, until they are soft and easy to press with your fingers, about 1 hour.

2. Make the stock: When the potatoes are cool enough to handle, scoop out the flesh into a medium bowl, cover with foil to keep warm, and set aside. Combine the skins with the rest of the stock ingredients in a stockpot, cover, and simmer over medium heat for 30 minutes (do not let it boil). Remove the potato skins and discard. There may be some bits of potatoes left in the stock, but that's fine.

3. Make the soup: Fit an electric mixer with the paddle attachment. Beat the potatoes on medium with ½ cup of the cream until fluffy but not completely smooth, leaving a few bits of potato throughout.

4. Whisk the remaining 2½ cups cream into the hot stock. With the mixer on low, gradually add the stock to the mashed potatoes a little at a time until all is incorporated. Taste the soup and add more salt and pepper if you wish. Return the soup to the pot and stir over medium heat until hot. Ladle the soup into individual bowls. Scatter the scallion greens on top. Add a dollop of sour cream, if you like. Cool any leftover soup to room temperature. Refrigerate, tightly covered, and enjoy within 2 days. Do not freeze this soup.

This soup is a more recent addition to Junior's menu. The secret of its wonderful flavor is the slow roasting of the squash with Spanish onions, olive oil, and seasonings. The roasted squash is then added to the soup pot, along with chicken broth, a little maple syrup, and a vanilla bean.

roasted butternut squash soup

MAKES 1½ QUARTS (6 FIRST-COURSE OR 4 LIGHT-MEAL SERVINGS)

1 large butternut squash (about 4 pounds)

1 extra-large Spanish onion, coarsely chopped

¼ cup olive oil

1 tablespoon kosher salt, plus more to taste

1 teaspoon freshly ground black pepper, plus more to taste

½ teaspoon ground ginger

1 quart (4 cups) chicken broth or stock (homemade or store-bought), or more if you wish your soup to be a little soupier

1½ tablespoons maple syrup, plus more to taste

One 5-inch vanilla bean or a splash of pure vanilla extract

1. Preheat the oven to 425°F. Peel and cut the squash into 1-inch cubes, then spread with the onion in a large roasting pan in a single layer. Drizzle with the olive oil and sprinkle with the salt, pepper, and ginger. Roast, uncovered, for 45 minutes, or until fork-tender, stirring occasionally to avoid burning.

2. Transfer to a large soup pot. Add the broth, maple syrup, and vanilla bean. Stir over medium-high heat just until the soup comes to a full boil.

3. Remove the vanilla bean. Carefully transfer the hot mixture to a food processor or blender and process for about 1 minute. (You may need to do this in batches.) Add a little more broth, salt, pepper, and maple syrup if you wish.

4. Ladle the soup into individual bowls and garnish as you like (see The Junior's Way). Let any leftover soup cool to room temperature. Refrigerate, tightly covered, and enjoy within 2 days. Do not freeze this soup.

The Junior's Way

Garnish the bowls of soup simply, by scattering some diagonally sliced scallion greens on top. Or get a little fancier. Mix some sour cream with a bit of heavy cream, plus a drop or two of water. Put the mixture in a squeeze bottle or use a grapefruit spoon, and make a few white dots on the surface of the soup. Swirl the dots with a toothpick, creating your own unique design.

"Trust me," Alan said one day. "This is the best clam chowder ever." He was right . . . it really is! Maybe it's because it is chock full of a whole quart of fresh clams, a half-pound of hickory-smoked bacon, and a pint of heavy cream.

new england clam chowder

MAKES ABOUT 2 QUARTS (8 MAIN-DISH SERVINGS)

½ pound thick-sliced hickory-smoked bacon, cut into ½-inch pieces

½ cup (1 stick) unsalted butter

2 pounds potatoes, preferably Yukon Gold, peeled and cut into ¾-inch dice

2 cups chopped onion

2 cups chopped celery

1 extra-large leek (white and light green parts only), washed well and thinly sliced (1 cup)

1 large clove garlic, minced

Kosher salt and freshly ground black pepper, to taste

½ cup all-purpose flour

3 cups whole milk

One 8-ounce bottle clam juice

1 tablespoon chopped fresh thyme

2 cups (1 pint) heavy whipping cream

1 quart (4 cups) shucked fresh clams (see The Junior's Way), preferably littlenecks, chopped (reserve any juice)

¼ cup finely chopped fresh parsley

1. In an 8-quart soup pot, sauté the bacon over medium heat until lightly browned and the fat has rendered. Remove the bacon and all but 2 tablespoons of bacon fat from the pot.

2. Melt the butter in the same pot, then stir in the potatoes, onion, celery, leek, and garlic. Add as much salt and pepper as you like. Increase the heat to medium high and cook, stirring a few times, until the potatoes, onion, and celery are crisp-tender, about 10 minutes.

3. While stirring constantly, sprinkle the flour over the mixture. Cook for 5 minutes, stirring frequently to prevent the vegetables from sticking. Add the milk, clam juice, reserved bacon, and thyme. Bring to a simmer over medium heat and cook until the potatoes are tender, about 20 minutes.

4. Add the cream, clams and their juice, and parsley. Bring back to a simmer and cook for 5 minutes more. Serve hot. Let any leftover soup cool to room temperature, then refrigerate, tightly covered, and serve the next day. Do not freeze.

The Junior's Way

Buy 1 quart of freshly shucked littleneck clams or littleneck clams in the shell. You need 3½ to 4 dozen for 1 quart of shucked clams. Sort through the clams. If slightly opened, tap on the counter. If they close, use them; if not, discard. Do not use any with a cracked shell. Steam in a covered pot in 1 inch of salted water until they open, 6 to 10 minutes. Discard any that do not open. Filter the broth through a doubled piece of cheesecloth; use in the chowder.

Way down in the state of Texas, they like to make their chili with cubes of beef, tomatoes, and lots of heat—and not much else. The heat traditionally comes from ancho chiles (see The Junior's Way on page 69). Junior's serves a great bowl of chili, so we've taken their recipe and made it with chunks of beef chuck that get more tender and flavorful as they simmer. Beans? You betcha—lots of them. And onions too. Serve over rice with a bottle of Tabasco on the side, which is a staple on every Texan's table.

texas bowl of red

MAKES ABOUT 2½ QUARTS (4 TO 5 MAIN-DISH SERVINGS)

3 to 3½ pounds beef chuck, trimmed of fat

1 tablespoon kosher salt, plus more to taste

1 teaspoon freshly ground black pepper, plus more to taste

¼ cup (½ stick) unsalted butter

2 large yellow onions, chopped (2 cups)

1 large red bell pepper, seeded and chopped (1½ cups)

3 large cloves garlic, minced

2 teaspoons ground ancho chile or 2 tablespoons chili powder

One 28-ounce can diced tomatoes (do not drain!)

One 15-ounce can kidney beans, rinsed and drained

One 15-ounce can pinto beans, rinsed and drained

2 cups beef broth, plus more if needed

2 tablespoons cider vinegar

1 tablespoon Worcestershire sauce

2 teaspoons brown sugar

Tabasco, to taste

continued

1. Cut the beef into 1½-inch cubes. Season with 1 teaspoon salt and ½ teaspoon black pepper. Brown on all sides in 2 tablespoons of the butter in a large Dutch oven over medium-high heat just until the pink disappears. Using a slotted spoon, remove to paper towels to drain.

2. Add the remaining 2 tablespoons butter to the drippings in the pan and heat until melted. Add the onion, bell pepper, garlic, ancho chile or chili powder, and the remaining salt, and black pepper. Cook, stirring, until the vegetables are tender, about 8 minutes.

3. Return the beef to the pot. Add the rest of the ingredients except the Tabasco and accompaniments. Bring to a boil, reduce the heat to low, and cover the pot. Simmer until the beef is fork-tender and the flavors are well blended, about 2½ hours. Remove the cover during the last half-hour of cooking. Stir occasionally and add more broth (important!) if needed to get the consistency you prefer.

continued

FOR THE ACCOMPANIMENTS
(optional)

Cooked white rice

6 scallions (green part only), cut ¼ inch thick on the diagonal, or coarsely chopped yellow onions

Shredded Cheddar cheese

4. Season to taste with the Tabasco. Serve over cooked rice and top with scallions and Cheddar if you like. If there's any chili left (hard to imagine!), let it cool to room temperature. Refrigerate, tightly covered, and enjoy within 3 days. This chili also freezes well, when properly packaged, for up to 1 month.

The Junior's Way

- Unlike some chili pots, this one needs to be covered during the entire cooking time in order to tenderize the beef chuck steak, leaving it moist and so soft you can cut it with a spoon.

- Ancho chile peppers are actually dried poblanos—the sweetest of the dried chiles, deep reddish brown in color, and long, flat, wrinkled, and heart-shaped. Instead of buying dried chiles, which you would need to rehydrate, then seed and mince, use ground ancho chile or chili powder instead, as they do at Junior's.

Sensational Sandwiches

"When my grandpa and his brother Mike operated the Enduro Sandwich Shops in the late 1920s in Manhattan, and in Brooklyn in the '30s," explains Alan, "all their customers needed was a good sandwich. Junior's has been famous for its sandwiches every since." And what sandwiches! "Meet the Reubens" says their menu, which lists four, including the Combo Reuben — slices of corned beef and pastrami piled high on onion rye bread along with plenty of sauerkraut and Swiss, then grilled to perfection and rushed to your table, all melted and hot. There's Junior's BLT, reinvented to include a thick layer of white-meat chicken salad, but of course you can make it the traditional way too, with just bacon. Here, too, is their version of the Philly Cheese Steak, topped off with slices of real American cheese . . . no Cheez Whiz® on this New York sandwich! The Po' Boy comes with both fried shrimp *and* fried oysters — but you can have it your way by making it with only one.

Enjoy a Junior's overstuffed, super-stuffed, sensational sandwich today!

This is one impressive sandwich! The first thing you notice is the amount of roasted turkey packed into every sandwich. Add to that plenty of bacon, lettuce, and tomatoes. We've given this Junior's Club a couple of new twists, adding slices of ripe avocado and Swiss cheese. But we haven't changed the bread . . . we've made it the traditional way, on toasted white. But of course you can make it on any kind of toasted bread you like. For the nicest looking sandwich, try to get three slices of bread that are the same size. Junior's grill master has stacked up a lot of clubs in his career, so he is a "pro" at cutting this mile-high sandwich into four triangles and moving them onto a plate. But this takes a lot of skill and practice, so cutting each sandwich into two triangles is just fine.

junior's club

MAKES 1 OVERSTUFFED SANDWICH

3 slices toasting white bread (about ³/₄ inch thick)

1 recipe Fast Mayonnaise Dressing (page 46)

Two ¹/₂-inch-thick slices tomato

6 iceberg or romaine lettuce leaves

Two or three 1-ounce slices Swiss cheese

4 slices thick-sliced hickory-smoked bacon, cooked until crisp and drained on paper towels

6 ounces thinly sliced roast turkey

¹/₂ ripe medium avocado, peeled, pitted, and thinly sliced

Sandwich picks or party toothpicks, 4¹/₂ inches long

1 dill pickle spear, for garnish (optional)

2 red bell pepper rings, for garnish (optional)

Broccoli florets, for garnish (optional)

1. Toast the bread on both sides. Spread 2 slices of the bread on one side with some of the mayonnaise dressing, then spread dressing on both sides of the third slice. Set one piece of toast on a plate, mayonnaise side up. Stack in this order: the 2 tomato slices, 3 lettuce leaves, and the 2 or 3 cheese slices.

2. Cover with the second slice of toast (the one with dressing on both sides). Top with the bacon, turkey, avocado slices, and the rest of the lettuce.

3. Top with the third slice of toast, mayonnaise side down, and secure with 4¹/₂-inch-long sandwich picks. (Look for them at a gourmet shop, a party store, or online.) Slice into two triangles and arrange on a plate. Offer a dill pickle, red pepper rings, and broccoli florets if you like. Serve with the rest of the mayonnaise dressing on the side.

You can always get a delicious sandwich at Junior's! Take this one . . . a long challah roll or Italian hero stuffed with a chicken cutlet that's pounded thin, battered, and fried up golden brown and crisp. It's then topped with marinara and mozzarella, and popped under the broiler until the cheese is melted. This is the sandwich to serve friends before the game!

chicken parm subs

MAKES 4 OVERSTUFFED SANDWICHES

1 recipe Junior's Spice (page 146)

1 recipe Marinara Sauce (page 142)
or one 24-ounce jar marinara sauce

FOR THE DIPPING BATTER

1¹/₂ cups all-purpose flour

2 tablespoons yellow cornmeal

1 tablespoon baking powder

1 teaspoon table salt

¹/₂ teaspoon ground white pepper

1 cup whole milk

2 extra-large eggs

1. Make the Junior's Spice and set aside.

2. Make the Marinara Sauce or heat up the store-bought sauce. While the sauce simmers, whisk together the dipping batter ingredients in a shallow bowl and refrigerate for 15 minutes.

3. Spread out the breadcrumbs on a platter. Sprinkle the cutlets on both sides with the Junior's Spice, about ¹/₂ teaspoon on each side or to taste, then dip them in the batter, letting any excess drip back into the bowl. Dredge the cutlets completely in the crumbs and place on a tray. Refrigerate for 15 minutes to set the coating.

4. For each cutlet you are frying, melt 2 tablespoons of the butter in a large skillet over medium-high heat. Pan-fry the cutlets, one or two at a time, depending upon the size of your skillet, until golden, crispy, and cooked all the way through, about 2 minutes per side. Transfer to a wire rack to drain while you fry the others. Add more butter before adding more cutlets to the skillet.

FOR THE SUBS

1 to 2 cups unseasoned dry breadcrumbs

Four 6-ounce skinless, boneless chicken cutlets, pounded ⅛ to ¼ inch thick

¼ to ½ cup (½ to 1 stick) softened unsalted butter, as needed

Four 7-inch challah rolls or 8-inch Italian heroes, split and separated

Olive oil, for drizzling

Twelve 1-ounce slices mozzarella cheese

Freshly grated Parmesan cheese, for serving

5. Preheat the broiler. Open the rolls and place soft side up in a large shallow pan. Lightly drizzle the insides with a little olive oil. On the bottom half of each roll, place one chicken cutlet (don't worry if it hangs over the sides) and spoon on about ⅓ cup of marinara sauce, spreading it over the cutlet. Arrange 3 slices of cheese on top, overlapping them. Broil the open subs until the cheese melts on the bottom halves and the top halves of the rolls are slightly toasted, about 5 minutes.

6. Transfer to individual serving plates and cover each bottom with the top of a roll, set slightly on the diagonal so the cheese, sauce, and cutlet are peeking out. Serve with the extra marinara sauce and Parmesan for sprinkling, if you wish.

The Junior's Way

Here are some tips that make pounding chicken or veal cutlets easy:

- Be sure the chicken cutlets are well chilled, right out of the refrigerator. Rinse them and pat them dry with paper towels.

- Working with one at a time, slide a cutlet into a heavy-duty, 1-gallon freezer bag and partially seal it, leaving a small gap in the top so air can escape. Protect your countertop by placing the bag on a cutting board.

- Using the smooth end of a tenderizing meat mallet or a rolling pin, pound the cutlet with even strokes, working from the center of the cutlet out toward the edge. Keep pounding until the cutlet is ⅛ to ¼ inch thick, turning the bag clockwise a couple of times to ensure uniform thickness.

- Be careful not to tear the bag or the meat!

The grilled cheese sandwich that Junior's offers in its restaurants is the same today as it was when Alan's Grandpa Rosen opened the doors of the first Junior's on Election Day in 1950. It's 5 ounces (yes, 5!) of American cheese on Texas toast (thick-sliced challah), served with a side of fries. It comes sizzling hot off the grill and is cooked to perfection—golden brown and crispy on the outside, warm and melted on the inside.

For this book, we wanted to give you a grilled cheese that's all grown up. Consider this a sophisticated cousin of Junior's traditional all-American grilled cheese. Instead of just American, there are three cheeses melted inside—American or Cheddar (your choice), Muenster, and Havarti—plus a bit of spice provided by a smear of Dijon. But, of course, you can make this same recipe our traditional way, too, with all American cheese. The kids love it!

the grown-up grilled cheese

MAKES 1 OVERSTUFFED SANDWICH

Two 3/4-inch-thick slices challah, white, rye, or other bread of your choice

4 to 6 tablespoons (1/2 to 3/4 stick) softened unsalted butter

1 tablespoon Dijon mustard, or to taste

Two 1-ounce slices American or yellow Cheddar cheese

Two 1-ounce slices Muenster cheese

One 1-ounce slice creamy Havarti (your choice of flavor, see The Junior's Way on page 78)

1. Spread one side of both slices of bread with a little butter and then a smear of Dijon, to your taste.

2. On 1 piece of bread, mustard side up, stack all of the cheese, alternating the types of cheese. Top with the second slice of bread, mustard side down.

3. Preheat a griddle or large skillet over medium-low heat (no hotter!). Add a large pat of butter. After it has melted, add the sandwich, weigh it down with a grill press if you have one, and grill until golden brown, about 5 minutes. (If you don't have a grill press, push down on the sandwich with a large metal spatula a few times while it is cooking, as the grill master does at Junior's.)

continued

4. Add a second pat of butter to the griddle or skillet, turn over the sandwich, and cook until the other side is golden brown and the cheeses are hot and melty on the inside, about 5 minutes more. Remove to a cutting board, cut in half on the diagonal, and serve immediately. At Junior's, you get French fries, too!

The Junior's Way

- Check the weight of the cheese slices you're using; they can vary between 1/2 ounce per slice for packaged sliced cheese to 1 ounce a slice for deli slices. This cheese sandwich typically uses 5 ounces of cheese.

- Junior's grilled cheese is served on thickly sliced challah but feel free to try other breads—sourdough, country white, seedless rye, pumpernickel, or seven grain. Junior's cuts 3/4-inch-thick slices of challah. These thick slices resemble Texas Toast, a white bread popular in Texas that is normally sliced 1 inch thick—twice the thickness of a normal slice of bread. You can also make this sandwich your way by using a different combination of cheeses—try Cheddar, smoked Gouda, and Gruyère or Monterey Jack with jalapeño, mozzarella, and Fontina.

- Buy creamy Havarti for this sandwich, if you can find it, as it is 60% butter-fat and melts better than regular Havarti, which is only 40% butterfat. The creamy variety is available plain or with caraway, dill, garlic and herbs, or jalapeño, letting you change up the flavor of your grilled cheese in yet another way!

Order a BLT at Junior's and an oversized sandwich on toasted challah arrives, layered with thick-cut hickory-smoked bacon, red-ripe tomato slices, and a large curly lettuce leaf. Order a Chicken Salad BLT and it comes with the addition of a generous layer of freshly made chicken salad. This could be the best BLT you have ever tasted!

junior's chicken salad BLT

MAKES 4 OVERSTUFFED SANDWICHES

1 recipe Junior's All-White-Meat Chicken Salad (page 80)

12 to 16 slices thick-sliced hickory-smoked bacon ($3/4$ to 1 pound)

Eight $1/2$-inch-thick slices challah or other bread of your choice

8 large crisp lettuce leaves

Eight $1/2$-inch-thick ripe tomato slices (about 3 extra-large)

Mayonnaise on the side

1. Prepare the chicken salad and refrigerate.

2. Fry the bacon in a large skillet over medium-high heat until it's done the way you like it, and transfer to paper towels to drain.

3. Toast the bread on both sides.

4. For each sandwich, spread a generous helping of chicken salad (1 to $1^{1}/2$ cups) on top of one piece of toast. Top with 1 or 2 lettuce leaves, 2 slices of tomato, and 3 or 4 slices of bacon. Cover the sandwich with the second slice of toast. Serve immediately while the bacon is still hot, with mayonnaise on the side.

JUNIOR'S TRADITIONAL BLT

Omit the chicken salad and increase the bacon to $1^{1}/2$ pounds to make 4 sandwiches. Use 6 slices per sandwich.

continued

junior's all-white-meat chicken salad

Enjoy this in Junior's Chicken Salad BLTs or served on a bed of lettuce as an entrée salad.

MAKES ABOUT 6 CUPS (ENOUGH FOR 4 SANDWICHES)

FOR THE SALAD

Juice of 1 large lemon

5 cups cubed ($^3/_4$-inch) cooked chicken breast (see The Junior's Way)

1$^1/_2$ cups finely chopped celery

1 cup thinly sliced scallions (white and light green parts)

1 to 2 tablespoons snipped fresh dill, to taste

$^1/_4$ to $^1/_2$ teaspoon garlic powder, to taste

Kosher salt and ground white pepper, to taste

FOR THE MUSTARD CREAM DRESSING

1 cup Hellmann's Real Mayonnaise (don't use light or nonfat)

$^1/_3$ cup sour cream (don't use light or nonfat)

1 tablespoon fresh lemon juice

1 to 2 tablespoons Dijon mustard, to taste

1. In a medium bowl, sprinkle the lemon juice over the chicken. Add the celery, scallions, dill, and garlic powder and toss to mix. Season to taste with salt and pepper.

2. In a small bowl, whisk all the dressing ingredients together. Spoon the dressing over the chicken mixture, starting with 1 cup and then adding more until the salad is as creamy as you like. Use a rubber spatula to mix until all the ingredients are well coated. Refrigerate, tightly covered, and enjoy the same day or the next. Do not freeze!

The Junior's Way

- For 5 cups of cooked chicken, buy 2 pounds boneless, skinless chicken breasts—the thicker ones, not the thinner cutlets. Season the chicken with kosher salt and ground white pepper and brush with some olive oil. Then either roast the breasts (at 450°F for 30 to 40 minutes, turning once) or broil (on high, 5 to 6 inches from the heat source for 10 to 12 minutes, turning once) until cooked through, then cut them into $^3/_4$-inch cubes.

- Sprinkling the chicken with lemon juice keeps the meat white, so don't skip this step!

*" 'To whiz or not to whiz'—that's the question when making a cheese steak
sandwich," explains Alan. "In Philadelphia, slathering on Cheez Whiz is
expected and always done. But not at Junior's! We use slices of bright yellow
American cheese instead." Here is Junior's take on the Philly cheese steak.
It comes on a challah roll about 8 inches long and is stuffed with slices
of grilled rib-eye steak so tender you can easily bite right through—plus
sautéed onions and peppers. And, naturally, it's topped off with three slices of
American cheese that melt from the heat of the sautéed peppers and onions
before you take a bite!*

new york cheese steak

MAKES 2 OVERSTUFFED SANDWICHES

1 to 2 tablespoons Junior's Spice
(page 146)

1 boneless beef rib-eye steak,
1½ inches thick (about 1½ pounds)

6 tablespoons (¾ stick)
unsalted butter

2 extra-large white onions, sliced
¼ inch thick and separated
into rings

2 cups green bell pepper strips
(about 2 large peppers), sliced
¼ inch thick

Two 8-inch oblong challah rolls
or other long soft rolls, split and
separated

Six 1-ounce slices American or
provolone cheese

1. Sprinkle the Junior's Spice all over the steak, as you like. Let stand for about
15 minutes at room temperature while you heat up an outside grill or broiler
and oil the rack or broiler pan: Use medium-hot coals or moderately high heat
for a gas grill or high for the broiler. If grilling, when the coals turn ash white,
it's time to put on the steak. The steak should be 5 or 6 inches from the heat
source no matter how you cook it.

2. If grilling, sear the steak over direct heat until it is nicely browned on both
sides, 4 to 5 minutes, turning it only once. Move the steak away from the coals
(or turn off one of the burners on the gas grill and set the steak over it), cover
the grill, and cook until it's as you like it. To sear and cook this 1½-inch-thick
boneless steak to rare takes a total of 8 to 9 minutes (120° to 125°F), 10 to
11 minutes for medium rare (125° to 130°F), 12 to 13 minutes for medium
(130° to 135°F), and 14 to 15 minutes for medium-well done (140° to 145°F).
Use an instant-read thermometer.

   If using the broiler, sear the steak on both sides, turning it only once. After
searing, lower the rack to the middle of the oven and continue broiling until
the steak is as done as you like. Use the grilling times as a guide. Check

continued

frequently, as it usually takes a little less time to broil this steak than to grill it. Remember, the temperature rises about 5° after cooking and before slicing.

3. Transfer the steak to a cutting board and let it rest for 5 to 10 minutes, then cut it on the diagonal into thin slices, about ⅜ inch thick.

4. While the steak is grilling and resting, melt the butter in a large skillet over medium heat. Add the onions and peppers and cook, stirring occasionally, until the onions are caramelized and the peppers are tender, 10 to 12 minutes. Keep hot.

5. Wrap the rolls in aluminum foil and warm on the grill or on the lowest rack in the oven while the steak is broiling.

6. For each sandwich, stuff a roll with half the hot steak slices, half the onions and peppers, and 3 slices of cheese. Overlap the cheese slices and arrange them so they are hanging over the sides of the bread and peeping out of the sandwich. While the sandwich is being brought to the table, the heat from the steak and vegetables will melt the cheese.

The Reuben sandwich and the Rosen family date back to when Alan's Grandpa Harry and his brother Mike ran the Enduro Sandwich Shoppes in the late 1920s in Manhattan. That began a long Rosen history of serving some of the best Reubens in New York—but not always with corned beef! Today you can walk into Junior's and still order the Original Reuben, made only with corned beef. But now you also have the option of a Turkey Reuben with melted Swiss and coleslaw, a Pastrami Reuben, and this one, the Combo Reuben, which is overstuffed with corned beef and pastrami. Feel free to make them any way you like. At Junior's, each Reuben comes with grilled sauerkraut and melted Swiss and is always on rye bread, hot off the grill, with potato salad on the side.

combo reuben

MAKES 1 OVERSTUFFED SANDWICH

1 recipe Junior's Russian Dressing (recipe on page 49)

¼ cup (½ stick) unsalted butter

2 slices rye bread

Four 1-ounce slices Swiss cheese

3 ounces very thinly sliced lean corned beef (about 10 slices)

3 ounces very thinly sliced lean pastrami (about 10 slices)

½ cup drained fresh sauerkraut

1. Make the Russian Dressing and refrigerate until needed.

2. Butter one side of both slices of bread. Melt the rest of the butter on a griddle or in a large skillet over medium heat. Place both slices of bread, buttered side down, on the hot griddle. Top each with 2 slices of cheese.

3. Microwave the corned beef and pastrami, in separate stacks, on high, for about 1 minute, just until the meat begins to steam (do not overheat).

4. When the bread has toasted and the cheese has melted, top one slice of bread with the stack of hot pastrami, then cover with the stack of hot corned beef. Top the other slice of bread with the sauerkraut. Flip the side with the sauerkraut on top of the one with the meat and grill for about 2 minutes, until the Reuben is hot throughout. Transfer to a cutting board.

5. Cut the sandwich The Junior's Way: First, slice the sandwich vertically into two pieces—one piece twice the width of the other. Slice the larger piece on the diagonal into two equal triangles. You now have three small overstuffed Reubens for each plate. Serve immediately, with the Russian Dressing on the side.

Folks living in Brooklyn know that the place to go for a terrific, traditional turkey dinner is Junior's. It always has been, ever since they opened their doors in 1950. In those days, one could get a Roast Maryland Turkey Dinner, with all the trimmings, for $2.00 . . . spend 75 cents more and you also got your choice of an appetizer and dessert, plus coffee, tea, or milk.

One of the best parts of roasting a turkey is enjoying the leftovers. This sandwich is a way to celebrate Thanksgiving, any day you wish, all year long.

thanksgiving on a roll

MAKES 1 OVERSTUFFED SANDWICH

One 6-inch round sandwich roll (with or without sesame seeds), split and separated

1 cup leftover gravy (see Giblet Gravy on page 125)

3/4 to 1 cup leftover stuffing (see Cornbread Stuffing on page 124 or Chestnut Stuffing on page 165)

6 to 8 ounces sliced leftover turkey, white and/or dark meat—your choice

3/4 cup leftover cranberry sauce

1. Preheat the oven to 275°F, wrap the roll in aluminum foil, and place in the oven until warmed, about 10 minutes. Split the roll.

2. Meanwhile, heat the gravy in a small saucepan over medium heat until hot; keep warm. Preheat the broiler.

3. On the bottom half of the roll, spoon the stuffing about ½ inch high, packing it a little to form the shape of the roll, then place in a broiler pan. Ladle over 2 to 3 tablespoons of gravy. Alongside in the same pan, make a stack of the turkey in the shape of the roll and ladle over another 2 to 3 tablespoons of gravy. Pop under the broiler, about 6 inches from the heat, until the gravy over both is bubbling and hot.

4. Transfer the bottom of the roll with the stuffing to a serving plate. Using a spatula, top the stuffing with the stack of turkey. Cover with the top half of the roll, placing it so that some of the turkey and stuffing are peeking out. Serve with the cranberry sauce on the side and extra gravy if you like.

OPEN ROAST TURKEY

Another sandwich variation at Junior's is their rendition of the traditional hot open-faced sandwich made with plenty of sliced turkey piled high on two slices of white bread, smothered with homemade gravy. Right before it's served, the sandwich is popped under the broiler until it's bubbling.

New Yorkers love their lobster rolls — all kinds have been popping up on menus around town. Junior's is no exception. Drop by during the summer months, look at the Specials card slipped inside your menu, and you're likely to find it. And not just any lobster roll . . . The Best Lobster Roll! It's simple and straightforward, like they make them Down East in Maine, and overstuffed with big chunks of fresh lobster meat tossed with just enough mayonnaise dressing to hold it together. It's piled high on a toasted buttered split-top hot dog bun.

Look for lobster meat in your local fish market. That's much easier and faster than steaming and shelling a live lobster!

"the best" lobster roll

MAKES 2 OVERSTUFFED LOBSTER ROLLS

1 recipe Junior's Old Bay®
Mayo (recipe on page 88)

2 cups bite-sized chunks fresh
lobster meat (see The Junior's Way
on page 88)

⅓ cup finely chopped celery

⅓ cup finely chopped white onion

Juice of 1 large lemon (about
3 tablespoons)

Kosher salt and ground white
pepper, to taste

Unsalted butter, at room
temperature

2 split-top hot dog buns

1. Make the Old Bay Mayo and refrigerate.

2. In a medium bowl, toss the lobster meat with the celery, onion, and lemon juice. Add 2 to 3 tablespoons of the Old Bay Mayo (just enough to hold the mixture together). Taste and add salt and pepper to taste. Cover the bowl with plastic wrap and refrigerate for at least 30 minutes, but no longer than a couple of hours, until the flavors have blended and the lobster is thoroughly chilled.

3. When ready to serve, spread some butter on both the outside and inside of the buns. Heat a nonstick medium skillet over medium heat. Open up the buns (without breaking them apart) and set them outer side down in the skillet. Toast until light golden brown, about 2 minutes. Flip over the buns and toast the insides until golden brown, another 2 minutes.

4. Stuff each of the buns with half the lobster filling, piling it high. Serve immediately with extra Old Bay mayo on the side.

continued

junior's old bay mayo

Junior's uses this mayonnaise to flavor their crab cakes. It's also a perfect complement for shrimp and lobster sandwich fillings and salads. When serving fish, place a spoonful on the plate and top with the hot fish fillet. The mayo melts from the heat of the fish and becomes a delicious sauce.

MAKES 1 CUP

1 cup Hellmann's Real Mayonnaise (don't use light or nonfat)

2 tablespoons fresh lemon juice

1 tablespoon Old Bay seasoning

1 teaspoon Worcestershire sauce

In a small bowl, stir all the ingredients together. Refrigerate, tightly covered, and use within a couple of days. Do not freeze.

The Junior's Way

- You need bite-sized chunks of lobster for this sandwich. If the lobster meat you find is in large chunks, use your hands to separate it into smaller pieces, just like you do when cracking and eating a whole lobster. A knife tears the delicate meat and makes it look more "commercial" and less authentic.

- As you work with the lobster meat, check closely and discard any cartilage or shells you find.

- If you can't find ready-to-eat lobster meat, most fish counters and seafood markets will steam a live lobster for you to carry home. And some markets with take it out of the shell, too, for an extra price!

"While visiting customers in New Orleans a few years ago, I fell in love with the Po' Boy! Every chance I got I discovered a different one, and ate them all over town. I loved them all! So I decided to give you my favorite version here. The classic New Orleans Po' Boy is usually stuffed with either fried oysters or fried shrimp. I like to make mine over-the-top by overstuffing it with both! I 'dress' my Po' Boy the authentic New Orleans way—with shredded lettuce, sliced tomatoes, pickles, and Cajun mayonnaise, served in a buttered hero or French bread loaf. Don't forget the bottle of Tabasco—it's a must!"

junior's shrimp & oyster po' boy

MAKES 2 OVERSTUFFED PO' BOYS

FOR THE CAJUN MAYONNAISE
1/2 cup Hellmann's Real Mayonnaise (don't use light or nonfat)

1 teaspoon Cajun seasoning, or to taste

FOR THE BATTER
3 extra-large eggs

1 cup all-purpose flour

1 1/2 teaspoons kosher salt

1 1/2 teaspoons baking powder

1/2 teaspoon ground white pepper

3/4 cup whole milk

1. In a small bowl, whisk the mayonnaise and Cajun seasoning together. Taste; add more seasoning if you like. Transfer to a sauce dish and refrigerate.

2. In a large bowl, whisk all the batter ingredients together; let stand at room temperature for 15 minutes.

3. While the batter chills, mix all the breading ingredients together in a shallow baking dish.

4. Working in small batches, prepare the seafood for frying—first the shrimp, then the oysters. Dredge each in the breading, working one by one, shaking off any excess. Next, submerge in the batter, turning the seafood with your hands to coat well, letting any excess batter drip back into the bowl. Dredge each in the breading again, pressing and patting to help it stick. Place on a wire rack set in a baking pan and refrigerate until the coating is set, about 15 minutes.

5. Meanwhile, preheat the oven to 200°F. Line a large shallow pan with paper towels and place a wire rack on top. Butter the rolls, wrap in foil, and place in the oven to warm.

FOR THE BREADING

1 cup all-purpose flour

2 tablespoons yellow cornmeal

1 1/2 tablespoons Old Bay seasoning

2 teaspoons paprika

1/2 teaspoon Cajun seasoning, or to taste

1 teaspoon kosher salt

FOR THE PO' BOYS

1/2 pound extra-large (16 to 20 count) shrimp, peeled and deveined with tails left on

1/2 pound shucked oysters, well drained

Softened unsalted butter, for the rolls

Two 8-inch oblong heroes or French bread loaves

Canola, peanut, or sunflower oil, for frying

FOR THE ACCOMPANIMENTS

Sliced tomatoes

Coarsely shredded lettuce

Dill pickle spears

Tabasco

6. Heat an inch of oil in a large frying pan (an iron skillet is great if you have one) over medium heat until hot (360° to 365°F) but not smoking! Fry the shrimp, then the oysters until puffy and golden brown, 3 to 4 minutes per side, turning only once. Remember not to overcrowd the skillet, as the shrimp and oysters need their frying space. Between batches, add more oil if needed, pouring it down the side of the skillet to warm it, then wait until the oil comes back to the right temperature before adding the next batch of seafood. (Don't fry the shrimp and oysters at the same time in the same skillet.) Transfer the fried seafood with a slotted spatula or spider to the wire rack, in a single layer, and keep warm in the oven while frying the rest.

7. Fill the warm rolls with the shrimp at one end, the oysters at the other. Serve immediately with the Cajun Mayonnaise and the accompaniments on the side for people to dress their sandwich just the way they like it.

Everyday Brunch

"Let's call a chapter Everyday Brunch," exclaimed Alan, "because we really do serve brunch at Junior's every day…in fact, all day long!" And what a brunch it is! You'll find several versions of Junior's Eggs Benedict—one served on corned beef hash, another on a juicy beef filet, and another with smoked salmon, all of them topped with creamy Hollandaise. There's a stuffed French toast, a delicious collision of Junior's #1 rated cheesecake and French toast. Or enjoy Junior's signature blintzes, chock full of creamy cheese filling and served with their famous fresh strawberry sauce. And what brunch would be complete without a quiche? Ours is bursting with eggs, bacon, Gruyère cheese, and cream (that's all you need!). Invite a few friends over and proudly serve brunch—the Junior's Way.

Leave it to Junior's to take Eggs Benedict and make it even better! The special ingredient is their corned beef hash, normally served with a poached egg on top. But here it gets the Benedict treatment, set on an English muffin and rich Hollandaise spooned over the top. Not only that, we've given you two other ways to go Benedict—over a grilled beef filet and topped with sautéed mushrooms and onions, or with thinly sliced smoked Nova salmon and fresh asparagus. Either way, it gets a generous helping of Hollandaise.

a different benedict

MAKES 4 SERVINGS

1 recipe Foolproof Hollandaise (page 97)

1½ pounds baking potatoes

1 pound corned beef, purchased from the deli counter or leftover

1 teaspoon minced garlic

1 teaspoon paprika

2 tablespoons unsalted butter

2 tablespoons vegetable oil

2 cups coarsely chopped yellow onion (2 large)

⅓ cup heavy whipping cream

Table salt and ground white pepper, to taste

½ teaspoon distilled white vinegar

8 extra-large eggs

4 English muffins, split and toasted right before serving

Chopped fresh parsley (optional)

Diced red bell pepper or diced roasted red pepper (optional)

1. Make the Foolproof Hollandaise and keep warm.

2. Peel and cut the potatoes into ½-inch dice. Cook in lightly salted boiling water until tender, about 4 minutes, then drain well.

3. Pulse the corned beef in a food processor until coarsely chopped. Add the garlic and paprika.

4. In a large skillet over medium, heat the butter and oil together; add the potatoes and onion and sauté until tender and lightly browned, about 5 minutes. Add the corned beef and cook, stirring, until the mixture has browned, about 5 minutes more. Stir in the cream. Season with salt and pepper to taste. Transfer to a dish and keep warm. Wipe out the skillet.

5. Fill the skillet half full with water, add the vinegar and about 1 teaspoon salt, and bring to a simmer. Crack each egg into a small cup, one at a time, and gently slide into the skillet. Depending on the size of your skillet, you can probably poach 4 eggs at a time. Let the water return to a boil, then reduce the heat to low and poach the eggs until the whites have set but the yolks are still soft, about 3 minutes after the water returns to a boil. Transfer the poached eggs to a bowl of hot water while you poach the rest; the water should be just hot enough to keep them warm, not to cook them further.

continued

6. To assemble the Benedicts, place one toasted muffin (2 halves) on each of 4 plates. Cover each half with a generous helping of hash, shaping it into a free-form patty in the pan with a metal spatula before lifting it onto the muffin. Top each muffin half with an egg. Spoon a generous amount of Hollandaise over each egg, letting it drip onto the hash and muffin. Generously sprinkle with parsley and/or red bell pepper if you wish and serve immediately.

STEAK AND EGGS BENEDICT

Omit the potatoes and instead sauté 12 ounces sliced mushrooms with the onion. Substitute eight 3-ounce beef filets for the corned beef hash. In a hot skillet over high heat, sear the filets, about 2 to 3 minutes per side for medium rare, turning once. Season with salt and pepper to taste. To assemble, set a filet on each muffin half, spoon over some of the mushroom and onion mixture, and top each filet with a poached egg. Spoon a generous amount of Hollandaise over each egg, letting it drip down over the filet, and garnish with parsley and diced red pepper as directed above.

NOVA BENEDICT

Substitute 24 trimmed fresh asparagus spears (about 1 pound) for the onion and potatoes (buy the thin spears if your market has them). Cook in boiling salted water until just tender and still bright green, about 5 minutes, then drain well. Sprinkle with the juice of 1 lemon, and season with salt and pepper to taste. Substitute 8 ounces very thinly sliced smoked Nova salmon lox for the corned beef. To assemble, arrange 3 asparagus spears on the bottom of each English muffin half, then top with a slice of salmon, folding it over to match the size of the muffin and allowing the asparagus spears to peek out from underneath. Cover each with a poached egg and spoon a generous amount of Hollandaise over each egg, letting it drip down onto the salmon and muffin. Omit the parsley; garnish with diced red bell pepper as directed above.

foolproof hollandaise

Here is a Hollandaise you can whirl up in minutes, with no worries of it separating before you're ready to serve it!

MAKES ABOUT 1²/₃ CUPS

1 cup (2 sticks) unsalted butter

6 extra-large egg yolks

3 tablespoons fresh lemon juice

½ teaspoon table salt

¼ to ½ teaspoon ground white pepper, to taste

1. Melt the butter in a small saucepan over low heat (don't let the butter brown) and keep warm.

2. Place the egg yolks, lemon juice, salt, and pepper in a blender and process on high for a few seconds to blend.

3. With the blender still on high, slowly add the melted butter in a steady stream through the hole in the lid. When the mixture turns into a thick, creamy sauce, it is ready. Keep warm until ready to use (see The Junior's Way).

The Junior's Way

To keep the sauce warm, pour it back into the saucepan, cover, and place in a warm oven (275° to 300°F) until you're ready to use it. The sauce will thicken slightly more upon standing.

Recently the New York Daily News announced: "Best of NY: Junior's in downtown Brooklyn has the best French toast . . . Junior's might be best known for its cheesecake but don't pass up the French toast. Caked in bits of cornflakes and fried to a golden brown hue, the challah is perfectly crisp on the outside without being mushy on the inside."

Daily News staff writers Jacob E. Osterhout and Amanda P. Sidman further explain the history: "Third-generation owner Alan Rosen claims the French toast recipe originally came from his uncle, who washed the thick yellow bread in egg, cream, and vanilla before dipping it in crushed cornflakes. The result is a breakfast delicacy that maintains a great texture without being overly sweet."

We've taken it one step further in this recipe. Before dipping and frying, we make a French toast "sandwich" and stuff it with (you guessed it!) Junior's cheesecake. You won't find this version on their menu, but you can make it easily at home. It's perfect for a weekend brunch with friends.

junior's cheesecake french toast

MAKES 6 FRENCH TOAST SANDWICHES

FOR THE CHEESECAKE STUFFING
Two 8-ounce packages PHILADELPHIA® cream cheese, softened

¼ cup heavy whipping cream

¼ cup sugar

1 tablespoon pure vanilla extract

1 to 2 teaspoons Grand Marnier®, or to taste (optional)

1. In a medium bowl, using an electric mixer fitted with the paddle attachment if your mixer has one, beat the cheesecake stuffing ingredients together on medium until blended.

2. In another medium bowl, whisk the batter ingredients together until frothy.

3. Cut the bread into twelve ½-inch-thick slices. Make 6 sandwiches by generously spreading 6 slices with the cream cheese mixture (about ⅓ cup each) and topping each with another slice of bread. Place the sandwiches in a single layer in a large shallow baking dish. Pour the batter over the sandwiches and let stand until saturated, 10 to 15 minutes, turning each sandwich over once.

FOR THE BATTER

8 extra-large eggs

$1/2$ cup heavy whipping cream

$1/4$ cup sugar

$1^1/2$ tablespoons pure
vanilla extract

$1/2$ teaspoon table salt

$1/2$ teaspoon ground nutmeg

FOR THE FRENCH TOAST

1 large loaf challah, brioche, or
other white toasting bread

$1^1/2$ to 2 cups cornflake crumbs

$1/4$ cup ($1/2$ stick) unsalted butter,
softened, plus more as needed

Maple syrup, warmed

4. Spread the cornflake crumbs on a plate and dredge the sandwiches in the crumbs to coat them on all sides.

5. Preheat the oven to 200°F, for keeping the batches warm while frying the others. In a large skillet, melt the $1/4$ cup butter over medium-high heat. Pan-fry the sandwiches in batches, turning each only once, until crisp and golden brown on both sides, about 8 minutes total. Transfer to a baking sheet and keep hot in the warm oven. Add more butter, 1 tablespoon at a time, between batches, if needed. Serve with warmed maple syrup.

The Junior's Way

The secret of this recipe is all in the soaking. Use a dish big enough so you can soak all six sandwiches in a single layer. Watch the soaking time carefully. Ten minutes total works the best and no more than 15 minutes, turning each sandwich only once. If you soak the sandwiches any longer, they may not stay together when frying.

When Alan serves a Sunday brunch for friends, quiche is always on the menu! Though you will not find quiche at Junior's, this one was created their way—with Gruyère cheese, smoked bacon, and a creamy egg custard.

quiche à la junior's

MAKES ONE 9½-INCH DEEP-DISH QUICHE

One disk All-Butter Pie Pastry (recipe follows)

Unsalted butter for the pan

½ pound thick-sliced hickory-smoked bacon (about 8 slices)

2 cups (8 ounces) shredded Gruyère cheese

2 tablespoons all-purpose flour

4 extra-large eggs

1½ cups heavy whipping cream

½ teaspoon table salt

¾ teaspoon ground nutmeg

½ teaspoon ground white pepper

The Junior's Way

This quiche can be baked the night before. Let cool on a wire rack, then stand up 6 toothpicks (wooden, not colored) in the filling, loosely wrap the quiche with foil, and refrigerate. The next day, remove the picks, rewrap in the foil, and reheat in a 300°F oven until piping hot, 15 to 20 minutes.

1. Prepare and chill the pastry. Preheat the oven to 400°F and generously butter a deep 9- or 9½-inch quiche dish with straight sides at least 2 inches high. On a lightly floured surface, roll out the pastry ⅛ inch thick and trim to a 17-inch circle. Transfer to the quiche dish, leaving a 2-inch overhang all around. Shape a 1-inch stand-up edge and flute. Prick the bottom and side with a fork, then freeze for 15 minutes.

2. Blind-bake the crust: Cut out a 12-inch circle of aluminum foil and butter one side. Cover the crust with the foil, buttered side down, pressing it securely over the bottom and all the way up to the fluted edge. Fill with at least 1 inch of pie weights or uncooked rice or beans. Blind-bake the shell until set and golden but not browned, about 10 minutes. If the edge of the crust begins to sink, gently press the foil against the side and add more weights. Remove the foil and weights, and return the crust to the oven to bake for 3 minutes more, just until set but not brown (remember, the crust bakes again after adding the filling). Cool on a wire rack. Reduce the oven temperature to 350°F.

3. Meanwhile, fry the bacon in a medium skillet over medium heat until almost crisp. Cool on a wire rack, then cut into ½-inch pieces. In a medium bowl, toss the bacon, cheese, and flour together, then spread out evenly in the pie shell.

4. In a large bowl, whisk the eggs, cream, salt, nutmeg, and pepper together until frothy. Pour over the cheese mixture in the pie shell, all the way up to the top. Cover the fluted edge with a strip of foil. Carefully place the quiche on a baking sheet to catch any drips and set it on the middle rack in the oven. Bake the quiche until puffed and golden brown, 35 to 40 minutes. Cool on a rack for 10 minutes, then serve in wedges right from the dish.

Prepare the All-Butter Pie Pastry (you may need both disks) and use to roll out 8 individual crusts to fit into 4½- or 5-inch tartlet pans, 1 inch high, preferably nonstick ones with removable bottoms. Butter them well! Skip the blind-bake step for these baby quiches. Prepare the filling as directed on page 100 and divide it among the 8 tarts. Bake at 400°F until a knife inserted in the center comes out almost clean, about 25 minutes.

all-butter pie pastry

This is as rich as it gets! Use it for quiches, your favorite chocolate or coconut cream pies, and fresh fruit pies. If you don't need the entire recipe, freeze the remaining disk for use later.

MAKES ENOUGH PASTRY FOR TWO 9- OR 10-INCH SINGLE-CRUST PIE, QUICHE, OR TART SHELLS, ONE DOUBLE-CRUST PIE SHELL, OR SIX 4½- TO 5-INCH TARTLET SHELLS

2½ cups all-purpose flour

1 tablespoon sugar

1 teaspoon table salt

½ teaspoon baking powder

1 cup (2 sticks) cold unsalted butter, cut into ½-inch cubes and frozen (see The Junior's Way)

⅓ cup ice water

1 tablespoon fresh lemon juice (this keeps the gluten from overdeveloping and ensures a tender crust)

1. Place the flour, sugar, salt, and baking power in a food processor. Process for a few seconds to mix. Add the butter and pulse until coarse crumbs form.

2. Combine the water and lemon juice. With the processor running, pour through the feed tube and process for 30 seconds more, until a dough forms.

3. Turn out the pastry onto a lightly floured work surface and divide into two equal parts. Shape each into a 6-inch disk, wrap in plastic wrap, and chill until firm, at least 1 hour or overnight. Roll out as directed in your specific recipe.

The Junior's Way

This pastry turns out best when you start with frozen butter. First cut the butter into ½-inch cubes, then freeze for at least 15 minutes, a couple of hours, or even overnight. The colder the butter, the flakier the baked crust will be. And like all crusts, handle the dough as little as possible.

"This is as good as it gets!" Alan exclaimed as he took his fourth forkful of this creation, followed by a fifth. Picture a warm, creamy, puffy bread pudding, straight from the oven, that tastes like it was made in a praline confectionary shop in New Orleans. You start with a loaf of challah, cut it into thick slices, and pour over a rich, creamy custard. Marble it with a buttery brown-sugar praline crunch filled with pecans and flavored with cinnamon. The secret is to refrigerate the pudding for several hours or overnight before baking; it's the long soak that makes this bread pudding the best you've ever tasted!

praline french toast bread pudding

MAKES 8 GENEROUS SERVINGS

One 1-pound loaf challah (preferably the braided one) or brioche

8 extra-large eggs

2 cups heavy whipping cream

1½ cups whole milk

1 cup granulated sugar

1 tablespoon pure vanilla extract

½ teaspoon table salt

½ teaspoon ground nutmeg

FOR THE PRALINE TOPPING

½ cup (1 stick) unsalted butter, softened

1 cup firmly packed dark brown sugar

¾ cup coarsely chopped pecans

1 teaspoon ground cinnamon

3 tablespoons maple syrup for drizzling

1. Generously butter a rectangular baking dish (13 x 9 x 2½ inches); use the prettiest one you have. Set out a large shallow pan for the water bath. Cut the bread across into ¾-inch-thick slices. If you are not using a braided bread, cut slices into four triangles each. Arrange bread slices in rows, leaning and overlapping them, if necessary.

2. In a large bowl, using an electric mixer, beat the eggs on high until light golden and slightly thickened, about 3 minutes. Beat in the cream, milk, granulated sugar, vanilla, salt, and nutmeg. Pour over the bread in the dish, lifting the bread up slightly to pour between the slices and letting the custard soak in (this is important; see The Junior's Way on page 104).

3. Using a pastry cutter or two knives, combine all praline topping ingredients, except syrup. Using your hands, spread the mixture over the top of the soaked challah, pushing some down between the slices. Cover with plastic wrap and refrigerate for at least 1 hour or preferably overnight.

continued

4. Preheat the oven to 350°F. Remove the plastic wrap and drizzle the maple syrup over the top. Place the dish in the center of a larger pan. Pour hot water into the pan until it comes 1 inch up the side of the baking dish. Bake until the pudding is puffy, souffléd, and golden brown, 35 to 40 minutes (don't let it overbake or get too brown). Touch it: The top should be spongy, not dry or crusty. The bread pudding is best served piping hot, right out of the oven.

The Junior's Way

- Drizzle the custard very slowly over the slices of challah, giving it time to soak into the bread. You're going to think there is no way the bread can absorb all of it; be patient—it will slowly soak it all up. Lightly press the bread down into the custard as you pour. Be sure to use all of the custard!

- When spreading on the praline topping, be sure to push it down between the slices of bread.

Blintzes are a tradition at Junior's . . . ones so tender and melt-in-your-mouth delicious that you can't eat just one. "Ever since my grandpa opened Junior's in the 1950s, folks knew where to come for the best blintzes in Brooklyn," says Alan. This recipe has the same cheese stuffing and Junior's Signature Fresh Strawberry Sauce they serve every day with their blintzes. But don't stop with this recipe, as delicious as it is. Try our variation for Sweet Blintzes, with a sweetened filling and Hot Chocolate Sauce drizzled over the top.

junior's cheese blintzes with fresh strawberry sauce

MAKES ABOUT TWENTY-FOUR 6-INCH BLINTZES (8 SERVINGS, 3 BLINTZES EACH)

1 recipe Junior's Signature Fresh Strawberry Sauce (page 108)

FOR THE BLINTZ WRAPPERS
2 1/2 cups all-purpose flour
1/2 cup granulated sugar
3 tablespoons cornstarch
1 1/2 teaspoons table salt
9 extra-large eggs
1 3/4 cups whole milk
1/2 cup water
1/2 cup (1 stick) unsalted butter, melted, plus more for cooking the wrappers and frying the blintzes
Vegetable oil for cooking the wrappers

continued

1. Make the Fresh Strawberry Sauce and refrigerate or leave out to cool to room temperature.

2. Make the blintz wrappers: In a small bowl, mix the flour, granulated sugar, cornstarch, and salt together. In a medium bowl, using an electric mixer, beat the eggs on high until light yellow and slightly thickened, then beat in the milk, water, and 1/2 cup melted butter. Reduce the speed to low and blend in the flour mixture all at once, just until any traces of white disappear. (Do not overbeat, or the blintzes could be tough.) Let the batter rest at room temperature for 20 to 30 minutes (important!).

3. Meanwhile, make the cheese filling (ingredients on page 106): In a medium bowl, using an electric mixer fitted with the whisk attachment, beat the cream cheese, cottage cheese, granulated sugar, and vanilla together on medium just until mixed. Refrigerate.

4. Cook the blintz wrappers: Preheat a 7- to 8-inch crêpe pan (preferably nonstick) over medium heat until a droplet of water sprinkled on the bottom dances. (Be careful not to overheat or the butter might burn.) Add a small dab

continued

FOR THE CHEESE FILLING

2 pounds (four 8-ounce packages)
PHILADELPHIA cream cheese (use
only full fat), at room temperature

2 cups large-curd cottage cheese

1⅓ cups granulated sugar

2 tablespoons pure vanilla extract

Sifted confectioners' sugar
Sour cream

of butter (about ¼ teaspoon), plus a few droplets of oil (this helps keep the butter from burning). Be sure the skillet is coated well. For each blintz, spoon ¼ cup of the batter into the pan (the amount of batter you need for each blintz depends on the size of your pan). Immediately tilt and swirl the pan so the batter coats the bottom lightly but completely. Swirl it around and around and quickly pour any excess batter back into the bowl. Cook for about 30 seconds, until the bottom of the crêpe is light golden brown (lift up the edge with a butter knife to see). Loosen the wrapper by shaking the pan, then gently turn the crêpe over with a rubber spatula (be careful not to tear it). If you're adventuresome, you might even try flipping one over by tossing it slightly in the air and catching it back in the pan. Cook the crêpe on the other side for only about 15 seconds, just until it's set (do not overcook or the wrappers will be hard to fill and fold). Turn the crêpe upside down onto a wire rack, so the lighter underside is up. Repeat with the remaining batter, making sure to add a little oil and butter to the pan before cooking each crêpe. The wrappers can be refrigerated for up to 2 days or frozen for up to 1 month. To store, stack them, separating each one with plastic wrap or waxed paper. Place in a zip-top plastic bag.

5. Assemble the blintzes: Working with one wrapper at a time, spoon 3 tablespoons of the filling in the center on the lightly cooked side (not the golden brown side) of each wrapper, then fold the edges over like an envelope (see The Junior's Way). If you're not ready to fry the blintzes, cover with plastic wrap and refrigerate for up to an hour.

6. Fry the blintzes: Preheat the oven to 200°F. In a large skillet over medium heat, melt 2 to 3 tablespoons butter (just butter this time, no oil). Place one-third to one-half of the filled blintzes (depending upon the size of your skillet), folded sides down, in the skillet. Fry the blintzes, turning each once, until golden on both sides and hot all the way through (this is important!), 4 to 5 minutes total. Transfer to a baking sheet and keep hot in the oven. Repeat with the rest of the blintzes, adding a little more butter between batches, 1 tablespoon at a time if necessary.

7. Serve the blintzes hot, three per person as they do at Junior's. Sprinkle them generously with confectioners' sugar and serve with the Fresh Strawberry Sauce and sour cream alongside. Once you have filled and fried these blintzes, serve them immediately (do not store).

SWEET BLINTZES

Make the blintzes as directed on pages 105–106, increasing the sugar in the cheese filling to 1⅔ cups. Serve drizzled with hot chocolate sauce and topped with a few sliced fresh strawberries and a dollop of sour cream. To make the sauce, melt 6 ounces semisweet chocolate and ¼ cup (½ stick) unsalted butter together in a small saucepan over medium-low heat. Stir in 2 tablespoons sifted unsweetened cocoa powder until smooth. Add ¼ cup granulated sugar and a dash of salt and stir until dissolved. Blend in 1 cup heavy whipping cream and 1 tablespoon light corn syrup and cook, stirring constantly, until the mixture pulls together into a sauce. Stir in 1 teaspoon pure vanilla extract, then remove from the heat and keep warm until ready to use.

continued

The Junior's Way

- Don't skip the step of letting the batter rest for 20 to 30 minutes before frying the blintz wrappers. This time is needed for the batter to pull together and thicken slightly.

- As you pour in the batter, swirl the pan to make sure the bottom is covered with it. Then continue to swirl and tilt the pan, letting some of the batter come up the side ¼ to 3/8 inch. This makes it easier to pick up an edge when turning the wrapper.

- This filling is so good you might be tempted to use more than 3 tablespoons for each blintz. But don't, because overstuffing can cause them to come unfolded during frying.

- The right fold is the key to making perfect blintzes. Spoon the filling in the center of a blintz wrapper, then fold the ends over like an envelope: first the top edge, then the left side, next the right side, and finally the bottom edge. Be sure the filling is completely enclosed (this is important!). Place the blintzes, folded sides down, in the skillet. As they fry, the heat seals the edges shut.

junior's signature fresh strawberry sauce

This sauce is very popular with Junior's regulars. It always comes with their cheese blintzes and the cheesecake too, if you ask. Why are the berries always plump, ripe, sweet, and delicious? Because each one is hand-picked by a dedicated member of their bakery staff.

MAKES 1 QUART

2 quarts ripe, fresh strawberries
1 cup cold water
2 cups sugar
1/4 cup cornstarch
1 teaspoon pure vanilla extract
1/4 teaspoon pure lemon extract
2 to 3 drops of red food coloring (optional)

1. Pick over the berries, discarding any over-ripe or under-ripe ones, then wash and hull them. Slice the berries vertically, from top to pointed end, 1/2 inch thick—no thinner! (This size keeps them plump and juicy in the sauce.) Place in a medium heatproof bowl.

2. Bring 3/4 cup of the water and all of the sugar to a boil in a medium saucepan over high heat and continue to boil, uncovered, for 5 minutes.

3. In a cup, dissolve the cornstarch in the remaining 1/4 cup water. Whisk into the boiling syrup and cook until it thickens and turns clear, about 2 minutes.

4. Immediately remove the syrup from the heat and stir in both extracts. Whisk in the food coloring if you wish. Drizzle the syrup over the berries and gently stir until they are coated. The sauce is best served cold or at room temperature. Store in the refrigerator, tightly covered, for up to 3 days or in the freezer for up to 1 month.

The Junior's Way

When cooking the cornstarch-thickened sauce (Step 3), watch it closely and remove from the heat immediately when it starts to thicken. If cornstarch is cooked too long, it will lose its thickening power, and the gel can break.

Any time of day, every day, you can get a stack of griddle cakes at Junior's. They're almost as big as the plate they're served on and come with plenty of melted butter and maple syrup. But for something different and a little healthier, bake up a batch of Blueberry Buckwheats. They're similar to the griddle cakes, but with buckwheat flour, lots of juicy berries, and a splash of honey. We've also added a variation for making regular griddle cakes from only all-purpose white flour, which bake up light, golden, and melt-in-your-mouth delicious.

blueberry buckwheats

MAKES TWELVE 5-INCH PANCAKES (6 SERVINGS, 2 CAKES EACH); YOU CAN DOUBLE THIS RECIPE

1 cup all-purpose flour

³/₄ cup buckwheat flour

3 tablespoons sugar

1 tablespoon baking powder

1 teaspoon table salt

¹/₂ teaspoon baking soda

2 extra-large eggs

1¹/₂ cups whole milk

¹/₂ cup (1 stick) unsalted butter, melted, plus more for the griddle and pats for serving

2 tablespoons honey

1 tablespoon pure vanilla extract

1 pint (2 cups) fresh blueberries, washed, dried, and stems removed

Maple syrup, warmed

Low-fat vanilla Greek yogurt

1. Preheat an electric griddle according to the manufacturer's directions for pancakes, usually about 400°F. If you do not have a griddle, preheat a large nonstick skillet over medium heat right before you're ready to cook the pancakes.

2. In a large bowl, mix both flours, the sugar, baking powder, salt, and baking soda together.

3. In another large bowl, using an electric mixer, beat the eggs on high until light yellow, about 3 minutes, then pour in the milk and beat for 2 minutes more. Blend in the melted butter, honey, and vanilla. Turn off the mixer, add the flour mixture all at once, and beat on low for about a minute, until blended and smooth (do not overbeat at this stage or the pancakes will be tough). Let the batter rest at room temperature for 15 minutes (it will "pull together" and thicken slightly). Preheat the oven to 200°F.

4. Smear the griddle with a little butter. For each cake, pour ¹/₄ cup of the batter onto the hot griddle, spacing the cakes about 3 inches apart (they will spread out as they cook). Evenly place 7 to 9 blueberries on each cake, pushing

continued

them down very lightly. Cook the cakes on the first side until just a few bubbles start to form and the cakes are firm enough to turn, 3 to 4 minutes. Flip them over and cook the other side until golden brown, about 2 minutes more. Transfer the cakes to a baking sheet and place in the warm oven while you cook the rest. Smear the griddle with a little more butter between batches.

5. Serve the cakes immediately with pats of butter, warm syrup, and a large spoonful of yogurt, and sprinkle generously with the extra blueberries.

BLUEBERRY GRIDDLE CAKES

Prepare the batter as for Blueberry Buckwheats, omitting the baking soda and buckwheat flour and increasing the all-purpose flour to 2¼ cups and the eggs to 3. When cooking these cakes, wait until the top sides are about half-filled with bubbles surrounding the blueberries and the cakes are firm enough to turn, about 3 minutes, then cook the other side about 2 minutes more. Makes sixteen 5-inch griddle cakes.

The Junior's Way

- Look for buckwheat flour in supermarkets, health-food stores, gourmet markets, or online. Store the flour in an airtight container in the refrigerator.

- Take time to evenly place about 7 to 9 blueberries on each cake, instead of mixing them into the batter. This makes the pancakes brown more evenly and easier to turn. Press each berry down very lightly.

- When cooking these buckwheats, be careful not to let them brown too much. Don't wait for the top to fill with bubbles, or the cake will be overcooked.

The potato pancakes known as latkes are traditionally served during Hanukkah, but at Junior's you can order them any day of the year, any time of day. They appear as an Old Word Favorite on the menu and come spread out on their own entrée plate, three large pancakes to a serving, with homemade applesauce and sour cream alongside. Be sure to make the applesauce the day before, so it's good and cold.

potato pancakes with homemade chunky applesauce

MAKES ABOUT TWELVE 4- TO 5-INCH PANCAKES (4 SERVINGS, 3 PANCAKES EACH)

1 recipe Homemade Chunky Applesauce (page 168)

2½ pounds Idaho potatoes

1 cup grated white onion (about 1 extra-large)

2 extra-large eggs

½ cup all-purpose flour

1 tablespoon baking powder

2 teaspoons table salt

½ teaspoon ground white pepper

1 tablespoon sugar

Vegetable oil, for frying

Sour cream

1. The day before you plan to make the pancakes, prepare the applesauce and refrigerate.

2. Grate the potatoes and onions together in a food processor using a medium grating disk (you will have about 6 cups), then transfer to a colander, lightly press out any excess liquid, and let the mixture drain in the sink or over a bowl for about 30 minutes. Spread the grated mixture out on a clean dish towel and roll up, jelly-roll style, squeezing out as much liquid as possible.

3. Preheat the oven to 200°F to keep the pancakes warm while cooking the rest.

4. In a large bowl, whisk the eggs until well beaten and frothy. Add the flour, baking powder, salt, pepper, and sugar and whisk until smooth. Stir in the potato-onion mixture just until distributed; do not overmix or your pancakes may be tough.

5. Warm about ¼ inch of oil in a large skillet over medium heat. For each 4-inch cake, scoop out about ¼ cup of batter, drop it into the skillet, and spread the batter out with the bottom of the ladle or with a pancake spatula or

continued

fork. Space the pancakes 1 inch apart in the skillet. Fry the cakes just until light golden brown (no darker!) on the first side, 3 to 4 minutes, then turn the cakes over and cook the other side for 3 to 4 minutes. Keep pressing them out with the spatula as they cook. The pancakes should be light golden brown and crispy on the outside, soft but cooked and done on the inside. Transfer the fried pancakes to a wire rack set on a baking sheet in the warm oven while cooking the rest of the cakes. Add a little more oil to the skillet as needed. Serve with cold applesauce and sour cream.

PARTY PLATTER MINI POTATO PANCAKES

Make the batter as directed for the regularsized cakes above. For each mini-cake, scoop out 1 tablespoon of batter. Fry as directed for regular-sized pancakes, cooking each side only for about 2 minutes, until golden and crispy. These mini-cakes make a beautiful display for the brunch table. Arrange them on your prettiest oval platter, overlapping the cakes in vertical rows, with small bowls of applesauce and sour cream on opposite ends. Makes about 4 dozen 2-inch mini-cakes.

The Junior's Way

- Russet potatoes, such as Idahos, make the best potato pancakes. They are low in moisture and high in starch, which helps to hold the batter together during frying. "Grate the onion and potatoes together, not separately, in your food processor," advises the chef. "This keeps the potatoes from discoloring."

- The secret to getting latkes thin and crispy is to fry them in a skillet, not on a griddle. While the pancakes are cooking, keep pressing and spreading out the shredded potatoes with the bottom of a ladle or a pancake spatula, but gently, so as not to tear them.

Belgian waffles are a daily offering at Junior's—guaranteed to be The Best you've ever tasted. They come to your table piping hot, with plenty of melted butter and syrup alongside. This recipe uses a similar rich waffle batter with lots of toasted pecans mixed in.

belgian toasted pecan waffles with maple butter

MAKES ABOUT FOUR 8-INCH SQUARE WAFFLES (4 SERVINGS); YOU CAN DOUBLE THIS RECIPE

FOR THE MAPLE BUTTER
(1½ CUPS)

1 pound (4 sticks) unsalted butter, softened

½ cup confectioners' sugar

1 teaspoon ground cinnamon

⅓ cup maple syrup, plus more if needed

1 to 2 tablespoons heavy whipping cream

FOR THE WAFFLES

2 cups all-purpose flour

⅓ cup granulated sugar

1 tablespoon baking powder

1½ teaspoons table salt

3 extra-large eggs

1¼ cups heavy whipping cream

1 cup whole milk

½ cup (1 stick) unsalted butter, melted

1 tablespoon pure vanilla extract

½ teaspoon maple flavoring (optional)

¾ cup finely chopped pecans, toasted (see The Junior's Way)

1. Make the maple butter: In a medium bowl, beat the butter with a wooden spoon until creamy. Blend in the remaining maple butter ingredients, adding just enough of the cream to make it spoonable. Transfer to a small serving dish and set aside at room temperature.

2. Prepare and preheat your waffle iron according to the manufacturer's directions.

3. Mix the waffle batter: In a large bowl, mix the flour, granulated sugar, baking powder, and salt together. In a medium bowl, using an electric mixer, beat the eggs on high until light yellow and slightly thickened, about 3 minutes. Beat in the cream, milk, melted butter, vanilla, and maple flavoring, if using, until well combined. Turn off the mixer and add the dry ingredients all at once to the egg mixture. Mix on low just until the dry ingredients disappear into the wet ones (don't worry if a few white specks of flour remain). Stir in the pecans. Let the batter stand at room temperature for 5 minutes. Preheat the oven to 200°F.

4. Cook the waffles in the waffle iron according to manufacturer's directions. Transfer the waffles to a baking sheet and place in the warm (200°F) oven while you cook the remaining waffles. Serve piping hot with the maple butter (and sliced strawberries if you like) and drizzle on some warm maple syrup.

If the waffles are not all eaten (hard to imagine!), freeze them for up to 1 week in zip-top plastic freezer bags. To reheat, use the oven, never your microwave, as that can make the waffles tough. Take the waffles out of the freezer, unwrap them, and place right on the middle rack of a preheated 350°F oven (this lets hot air circulate around the waffles and re-crisps them). Heat just until piping hot, about 8 minutes. Enjoy, hot out of the oven!

The Junior's Way

- To prevent the waffle batter from sticking to the waffle iron, be sure to season the waffle plates with a little oil, according to the manufacturer's instructions. Important: Wait until your iron has completed preheating before adding the waffle batter.

- After cooking each batch, wait until the waffle iron's "ready" light indicates it has preheated before spooning in more batter.

- To toast the pecans, spread the chopped nuts in a single layer in a rimmed baking sheet. Toast in a preheated 350°F oven for 10 to 15 minutes, tossing them a couple of times (this helps them to brown evenly). Remove the nuts from the oven just as they begin to darken a little and you can smell "toasted pecans" in the air. Cool the nuts before stirring them into the waffle batter.

Daily Specials

"Welcome to Junior's in Brooklyn! Our special today is Maryland Crab Cakes. Try them . . . you'll be glad you did!" Whichever day of the week you walk into Junior's, you'll find an insert in your menu listing the specials, which change from season to season. But every day is a special day at Junior's—and many items are so special they're always on the menu, every day! You can have their Baked Meat Loaf with delicious Mushroom Gravy one day (you get a whole little meat loaf, not just slices like in most restaurants), or Southern Fried Chicken, either half a bird or boneless chicken cutlets that have been pounded thin, then fried to crispy, crunchy perfection. Every day is Thanksgiving at Junior's, too—enjoy the Roast Turkey Special with Giblet Gravy and your choice of Chestnut Stuffing or Cornbread Stuffing. You'll also find Junior's Roumanian Tenderloin Steak smothered with onions, grilled salmon for a party, and baby back ribs for a barbeque. Here you'll find recipes for these—and much more. Go ahead . . . pick your favorite and make your Junior's special for dinner tonight!

The regulars know you can always order fried chicken, just like folks have been doing ever since Junior's opened its doors in 1950. Back then, just $2.50 could buy you a whole chicken dinner! Though the price has changed, the way Junior's fries chicken has not. Order chicken your way: half-a-chick or a pounded boneless chicken breast, battered, breaded, and fried Southern style. It will come out of the kitchen in all its glory: golden, crispy on the outside, juicy on the inside, and still sizzling! The secret? Dip the chicken in the batter, then roll it in their special breading, which has just enough yellow cornmeal to give each piece that delicious golden color and crunch.

southern fried chicken

1½ pounds skinless, boneless chicken breasts or thighs or 3 pounds bone-in skin-on chicken pieces, rinsed and dried

Kosher salt and freshly ground black pepper

Cajun or Creole seasoning (optional)

FOR THE DIPPING BATTER

5 extra-large eggs

1½ cups whole milk

2 cups all-purpose flour

2 tablespoons yellow cornmeal

1 tablespoon kosher salt

1 tablespoon baking powder

1 teaspoon ground black pepper

continued

MAKES ABOUT 4 SERVINGS

1. Place the boneless breasts or thighs between sheets of wax paper and, using a meat mallet, pound them out to ⅛- to ¼-inch thickness. If using chicken pieces, set them out. Sprinkle both sides with as much salt, pepper, and Cajun seasoning (if using) as you like.

2. Make the dipping batter: In a large bowl, whisk the eggs and milk together until frothy. Add the remaining batter ingredients and whisk until blended and smooth. Let stand for 15 minutes. Meanwhile, mix all the breading ingredients together in a shallow baking dish (a 13 x 9-inch one is perfect).

3. Working with one piece of chicken at a time, dip first in the batter, letting any excess drip back into the bowl, then roll in the breading, coating it well on both sides. Transfer to a tray and continue until all the pieces are coated. Refrigerate for about 15 minutes, until the coating is set.

continued

2 cups all-purpose flour

1 tablespoon yellow cornmeal

1 tablespoon fried chicken seasoning or Cajun seasoning, more to taste

1 tablespoon dried thyme

1 tablespoon paprika

2 teaspoons kosher salt

1 teaspoon freshly ground black pepper

Canola or vegetable cooking oil (not olive oil), for frying

4. Meanwhile, in a large frying pan (use an iron skillet if you have one), heat 1 inch of oil over medium heat until hot but not smoking, 325° to 350°F (no higher, as the oil can break down and burn). Gently slide the chicken into the hot oil. Cook only a few pieces at a time; otherwise the temperature of the oil will drop and the coating will absorb oil instead of frying up crispy. And remember, avoid overcrowding the skillet, because each piece needs its own frying space to cook evenly.

5. Cook the boneless chicken, turning only once, until golden and cooked all the way through, 3 to 4 minutes per side for boneless breasts and 4 to 5 minutes per side for boneless thighs. Cook the bone-in pieces for 8 to 10 minutes total for white meat, 12 to 13 minutes total for dark meat. The bone-in pieces of chicken are done when the juices run clear at the thickest point at the bone. Between batches, if you need to add more oil, carefully and slowly pour it down the side of the skillet and wait until the oil comes back to frying temperature before adding the next batch of chicken. Drain the cooked chicken on a wire rack (not on paper towels). The chicken is best served while still hot, but is still delicious at room temperature. If there is any chicken left over, refrigerate in a zip-top plastic bag and enjoy the next day. Do not freeze.

The Junior's Way

If you've always wondered how to batter and fry delicious Southern fried chicken, this is it. Be sure the batter is thick, but not too thick or it will fall off during frying. Watch the batter closely. It can thicken as it stands, so add a little extra milk if you need to.

Every day is Thanksgiving at Junior's! Whatever the month or day of the week, you can order the Roast Turkey Chef's Special. If you order it on Thanksgiving at one of Junior's restaurants, it comes with a chestnut stuffing, gravy, and cranberries. We've made this traditional meal the Southern way with Cornbread Stuffing, but you'll find Junior's Chestnut Stuffing on page 165.

roast turkey with cornbread stuffing and giblet gravy

One 12- to 16-pound fresh or thawed frozen whole turkey

Kosher salt and ground white pepper

6 tablespoons (3/4 stick) unsalted butter, softened

FOR THE TURKEY SEASONINGS

6 large carrots, cut into 2-inch pieces

3 ribs celery with leaves, cut into 3-inch pieces

2 extra-large white onions, cut into 10 large wedges total

1 large bunch fresh curly parsley, thicker part of the stems trimmed off

About 25 (total) 6-inch sprigs fresh rosemary, sage, and thyme

4 to 6 cups turkey or chicken broth (homemade or store-bought)

continued

A 12-POUND TURKEY MAKES 12 SERVINGS, A 16-POUND TURKEY, 16 SERVINGS; 1 QUART GRAVY

1. Preheat the oven to 325°F. Remove the neck and giblets from the cavity of the turkey and save in the refrigerator for making the gravy (discard the gizzard). Wash the turkey under cold running water inside and out, then pat dry with paper towels. (Or use cold salt water to wash the bird if you wish, like they do at Junior's.) Season with salt and pepper, inside the cavity and on the skin of the bird, as much as you like. With your hands, work the softened butter under the skin of the breast, taking care not to rip it. Set in a large roasting pan.

2. Place inside both the body and neck cavities of the bird some of the carrot, celery, and onion pieces and a few sprigs each of parsley, rosemary, sage, and thyme. "Close" the body cavity by stuffing in the bunch of parsley in both the neck and body cavities. Truss the bird. Scatter the remaining vegetables and the herbs in and around the turkey. Pour enough broth in the pan to come up the sides about 2 inches.

3. Make the basting sauce (see the ingredients on page 123): Melt the butter in a small saucepan, then whisk in the rest of the basting sauce ingredients until they pull together into a sauce. Brush all over the bird and sprinkle with paprika. Keep the rest of the basting sauce warm.

continued

FOR THE BASTING SAUCE

1 cup (2 sticks) unsalted butter, melted

¼ cup turkey stock

Splash of dry white wine (or more stock), 2 to 3 tablespoons

Ground white pepper, to taste

Paprika

1 recipe Cornbread Stuffing (recipe page 124)

1 recipe Giblet Gravy (reserve the drippings from the turkey; recipe page 125)

4. Place the turkey in the oven; brush often with the basting sauce and the drippings from the bird, about every 30 minutes. Check the pan drippings too, adding more broth as needed. If certain parts, such as the wing tips, brown too fast, protect them with pieces of aluminum foil. The turkey is ready to come out of the oven when a meat thermometer inserted into the thigh, just above the drumstick and away from the bone, reaches 160° to 165°F and the juices run clear at the joint. This will usually take 3 to 3½ hours for a 12-pound bird and 4 to 4½ hours for a 16-pound bird. Remember, the temperature will rise at least 5 degrees after the turkey is removed from the oven, so watch carefully the last half hour and do not overbake. Let the bird rest while baking the stuffing. Using a slotted spoon, transfer the roasted vegetables from the bottom of the pan to a serving dish and keep warm. Discard the vegetables inside the bird. And be sure to save the drippings for the gravy!

5. While the turkey is roasting, prep the Cornbread Stuffing for baking. Refrigerate until it is ready to go into the oven. After the bird is done, increase the oven temperature to 350°F and bake the stuffing as directed.

6. When the turkey is done roasting, strain and measure the drippings in the roasting pan, adding extra broth to make 4 cups. Make the Giblet Gravy. Serve hot with the turkey and stuffing.

The Junior's Way

Turkeys are roasted every day at Junior's, dozens at a time! Before putting them in the oven, they are washed in salt water (their version of brining), then flavored simply, with salt, pepper, and a little garlic powder—not stuffed with anything. In this recipe, we have used fresh vegetables and herbs to flavor the bird during roasting, plus extra in the roasting pan to flavor the pan juices you'll use to make the gravy. To keep the bird moist during roasting, we've stuffed some butter under the skin, then whisked up a sauce for basting of more butter, a little stock, and some white wine for a little extra flavor.

continued

cornbread stuffing

If you like more crunch, stir in toasted pecans. You need to bake the cornbread for this the day before—or even weeks ahead and freeze if you wish. Defrost at room temperature before using in this recipe.

1 recipe Skillet Cornbread (page 192)

2 cups white country bread with crusts, torn into 1-inch pieces

1 pound bulk pork sausage, thawed if frozen

1/2 cup (1 stick) unsalted butter, plus more for the pan

1 1/2 cups coarsely chopped celery

1 1/2 cups coarsely chopped onion

1 cup cubed (1/2-inch) peeled and cored apple, such as Rome Beauty (1 large)

1 cup coarsely chopped pecans (optional), toasted (see The Junior's Way on page 115)

1 cup minced fresh curly parsley, plus more for garnish

3 tablespoons snipped mixed fresh herbs (rosemary, sage, and thyme)

Kosher salt and coarsely ground black pepper, to taste

4 extra-large eggs

1 cup hot turkey or chicken broth (homemade or store-bought); more as needed

Paprika

1. The day before you'll be preparing the stuffing, make the Skillet Cornbread. When it is cool enough to handle, coarsely crumble into a large bowl. You need 10 cups. In a large bowl, toss the crumbled cornbread and torn white bread together, cover with plastic wrap, and let stand at room temperature until ready to use in the stuffing the next day.

2. The next day, in a large skillet, brown the sausage over medium heat until no longer pink, about 5 minutes, stirring often to prevent sticking and over-browning. Using a slotted spoon, transfer the sausage to the bowl with the cornbread mixture.

3. Melt the butter in the hot drippings, then add the celery and onion and sauté until tender, about 5 minutes. Transfer to the bowl with the cornbread mixture. Also add the apple, toasted pecans if using, parsley, and the herbs. Season with salt and pepper, as you like.

4. In a medium bowl, beat the eggs with an electric mixer fitted with the wire whisk attachment on medium high until light yellow and frothy. With the mixer still running, pour in the hot broth. Stir into the stuffing. Add a little more hot broth if needed to pull the stuffing together.

5. Transfer the stuffing to a buttered 13 x 9-inch baking dish and sprinkle generously with paprika. Cover with aluminum foil, set the dish in a larger pan, and fill that pan with hot water to come halfway up the side of the dish. Bake at 350°F until light, fluffy, and piping hot (165°F in the center when measured with an instant-read thermometer), 40 to 45 minutes, removing the foil during the last 10 minutes to allow it to brown a little. Sprinkle with chopped parsley and serve with the roast turkey and gravy.

giblet gravy

Here's the special gravy Junior's makes every day for their turkey dinners. The drippings from the bird create a deep golden brown gravy that is full of flavor.

MAKES ABOUT 3 CUPS GRAVY

Giblets from turkey (liver, heart, and neck; do not use the gizzard)

4 cups reserved drippings from roasting the turkey or turkey or chicken stock (store-bought)

1/2 cup all-purpose flour

2 teaspoons paprika

1 teaspoon kosher salt, or to taste

1/2 teaspoon coarsely ground black pepper, or to taste

6 tablespoons fat skimmed from stock, or 3/4 stick unsalted butter

1 teaspoon minced garlic

Few drops of Kitchen Bouquet® (optional)

1. Cook and chop the giblets (see The Junior's Way). Measure the drippings; if you do not have at least 4 cups, add a little store-bought stock. Heat in a medium saucepan over medium heat; reduce the heat to very low and keep at a simmer.

2. In a small bowl, mix the flour, paprika, salt, and pepper together.

3. Melt the turkey fat or butter in a large heavy saucepan over medium-high heat until bubbly and light golden. Add the garlic and sauté for about 1 minute until soft. Reduce the heat to medium. Whisking constantly, slowly add the flour mixture until a thick paste (called a roux) forms and begins to bubble around the edge of the pan. Add the simmering stock, a little at first, then slowly add the rest, and continue to whisk until the gravy thickens. The gravy should be a rich, deep golden brown. If the color is not what you like, take a tip from Junior's and add a little Kitchen Bouquet.

4. Remove the gravy from the heat and stir in the giblets. Taste and add more salt and pepper if desired. Serve immediately. Refrigerate any leftover gravy in an airtight container and use the next day (do not freeze).

The Junior's Way

To cook the giblets, half-fill a stock pot with water and add 1 teaspoon kosher salt. Refrigerate the liver, discard the gizzard, and add the remaining giblets to the pot. Bring to a boil over high heat, reduce the heat, and simmer for 1 hour. Add the liver and simmer about 30 minutes more. Drain in a colander and let cool. Remove the meat from the neck and discard the bones. Chop the neck meat and the rest of the giblets by hand or in a food processor. Set aside until ready to add to the gravy in step 4.

Here's one of Junior's most popular steaks that's always on the menu; it's served as a plated lunch or dinner with sautéed onions, mashed potatoes, and gravy. Or you can order it as a sandwich on a hero roll. It's made using skirt steak, which is cut from the lower part of the brisket of beef. Skirt steak can be a chewy cut; to keep it tender, cook it only to medium rare or medium (no more!), searing it quickly over very high heat until it's almost crusty on the outside and hot red or pink on the inside. Most important, always slice this steak thin and on the diagonal, as the chef does at Junior's.

roumanian tenderloin steak

MAKES 4 SERVINGS

1 to 2 tablespoons Junior's Spice (page 146), to your liking

1 1/4 to 1 1/2 pounds skirt steak

2 extra-large white or Spanish onions

1/4 cup (1/2 stick) unsalted butter

1 teaspoon sugar

Kosher salt and coarsely ground black pepper, to taste

The Junior's Way

Slice skirt steak thin (1/2 to 3/4 inch thick), as they do at Junior's, across the grain on the diagonal. It's guaranteed to be very tender and delicious!

1. Make Junior's Spice and sprinkle all over the steak, as little or as much as you like. Let stand for about 15 minutes at room temperature while you heat up the outside grill or broiler and oil the rack or broiler pan: Use hot coals or high heat for a gas grill or high for the broiler.

2. Meanwhile, sauté the onions: Peel and halve the onions lengthwise, then cut into 1-inch-wide strips. Melt the butter in a large skillet over medium-high heat. Add the onions, sugar, and salt and pepper to taste. Sauté until translucent and tender, about 8 minutes. Keep warm.

3. When the coals turn ash white, it's time to put on the steaks. The steaks should be about 5 inches from the heat source no matter how you're cooking them. Alternatively, these steaks also cook well in a cast-iron skillet heated over high heat until it's very hot.

4. Grill, broil, or pan-fry the steaks for 1 or 2 minutes per side (remember, this steak is very, very thin!). When the steaks are crusty on the outside and medium-rare or medium on the inside, they are ready. Transfer them to a cutting board and let them rest for 5 to 10 minutes. Slice across the grain and on the diagonal, 1/2 to 3/4 inch thick. These are best served right away—with plenty of sautéed onions alongside!

It happens every day at Junior's . . . 50 pounds, sometimes as many as 100 pounds, of beef brisket are slow-cooked in the oven for 4 to 5 hours. They become so tender they almost fall apart, yet hold together just enough so they can be sliced. They also have that wonderful roasted flavor, unlike briskets boiled on top of the stove. Save the vegetables and pan drippings and stir up a tasty gravy to ladle on top. Also daily, Junior's tosses slices of this brisket in their famous barbecue sauce and stuffs them into soft rolls, for a finger-lickin' sensation (see our variation on page 128). When served inside mini-slider buns, these turn into hearty appetizer sliders, perfect for pleasing a crowd.

junior's brisket
with roasted vegetables in delicious country gravy

MAKES 6 TO 8 GENEROUS SERVINGS AND 4 CUPS DELICIOUS GRAVY

FOR THE BRISKET

One 4- to 5-pound fresh brisket of beef (preferably first cut; see The Junior's Way on page 128)

1 tablespoon kosher salt, or more to taste

1 teaspoon ground white pepper, or more to taste

1 pound carrots, peeled and sliced crosswise (4 cups)

3 cups sliced (½ inch thick) celery

3 extra-large white onions, sliced ¼ inch thick

6 large cloves garlic, minced

continued

1. Preheat the oven to 350°F. Rub the brisket all over with the salt and pepper and place it, fat side down, in a roasting pan. Pour in enough water to come two-thirds up the sides of the brisket. Arrange the carrots, celery, onions, and garlic around the brisket. Cover tightly with foil and roast for 2 hours, basting frequently with the pan drippings.

2. After the first 2 hours, discard the foil, flip the brisket fat side up and leave it that way during the rest of the roasting. If necessary, add a little extra water while it cooks to keep the liquid two-thirds up the sides of the brisket. Keep cooking until the brisket is browned and fork-tender! This will take at least 4 hours, maybe longer, depending upon the shape and thickness of the meat.

continued

FOR THE DELICIOUS COUNTRY GRAVY

½ cup (1 stick) unsalted butter

3 large garlic cloves, minced

½ cup Gold Medal Wondra® or all-purpose flour

5 cups strained pan drippings (save the vegetables!)

The Junior's Way

- For this recipe, look for the "first cut" of beef brisket, which is from the breast section of the animal, beneath the first five ribs. It's very flavorful, but not a tender cut, so it requires long, slow cooking.

- Roast brisket the way the chefs do at Junior's: Place it in an open roasting pan . . . no cover needed! Roast long and slow, basting often, until the brisket is fork-tender.

- The secret for making it tender? Keep plenty of drippings in the pan at all times to come two-thirds up the brisket.

- Remember, always slice brisket against the grain, on the diagonal . . . this makes it even more tender and juicy!

3. Transfer the brisket to a cutting board, let it rest for 10 minutes, then cut it across the grain on the diagonal (very important!) into slices ½ inch thick. Transfer to a serving platter and keep hot. Strain the drippings into a bowl, reserving the vegetables.

4. Meanwhile, make the gravy: Melt the butter in a large skillet over medium-high heat, add the garlic, and cook until it begins to soften, but not brown. Reduce the heat to medium. Whisk in the flour and cook, stirring constantly, until the mixture bubbles all over, about 2 minutes. Gradually pour in the strained drippings and continue cooking and whisking until the gravy thickens. Stir in the reserved vegetables and gently stir until hot. Ladle the gravy over the sliced brisket and serve hot.

BRISKET MELT

Here's another overstuffed, over-delicious Junior's sandwich that's always on the menu! For each sandwich, split an 8-inch onion loaf or Italian hero roll. Melt 2 tablespoons unsalted butter in a medium skillet over medium-high heat. Add about ¾ cup onion rings (¼ inch wide) and ¾ cup green bell pepper strips (¼ inch wide), and cook, stirring, until tender. On the bottom of the roll, stack 6 to 8 slices of beef brisket and top with the sautéed onions and peppers. Arrange three 1-ounce slices mozzarella cheese on top, overlapping them. Pop under the broiler until the onions and peppers are sizzling and the cheese has melted, about 3 minutes (watch closely!). Leave the sandwiches open-faced or close them shut; either way, serve them while they are still sizzling!

On August 17, 1981, a fire destroyed most of Junior's, including its records and memorabilia. Only one menu from the '50s survived: the Sunday dinner menu from October 28, 1956. The Sizzling Platter featured that day was Charcoal Broiled Prime Filet Mignon Steak, priced at $2.75 à la carte. For 75 cents more, you could enjoy the complete dinner: a thick-cut filet, French fried onion rings, carrots and peas, and a baked Idaho potato. What a way to feast on a Sunday!

These days, you are more likely to see a 24-ounce T-bone steak or a 20-ounce sirloin on Junior's menu. But we wanted you to have a recipe for a smaller steak, so here's one for a filet mignon.

charcoal-broiled prime filet mignon steaks

MAKES 4 SERVINGS

1 recipe French Fried Onion Rings (page 167)

1 recipe Junior's Spice (page 146)

4 beef prime filet mignon steaks, whatever thickness you prefer, from 1½ to 2½ inches

1. Prepare and batter the onion rings, then refrigerate to set the coating.

2. Meanwhile, make the Junior's Spice and sprinkle as much as you like all over the steaks on both sides. Let stand for about 15 minutes at room temperature while you heat up the outside grill or broiler and oil the rack or broiler pan; use medium-hot coals or moderately high heat for a gas grill or high for the broiler. If you're grilling, when the coals turn ash white, it's time to put on the steaks. The steaks should be 5 or 6 inches from the heat source no matter how you're cooking them.

3. If grilling, cook the steaks over direct heat, turning them only once. Cover the grill and cook until they're the way your guests prefer them, using an instant-read thermometer to check the internal temperature of each. As

continued

- When buying filets mignon, choose the best quality you can afford. Prime is the best, as these steaks have been aged longer and have more marbling and flavor; choice is good too—and less expensive. One 1½-inch-thick steak weighs 8 ounces; it's the size that's most readily available in supermarkets. A 2-inch-thick filet clocks in at 10 ounces; a man-sized 2½-inch-thick steak normally weighs 12 ounces —all beef, all meat. Our recipe has cooking instructions for all three. Another way to have it your way is to buy a half or a whole beef tenderloin and cut the steaks yourself, each the thickness your diners prefer.

- Remember, less is more for these steaks—that is, the less seasoning, less turning, less puncturing with a fork (use tongs!), the better these steaks will turn out.

a guide, cook the first side 1 to 2 minutes more than the second. Cook a 1½-inch-thick filet mignon to 125° to 130°F for medium-rare, 10 to 11 minutes total; 130° to 135°F for medium, 12 to 13 minutes; 140° to 145°F for medium-well, 14 to 15 minutes total. To cook 2-inch-thick filets, you will generally need a total of 1 to 2 minutes more per side, and for 2½-inch-thick filets, a total of 3 to 4 more minutes per side. Remember, the temperature will rise about 5° while the steaks rest a few minutes before slicing.

If using the broiler, sear the steaks on both sides, turning them only once. After searing, lower the rack to the middle of the oven and continue broiling until the steaks are as done as you like, using the grill times and temperatures as a guideline. Check frequently, as it usually takes a little less time to broil these steaks than to grill them.

4. While the steaks are cooking, begin frying the onions. Keep them warm as directed (page 167) as you finish each batch.

5. Transfer the steaks to a cutting board and let them rest for 5 to 10 minutes, then cut into thin slices on the diagonal. Serve immediately with the onion rings.

Here's a great home-cooked dish that's special enough for company. Although these short ribs are not on the menu, they are certainly in the Junior's style— home-cooked, delicious, juicy, and so tender the meat is falling off the bone. And the flavor . . . deep, rich, and down-home.

oven-braised short ribs

MAKES 6 HEARTY SERVINGS

FOR THE RIBS

1 tablespoon paprika

1 tablespoon plus 1 teaspoon kosher salt, plus more to taste

2 1/2 teaspoons coarsely ground black pepper, plus more to taste

6 bone-in short ribs (about 6 pounds), about 5 inches long

2 tablespoons unsalted butter

2 tablespoons vegetable oil

1 1/2 pounds carrots, peeled and cut into 1-inch rounds

6 ribs celery, trimmed and cut into 1-inch pieces

2 large red onions, coarsely chopped

6 large cloves garlic, quartered

One 28-ounce can peeled whole tomatoes, with their juice

4 cups beef stock or broth (store-bought or homemade), plus more if needed

1/4 cup dry red wine (optional)

1 cup coarsely chopped fresh curly parsley

Leaves from 10 sprigs fresh thyme, chopped

Leaves from three 4-inch sprigs fresh rosemary, chopped

1 pound small whole onions (24 to 28), peeled (see The Junior's Way)

1. Preheat the oven to 350°F. In a small bowl, mix the paprika, 1 tablespoon of the salt, and 2 teaspoons of the pepper and rub all over the ribs.

2. Heat the butter and oil together in a large Dutch oven over medium-high heat, adding a little more of each, if needed, to cover the bottom of the pot. Brown the ribs on all sides and remove to a plate.

3. Add one-third of the carrots, one-third of the celery, and all of the red onions to the pot, sprinkle with 1 teaspoon salt and 1/2 teaspoon pepper, and cook, stirring a few times, until the onions are translucent, about 5 minutes, adding a little more butter and oil if needed. Stir in the garlic and cook for 3 minutes more, stirring.

4. Return the ribs to the pot and add the tomatoes and their juices, the stock, wine if using, parsley, thyme, and rosemary. Bring to a full boil.

5. Cover the pot and transfer to the oven. Cook for 1 1/2 hours, remove the pot from the oven, and stir in the remaining carrots and celery, along with the peeled white onions. Taste and add more salt and pepper if you like. Return the covered pot to the oven and continue to cook until the vegetables are tender and the ribs are juicy and fork-tender, about 1 1/2 hours more.

FOR THE NOODLES AND GRAVY

12 ounces extra-broad or extra-wide egg noodles

Unsalted butter as needed

Kosher salt and coarsely ground black pepper

Pot juices from roasting the ribs

1/2 cup Wondra flour, or more if needed

3/4 cup cold water

Finely chopped fresh curly parsley, for garnish

6. When the ribs are ready, cook the noodles according to the package directions. Toss with butter and salt and pepper to your liking. Make a bed of noodles on a large serving platter. Arrange the ribs and vegetables on top. Keep warm while you make the gravy.

7. Bring the juices left in the pot to a simmer, adding more stock as needed to make 4 cups. In a small bowl, whisk together the flour and water, then slowly whisk into the stock. Continue to whisk constantly until the gravy thickens, about 4 minutes. Whisk in 2 tablespoons butter until it melts, then season to taste with salt and pepper. Ladle some gravy over the ribs and vegetables and pour the rest into a sauceboat to serve alongside. Sprinkle parsley over all. Refrigerate any leftovers, tightly covered, and enjoy the next day, or freeze for up to 2 weeks.

The Junior's Way

- When buying short ribs for this recipe, choose the bone-in English-cut ones, which are cut parallel to the bone and measure about 5 inches long.

- When using sprigs of fresh thyme and rosemary, it's much faster to throw the sprigs right into the cooking pot, if you like, instead of taking time to pull off the leaves and chop them. When the dish is done, lift the sprigs out with a slotted spoon or a spider.

- Here's a quick tip for peeling small onions: Drop them into a pot of boiling water, turn off the heat, and let stand for 8 to 10 seconds, just until their skins loosen. Quickly, drain in a colander and run cold water over them. Trim off the tips of both ends, leaving just enough to hold the little onions together. Starting at the wider end of each onion, push with your fingers until the onion pops out from its skin. Using the tip of a sharp paring knife, cut a small cross in the wide end of each onion, which helps them cook evenly and prevents them from bursting during roasting.

This roast just shouts, "Company's coming!" The king of roasts, it is guaranteed to impress. When buying the roast, you now have a choice in many markets between moister wet-aged prime beef, which most folks prefer, or the pricier dry-aged, which is the more intensely flavored beef served in steakhouses. Although you won't find prime rib on the menu at Junior's, we wanted to give you this recipe, as it's entertaining at its best!

company prime rib of beef au jus

MAKES 6 SERVINGS

1 standing prime rib of beef roast, with 3 ribs (6 to 7 pounds)

³/₄ cup (1¹/₂ sticks) unsalted butter, softened

1 recipe Junior's Spice (page 146; use as much as you wish)

4 to 5 extra-large white onions

10 to 12 sprigs fresh rosemary (6 inches long)

12 to 15 sprigs fresh thyme (6 inches long)

FOR THE AU JUS

Pan drippings from roast

2 to 4 tablespoons Wondra or all-purpose flour

4 cups beef broth (preferably homemade but store-bought also works)

Kosher salt and freshly ground black pepper

1. An hour before you plan to start roasting, rinse and pat the roast dry with paper towels. Using your hands, smear about ¹/₂ stick of the softened butter all over the roast, leaving a very thin coating (this holds the spice during roasting). Sprinkle generously and evenly with Junior's Spice. Place in a large roasting pan and let stand at room temperature for 1 hour.

2. Peel and halve the onions crosswise and cut each half into 3 wedges. Scatter the onions around the roast and sprinkle them with Junior's Spice. Scatter the herb sprigs on top of the roast and onions. Melt the remaining butter and drizzle over the onions.

3. Meanwhile, preheat the oven to 450°F. Place the roast on the center rack and let it sear at this high temperature for 20 minutes. Lower the oven temperature to 325°F and continue roasting until a meat thermometer inserted in the center away from the bone registers 110°F for rare (it will rise to 120°F upon standing), 120°F for medium-rare (130°F upon standing), and 130°F for medium (140°F upon standing). Transfer to a cutting board and let stand (without covering!) while you make the au jus. Arrange the roasted onions and sprigs of herbs around the edge of a serving platter.

continued

4. In the same pan, heat the drippings over medium heat, scraping up any crusty caramelized bits from the bottom of the pan. Whisk in the flour to make a roux, the amount depending upon how thick you like your gravy (remember, though, you are making slightly thickened au jus, not a thick gravy). Whisk in the broth, increase the heat to high, and boil to reduce the sauce until the flavor intensifies and it's as thick as you like, about 10 minutes. Season to taste with salt and pepper. Pour into a sauceboat. Slice the prime rib, place in the center of the serving platter, and serve hot with the au jus.

The Junior's Way

- Here's a tip to make serving this roast a snap: Ask your butcher to remove the roast from the rib bone and tie it back on for roasting. And for extra moistness, ask him to tie a thin layer of fat around the outside, if you like. The rib bones become the roast's own roasting rack and keep it standing up during cooking, not falling to its side in the pan juices. It also allows the juices from the fat to move down through the meat, flavoring it even more as it cooks. When you're ready to serve, snip off the strings and slice the roast the thickness you wish. The meat will fall away from the bone into perfect slices for serving.

- Use a meat thermometer (the instant-read type is preferred by the chefs) to determine when the roast is done. Insert into the center of the roast. Avoid touching a bone, as this gives a false reading. Bring the roast out of the oven about 10 degrees below your target temperature, as it will continue to cook as it stands, its internal temperature usually rising another 10 degrees.

One never leaves Junior's hungry . . . everything you order seems to come in super-sized helpings. When Alan suggested we make this recipe for 3-inch meatballs, it seemed the perfect idea. These will certainly impress your friends and family! Each person gets three giant meatballs, slathered with homemade marinara and topped with mozzarella and Parmesan. Enjoy supper!

a different meatball marinara

MAKES 6 SERVINGS (18 SUPER-SIZED MEATBALLS)

2 tablespoons olive oil

1 large white onion, chopped (1 cup)

2 teaspoons minced garlic

1½ pounds ground beef chuck (80% to 82% lean)

1 pound ground pork

½ pound ground veal

1 tablespoon kosher salt

2 teaspoons dried Italian herb seasoning

1 teaspoon coarsely ground black pepper

¾ cup freshly grated Parmesan cheese, plus more for serving

½ cup Italian-seasoned dry breadcrumbs

⅓ cup whole milk

½ cup finely chopped fresh flat-leaf parsley

2 extra-large eggs, whisked

1 recipe Marinara Sauce (page 142)

Vegetable oil

1 pound spaghetti

2 cups (8 ounces) shredded mozzarella cheese

1. Heat the olive oil in a medium skillet over medium-high heat. Add the onion and garlic and sauté until translucent but not brown. Transfer to a large bowl and mix with the beef, pork, and veal using either your hands or a wooden spoon.

2. Add the salt, Italian seasoning, pepper, Parmesan, breadcrumbs, milk, and parsley and mix thoroughly. Stir in the eggs just until incorporated (do not overmix, as that could make the meatballs tough). Shape into eighteen 3½-inch meatballs, set on a tray, and refrigerate for about 30 minutes to let them firm up. (When cooked, the meatballs will shrink down a little, to 3 inches.)

3. Meanwhile, make the Marinara Sauce and keep warm.

4. Heat ¾ inch of vegetable oil in a large skillet over medium-high heat until hot but not smoking. In batches, brown the meatballs on all sides, turning frequently; it will take 8 to 10 minutes per batch. As the meatballs finish browning, transfer them to the pot of sauce.

5. Simmer the meatballs in the sauce until cooked through, about 15 minutes, stirring occasionally and carefully (you don't want the meatballs to break apart).

continued

6. Meanwhile, cook the spaghetti according to the package directions. Drain and toss with 1 tablespoon vegetable oil. Divide the pasta among six serving plates. Top each with 3 meatballs. If you like, cut the meatballs into quarters, then ladle over some of the marinara and sprinkle with the mozzarella. Serve immediately with a dish of extra grated Parmesan, if you like.

MEATBALL SUB PARMESAN

This is the perfect way to use up any leftovers. First, reheat the meatballs in the sauce and preheat the broiler on high. Split a 7-inch challah loaf or an 8-inch round Italian hero roll. Place the roll, soft side up, on a broiler-safe pan. On the bottom half of the roll, place two meatballs (or three if you're really hungry!), spoon on about $1/3$ cup of marinara, covering the meatballs, and arrange 3 slices of mozzarella cheese on top. Drizzle some olive oil on the top half of the roll. Broil the open sub until the cheese melts and the top of the roll is slightly toasted, about 5 minutes. Cover the sandwich with the top of the roll set slightly on the diagonal so the meatballs, sauce, and the pointed ends of the cheese slices are peeking out.

The Junior's Way

Be sure to buy all three ground meats for these meatballs in the different amounts specified. Each one contributes in its own way to the flavor, texture, and firmness needed to shape, brown, and cook these large meatballs without them falling apart.

Leave it to Junior's to WOW their customers in every way possible. Like serving a whole individual loaf (not just slices!) to everyone ordering their Baked Meat Loaf. Junior's makes theirs from fresh-ground beef chuck, which means each loaf will have lots of real beef flavor and be extra juicy. Each loaf comes out of the kitchen with plenty of fresh mushroom gravy spooned over the top. Best of all, these loaves are always on the menu at Junior's every day. And these little loaves freeze great!

baked individual meat loaves with mushroom gravy

MAKES 6 MINI MEAT LOAVES

3 pounds ground beef chuck (80% to 82% lean)

1/4 cup (1/2 stick) unsalted butter

2 large white onions, chopped (2 cups)

1 1/2 tablespoons kosher salt

1 1/2 teaspoons coarsely ground black pepper

2 teaspoons dried oregano

1/2 cup Italian-seasoned dry breadcrumbs

2/3 cup ketchup

2 tablespoons Worcestershire sauce

1/2 cup chopped fresh parsley, plus more for garnish

1/2 teaspoon onion powder

3 large cloves garlic, minced, or 1/4 teaspoon garlic powder

3 extra-large eggs

1 recipe Mushroom Gravy (page 140)

1. Preheat the oven to 350°F. Butter 6 mini-loaf pans (5 x 3 x 2 inches). Put the ground beef in a large bowl.

2. Melt the butter in a large skillet over medium heat. Add the onion, salt, pepper, and oregano and cook, stirring a few times, until the onion is translucent but not browned, about 8 minutes. Add to the beef. Add the breadcrumbs, ketchup, Worcestershire, parsley, onion powder, and garlic and mix well with your hands. Whisk the eggs until frothy and mix into the meat mixture.

3. Fill each mini-pan with about 2 cups meat mixture. Or shape into 6 mini-loaves (see The Junior's Way on page 140).

4. Bake until an instant-read thermometer inserted into the center of each one registers 155° to 160°F and the meat is cooked through, 30 to 40 minutes. Let rest in the pans for 10 minutes before removing and serving. Refrigerate any leftover meat loaf and gravy separately, tightly covered, and serve within 2 days. These meat loaves also freeze well; wrap each loaf in plastic wrap, then insert into a zip-top freezer bag, freeze, and use within 3 weeks. Do not freeze the gravy.

continued

5. While the meat loaves bake, make the Mushroom Gravy. Serve each mini-meat loaf with plenty of gravy spooned over the top and a sprinkling of fresh parsley, if you like.

The Junior's Way

If you don't have mini-meat loaf pans, shape them by hand into mini-rectangular loaves measuring 5 inches long, 3 inches wide, and 2 inches high; use one-sixth of the meat loaf mixture (about 2 cups) for each one. Place the loaves in a large shallow roasting pan with 1-inch sides.

½ cup (1 stick) unsalted butter, plus 2 tablespoons for finishing

1 pound white button mushrooms, trimmed and sliced vertically ¼ inch thick

2 large cloves garlic, minced

2 teaspoons kosher salt, plus more to taste

1 teaspoon coarsely ground black pepper, plus more to taste

½ cup all-purpose flour

2 teaspoons paprika

1 quart (4 cups) beef stock or broth (store-bought or homemade)

mushroom gravy

This gravy is perfect for serving with Junior's meat loaves. It just might be the best mushroom gravy you've ever had!

MAKES 1 QUART (4 CUPS) GRAVY

1. Melt ¼ cup (½ stick) of the butter in a large deep skillet or saucepan over medium-high heat until bubbly and sizzling, but not browned.

2. Add the mushrooms, garlic, 1 teaspoon of the salt, and ½ teaspoon of the pepper, and sauté until the mushroom liquid has evaporated and the mushrooms start to brown, about 10 minutes. Using a slotted spoon, transfer the mushrooms to a bowl.

3. In a small bowl, mix the flour, paprika, the remaining 1 teaspoon salt, and remaining ½ teaspoon pepper. Add the remaining ¼ cup (½ stick) of butter to the pan. Reduce the heat to medium and whisk in the flour mixture. Cook for 3 minutes, stirring constantly. Watch carefully and do not burn the roux!

4. Whisk in 1 cup of the stock. After it's incorporated, add the remaining stock and bring to a simmer. When bubbles form around the edge and the gravy reaches a slow boil, reduce the heat to low. Simmer gently for about 20 minutes. You may need a little more stock or a little water to reach the thickness of the gravy you wish. Add the remaining 2 tablespoons butter and whisk until it has melted and is blended throughout. Taste the gravy and add more salt and pepper if you like. Gently stir in the sautéed mushrooms and heat through before serving. The gravy is best served the day you make it. Do not freeze.

One of the most popular Chef's Specialties at Junior's is Chicken Parmigiana, always served with a generous side of Linguine Marinara. We've turned the recipe into the even more special Veal Cutlet Parmigiana, which appeared on Junior's menu in the 1950s, served with Spaghetti à la Junior's, carrots, and peas for $2.00. Try our Chicken Parmigiana variation, too!

veal cutlet parmigiana

MAKES 4 SERVINGS

1 recipe Marinara Sauce
(page 142)

FOR THE DIPPING BATTER

3 extra-large eggs

1 cup whole milk

1$\frac{1}{2}$ cups all-purpose flour

2 tablespoons yellow cornmeal

1 tablespoon baking powder

1 teaspoon table salt

$\frac{1}{2}$ teaspoon ground white pepper

FOR THE CUTLETS

1 recipe Junior's Spice (page 146), use as much or as little as you wish

2 cups unseasoned dry breadcrumbs

1 tablespoon dried oregano

4 thin-sliced veal cutlets (scallopine), pounded to $\frac{1}{8}$ to $\frac{1}{4}$ inch thick (about 4 ounces each)

8 ounces linguine

3 tablespoons unsalted butter, plus more if needed

Twelve 1-ounce slices mozzarella cheese

Freshly grated Parmesan cheese, for sprinkling

Snipped fresh basil, for garnish

1. Make the Marinara Sauce and keep warm.

2. While the sauce simmers, make the dipping batter. In a large bowl, whisk the eggs and milk together until frothy. Add the remaining batter ingredients and whisk until blended and smooth. Let stand for 15 minutes.

3. To prepare the cutlets: Make the Junior's Spice. Spread out the breadcrumbs on a large platter and toss with the oregano. Sprinkle the cutlets on both sides with the spice, 1 teaspoon on each side, or to your liking. Dip the cutlets in the batter, letting any excess drip back into the bowl, then coat completely with the breadcrumbs. Set the cutlets on a tray and refrigerate for 15 minutes to set the coating.

4. Meanwhile, cook the linguine according to the package directions and drain. Toss with some marinara sauce and keep warm.

continued

The Junior's Way

Ask your butcher to pound the veal cutlets to $\frac{1}{8}$ to $\frac{1}{4}$ inch thick. Or pound them yourself by following The Junior's Way tips on page 75.

5. Heat the butter in a large skillet over medium-high heat. Fry the cutlets, one or two at a time, depending upon the size of your skillet, until golden, crispy, and cooked through, about 2 minutes per side.

6. Place the cutlets in a large pan in a single layer or in individual au gratin dishes. Spoon about ¼ cup marinara sauce on top of each cutlet and cover with three slices of mozzarella. Broil until the cheese melts. Sprinkle with the Parmesan and serve with the linguine on the side. Garnish with the fresh basil.

JUNIOR'S CHICKEN PARMIGIANA
Substitute four 6- to 8-ounce boneless skinless chicken breasts, pounded ⅜ inch thick, for the veal. Prepare as directed for Veal Cutlet Parmigiana.

marinara sauce

There are tomato sauces of all kinds, then there's Junior's Marinara Sauce— thick enough to stand up on spaghetti and coat it evenly, with small bites of tomato throughout and the flavor of fresh basil to round it all out.

MAKES 5 CUPS

1. Heat the oil in a large saucepan over medium-high heat. Add the onion and cook until it softens. Add the garlic and sauté until light golden brown, about 2 minutes.

2. Crush the tomatoes with your hands and add to the pot with their juices. Bring to a gentle boil, add the salt, and simmer until the flavors are blended (see The Junior's Way), about 45 minutes. Remove from the heat, stir in the basil, taste, and season with salt and pepper to taste.

The Junior's Way

The secret of the sauce is to slowly simmer it—don't let it boil. Stir occasionally to make sure it doesn't stick in the pot. And watch it carefully; when the oil begins to separate from the sauce, take it off the heat—the sauce is done.

½ cup olive oil
¾ cup chopped white onion
3 cloves garlic, thinly sliced
Two 28-ounce cans whole tomatoes (Italian variety preferred)
1 to 2 teaspoons kosher salt
½ cup snipped fresh basil
Freshly ground black pepper, to taste

Leave it to Junior's to know how to serve the juiciest, tastiest, tenderest baby back ribs ever! First, they season the racks of ribs with a mix they call Junior's Spice. It has only four ingredients, but that's all that's needed: garlic, paprika, kosher salt, and black pepper. Then they bake the ribs long and easy (only a little watching is required!) on a rack set over a pan of water that's been seasoned with Liquid Smoke and cloves of garlic. Now comes the sauce — nothing fancy, just down-home goodness. Before reaching the table, the ribs are sizzled under the broiler or on a grill until the sauce caramelizes and glistens. You'll never fix barbecued ribs any other way again!

bar-b-q baby back ribs

MAKES 5 GENEROUS SERVINGS

Generous splash or two of Liquid Smoke

4 cloves garlic, peeled

1 recipe Junior's Spice (page 146)

2 racks baby back ribs (about 4 pounds total)

1 recipe Junior's BAR-B-Q Sauce (page 24)

1. Preheat the oven to 400°°F and fit a large baking pan with a wire rack. Add ½ inch of water to the pan and season it with a few splashes of Liquid Smoke and the garlic.

2. Mix up the Junior's Spice and rub as much as you wish over both sides of the racks of ribs, making sure the spices stick to the meat. Place both racks of ribs on the rack, bone side down. Cover the pan with aluminum foil, sealing it tightly all around the sides.

3. Bake for about 2 hours, checking occasionally that the water is still at the same level; add more if needed. The ribs are done when they are very tender, but the meat is not falling off the bone. While the ribs cook, make the sauce.

4. During the last hour of cooking, paint the ribs with the sauce a couple of times, using a pastry brush. Be sure to reseal the foil cover tightly each time.

5. When the ribs are fully cooked, paint the ribs, completely and generously, with the sauce. Grill the ribs over medium-hot coals or broil on high 5 or 6 inches from the heat, turning the ribs once, until caramelized and glistening, 3 to 4 minutes per side, brushing with more sauce as they cook.

continued

junior's spice

From baby backs to burgers any time or steak on the grill, Junior's flavors them with this mixture they call Junior's Spice. The amount you use is up to you. Be sure to coat both sides of burgers and steaks evenly. It stores well in an airtight container in your pantry, so double the recipe if you like.

3 tablespoons kosher salt

2 tablespoons paprika

1 tablespoon granulated garlic

1 tablespoon coarsely ground black pepper

MAKES ⅓ CUP

Mix all of the ingredients together and use the amount you like based on how spicy you like your food. Store in a tightly covered glass jar at room temperature and use within 2 weeks.

The Junior's Way

Be sure to cook the ribs through and through in the oven. And watch them closely when they go under the broiler or on the grill—leave them there only just until the sauce caramelizes and browns. Chef Adam Marks at the Junior's flagship in Brooklyn explains: "It takes only a few minutes to finish the ribs off for service, whether you use the grill or the broiler. The ribs are done when there's still a little bite to them and the ribs are nice and tender on the inside and caramelized on the outside. You should be able to pick them up and eat them—without the meat falling off the bone."

Holidays are big days all year long at Junior's, especially in December when the kitchens are overflowing with smoked hams coming out of the ovens and on their way to holiday party buffets. Our recipe uses apple cider for basting, plus a splash of brandy if you like. During the last half-hour of cooking, the ham gets a coating of a sweet and spicy honey glaze, then returns to the oven until it's bubbling and glistening. Bake up the Quick Cheese Biscuits on page 186 to serve with this. For a buffet, cut the biscuits 1¼ inches wide.

honey-glazed ham on the bone

MAKES 14 TO 16 SERVINGS FOR A 14-POUND HAM, 22 TO 24 SERVINGS FOR A 22-POUND HAM

1 fully cooked smoked whole ham on the bone (14 to 22 pounds)

¼ cup whole cloves

3 cups apple cider

⅓ cup Calvados (apple brandy) or cherry brandy (optional)

¼ cup maple syrup

FOR THE HONEY GLAZE

2 cups firmly packed dark brown sugar

3 tablespoons honey

½ cup orange marmalade

2 to 3 tablespoons all-purpose flour

2 tablespoons Dijon mustard

1 teaspoon ground cinnamon

½ teaspoon ground nutmeg

Cider or brandy, as needed

1. Preheat the oven to 325°F. Trim most of the tough skin away from the ham, but not the thin layer of fat underneath. Leave a little of the thick skin on the narrow shank end to protect the bone. Using a small paring knife, score the fat diagonally in a diamond pattern, being careful not to cut into the meat, and stud each diamond in the center with a clove.

2. Line a large roasting pan with aluminum foil and place the ham, fat side up, in the pan (a rack is not needed). Pour 1 cup of the cider and enough water in the pan to come up the side of the ham about 1 inch. Combine the remaining 2 cups cider and the brandy, if using, and pour about a third of this mixture over the ham. Drizzle the maple syrup all over the top.

3. Bake the ham, uncovered, until an instant-read thermometer inserted in the center away from the bone registers 135° to 140°F—not any higher, as the ham can get dry. Figure about 10 minutes of cooking time per pound; this equals a total of 1½ to 1¾ hours for a 10-pound ham, 2 to 2¼ hours for a 14-pound ham, 2½ to 2¾ hours for a 16-pound ham, and 3¼ to 3½ hours for a 20- to 22-pound ham. Check the ham every 30 minutes. Add more water to keep the bottom of the pan covered. Baste the ham with the remainder of the cider mixture frequently. Loosely place a foil tent over any area that is browning too fast.

continued

4. While the ham is baking, mix the honey glaze ingredients together in a medium bowl until smooth. The glaze should be a stiff smear but not so thick that it tears the fat, so add a little more cider (or brandy!) to get the right consistency. About 30 minutes before the ham is done, remove it from the oven and carefully, using a sharp pointed knife, remove the cloves, leaving a few around the shank end for decoration. Using a rubber spatula, gently spread the glaze over the ham.

5. Continue baking the ham at 325°F until the surface is browned, glazed, and glistening, about another 15 minutes (watch it carefully so it does not overcook and overbrown). Transfer the ham to a cutting board and let stand for 15 minutes before slicing.

HONEY-BAKED HALF A HAM

This same recipe can be used to bake a half of ham on the bone, 9 to 12 pounds (see The Junior's Way); just use half the amount of the glaze. Prepare the ham with the cloves and place it, meat side down, in the pan for 45 minutes. Then return the ham on its side for the rest of the baking. The last half-hour, brush the glaze all over the ham, including the meat side. For a 9-pound half ham, roast to 135° to 140°F, about 1½ hours; for a 12-pound half ham, about 2 hours. Makes 9 to 12 servings for a 9-pound ham, 12 to 16 servings for a 12-pound ham.

The Junior's Way

- For this recipe, buy a *fully cooked* smoked ham, on the bone. Baking time is 10 minutes per pound. Whole smoked hams, which weigh 16 pounds or more, are perfect for buffets; plan on about half a pound per person.

- If feeding fewer folks, half a ham is often plenty, as it weighs in around 9 to 12 pounds. It's available in two shapes—the shank and the butt. The shank end is generally the larger, more tapered end. Visually, it looks the most like a ham, is easier to carve, and generally has the most meat. The butt end of the ham is often the smaller, rounder cut, with an irregular shape, and is harder to carve, but some believe it is the most flavorful. Follow our Honey-Baked Half a Ham variation to prepare either cut.

This is about as down-home as it gets! And although Junior's doesn't serve a ham steak, this certainly is "supper in the Junior's Way." A 3-pound steak is plenty to serve six hungry folks. Toss it into a hot cast-iron skillet, sear it on both sides, and finish it off with red-eye gravy; a Southern standby, it's made right in the skillet from the ham drippings and strong black coffee. This is delicious served with Quick Cheese Biscuits (page 186) or buttered grits.

iron skillet ham steak
with red-eye gravy

MAKES 4 TO 6 SERVINGS

One 2½- to 3-pound ham steak, about 1¼ inches thick

¼ cup firmly packed light brown sugar

¼ cup (½ stick) unsalted butter

FOR THE RED-EYE GRAVY

1 cup strong coffee

¼ cup water

1 teaspoon concentrated beef soup base or beef bouillon granules or 1 beef bouillon cube (optional)

¼ cup (½ stick) unsalted butter, softened

1. You need a center-bone ham steak, 1¼ to 1½ inches thick, for this recipe. Ask your butcher to cut it. Most prepackaged ham steaks are too thin for this recipe. Rub the brown sugar all over the steak, including the sides.

2. Preheat a 12-inch cast-iron skillet over medium-high heat until very hot. Drop 2 tablespoons of the butter into the skillet, wait for it to sizzle, then put in the steak. Cook until golden brown around the edges, 2 to 3 minutes. Remove the steak from the pan, add the remaining 2 tablespoons butter, and swirl to coat the bottom. Return the steak to the pan, flipping it over, and cook the other side until it is golden brown and the steak is heated through, another 2 to 3 minutes. Remove the steak to a platter and keep warm. Do not wipe out the skillet.

3. Make the red-eye gravy: In a 2-cup measuring cup, whisk the coffee, water, and soup base (if using) together until the soup base has dissolved. Pour slowly into the skillet while scraping up the browned bits from the bottom of the pan with a wooden spoon. Heat over medium heat until bubbly, then whisk in the butter and cook for a minute or two until the mixture comes together into a gravy. Serve alongside the ham steak. Refrigerate any leftover ham in a zip-top plastic bag and gravy in an airtight container and enjoy the next day. Do not freeze the ham steak or gravy.

"I love cooking for friends," Alan told me one day. "And salmon is one of my favorites. Buy a large fillet the same day you're cooking, drizzle it with a good olive oil, a splash of lemon juice, and seasonings. And let the grill do the rest. Or pop it under the broiler, if it's too cold or too rainy outside, or you don't have a grill. This same combination, with a little fresh garlic added, works great on lobster tails too, as they can grill right alongside the salmon. I often grill the whole dinner . . . shrimp or clams for appetizers, plus grilled vegetables or corn on the cob."

salmon for friends

MAKES 6 TO 8 SERVINGS

1 large skin-on salmon fillet, about 2 inches thick (about 3 pounds)

1/3 cup fresh lemon juice

2 teaspoons paprika

2 teaspoons kosher salt, or to taste

1 teaspoon freshly ground black pepper, or to taste

1 cup good olive oil

Vegetable oil

ACCOMPANIMENTS

Fresh lemon slices (optional)

Fresh dill sprigs (optional)

1 cup (2 sticks) softened unsalted butter mixed with 2 to 3 tablespoons finely chopped fresh chives (optional)

1. Rinse and pat dry the salmon and remove any pin bones (tweezers work great!). Place on a platter, skin side down.

2. In a small bowl, whisk the lemon juice, paprika, salt, and pepper together. Continue whisking while you slowly drizzle in the olive oil. Set aside half of this flavored oil to use after grilling. Brush the other half of the flavored oil all over the salmon, and refrigerate until ready to cook.

3. Fire up a grill or heat the broiler and brush the grilling rack or grate with vegetable oil (important!). Use medium-hot coals or moderately high heat for a gas grill, or high for the broiler. When the coals turn ash white, it's time to put on the salmon. (Tip: The coals are ready when you can hold your hand about 1 inch above the grill grate for 3 seconds.) The rack should be 5 to 6 inches from the heat, no matter whether you're grilling or broiling. Place the salmon, skin side down, on the grilling rack and cover the grill. Or place under the broiler, flesh side up. Grill or broil until the flesh flakes easily with a fork, 10 to 15 minutes, brushing once or twice with the flavored oil.

continued

4. Using a large spatula, transfer the fish from the grill or broiler pan to a large serving board and peel away the skin (this is easy once the salmon is cooked). Wash the basting brush, then use it to quickly brush the salmon with the reserved flavored oil. Let it rest for about 5 minutes, then slice thinly, about ¾ inch thick, with a long, thin sharp knife.

5. Serve the salmon hot, right on the slicing board, garnished with the lemon slices and dill sprigs if you like, plus chive butter alongside. Refrigerate any leftovers, tightly covered, and enjoy the next day. Do not freeze.

LOBSTER TAILS ON THE GRILL

These are a favorite of Alan's to serve at his backyard barbecues in the summer. Buy one lobster tail, 7 to 8 ounces each, per person, if you can find them this size. If your market has only 4-ounce tails, buy two for each guest. If the tails are frozen, thaw them at room temperature (not in a microwave!). Heat up the grill or the broiler as for the salmon. Prepare each lobster tail by turning it so the hard shell side is facing you. Using kitchen shears, cut lengthwise down the center of the shell, exposing the meat but not cutting through it, all the way to the tail fan. Make the flavored olive oil sauce as for the salmon in step 2 on page 151, adding 1 teaspoon minced garlic. Brush it generously over the lobster meat and refrigerate the tails while you fire up the grill or heat up the broiler. Grill or broil the lobster tails, cut side down, over medium-high heat, 5 to 6 inches from the heat source, until the shells turn bright red, about 5 minutes. Turn over the tails and spoon some flavored olive oil over each, then grill until the meat is white and opaque, another 3 to 4 minutes. (If you are cooking the smaller 4-ounce tails, they need only a total of 5 minutes of grilling.) Serve immediately with melted butter, lemon slices, and fresh dill if you like.

Crab cakes are often one of the Daily Specials at Junior's. They're served just the way you like them—chock full of lump crabmeat, with just enough breadcrumbs and mayonnaise added to hold them together. They come to the table set on a glistening pool of Roasted Red Pepper Sauce with a generous spoonful of smoky-good Grilled Corn Salsa alongside.

maryland crab cakes

MAKES 2 SERVINGS, TWO 4-OUNCE CRAB CAKES EACH; RECIPE MAY BE DOUBLED

1 recipe Roasted Red Pepper Sauce (page 155)

1 recipe Grilled Corn Salsa (page 155)

1 pound lump crabmeat (4 cups)

1/3 cup unseasoned dry breadcrumbs

1/4 cup minced fresh parsley

1/2 cup Old Bay Mayo (page 88)

Tabasco, to taste (optional)

3 tablespoons unsalted butter, plus more if needed

1. The day before serving, make the Roasted Red Pepper Sauce and Grilled Corn Salsa. Reheat the pepper sauce before serving.

2. Place the crabmeat in a large bowl and work through it with your fingers, discarding any shells. Gently toss with the breadcrumbs and parsley, then stir in the Old Bay Mayo. Add Tabasco if you like. Shape into four cakes, each about 3½ inches in diameter and 1 inch high. Set on a tray and refrigerate for 30 minutes to firm them up before frying.

3. Melt the butter in a large heavy skillet over medium-high heat. Fry the crab cakes until golden brown and firm, about 3 minutes per side, carefully turning them only once.

4. To serve, spread about ¼ cup Roasted Red Pepper Sauce on each plate and arrange 2 crab cakes on top. Scatter a generous ¼ cup Grilled Corn Salsa alongside.

continued

roasted red pepper sauce

Once you taste this sauce, you'll find other foods it works with, such as roast pork, grilled steaks, pork chops, and baked ham.

MAKES ABOUT 1½ CUPS SAUCE

2 cups drained roasted red peppers, from a can or jar

½ cup chopped white onion

1 cup dry white wine

3 tablespoons red-wine vinegar

2 teaspoons minced garlic

1 tablespoon Wondra or all-purpose flour

¼ cup heavy whipping cream

1. Place all the ingredients, except the flour and cream, in a medium saucepan and bring to a boil over medium heat. Continue to boil until the sauce has reduced about one-third in volume, about 15 minutes. Remove from the heat.

2. Stir the flour into the cream and whisk into the sauce until incorporated.

3. Pour the mixture into a blender and purée until smooth. Best served hot or warm. If you have any leftover, refrigerate in an airtight container and use within a few days.

grilled corn salsa

In addition to enjoying this with Junior's crab cakes, try it with roast turkey, honey-baked ham, or grilled steak.

MAKES 1 QUART (4 CUPS) SALSA

4 ears fresh corn, shucked with silks removed, or one 10-ounce package frozen corn kernels, thawed and drained on paper towels

Garlic oil or olive oil

Kosher salt and freshly ground black pepper

½ cup drained roasted red peppers, from a can or jar, cut into ¼-inch dice

¾ cup finely diced (¼-inch) red onion

½ cup chopped fresh parsley

1 teaspoon lemon pepper seasoning

3 tablespoons fresh lime juice

1. Lightly coat the corn with oil, season to taste with salt and pepper, and cook, turning frequently on a griddle over medium-high heat, until golden brown and tender. Cool, then cut the kernels off the cob. (Alternatively, sauté the thawed frozen corn kernels in a skillet with a splash of garlic oil, salt, and pepper.)

2. Toss the corn kernels with the remaining ingredients. The salsa is best if made the day before serving. Refrigerate in an airtight container for up to 1 week.

Although these shrimp are not on the menu, Junior's is well known for its seafood entrées. This one is fast to fix—and delicious! Buy jumbo shrimp if you can find them. You can save yourself some preparation time if you buy already peeled and deveined shrimp. About half an hour before you're ready to eat, quick-fry the shrimp with the onions and red bell peppers in the curry powder, then toss them with fresh tomatoes and scallions. Serve over hot rice . . . it's a super supper in less than 30 minutes.

curried jumbo shrimp

MAKES 6 SERVINGS

2 pounds jumbo shrimp (21/25 count)

3 cups uncooked white rice

3 tablespoons unsalted butter or vegetable oil, such as peanut or canola

2 tablespoons curry powder

³/₄ teaspoon turmeric

2 large onions, cut in half, then each half cut into ¹/₄-inch-thick half-moons (2 cups)

2 large red bell peppers, seeded and cut into ³/₄-inch dice (1¹/₂ cups)

1¹/₂ tablespoons minced garlic

Kosher salt

¹/₂ cup chicken stock or broth (homemade or store-bought)

1 tablespoon cornstarch

2 large ripe tomatoes, cut into ³/₄-inch dice (1¹/₂ cups)

1¹/₂ cups sliced scallions (white and green parts), cut on the diagonal into 1-inch pieces

¹/₈ to ¹/₄ teaspoon minced seeded fresh hot pepper (such as Scotch bonnet; optional)

1. Buy 2 pounds of fresh or frozen shrimp for this recipe. Look in your fish market or the seafood section in your supermarket for jumbo, 21/25 count, which is 21 to 25 shrimp per pound. The smaller the count number, the larger the shrimp. Tip: 1 pound shrimp in shells equals ¹/₂ pound shelled and deveined. Peel and devein the shrimp if necessary. Cook the rice according to the package directions and keep warm.

2. In a large skillet, melt the butter over medium heat, stir in the curry powder and turmeric, and cook, stirring, for 1 to 2 minutes, until fragrant; be careful not to burn the spices. Add the onions and bell peppers and sauté for about 2 minutes, then add the garlic and 1 teaspoon salt and sauté until crisp-tender, about 1 minute more. Stir in the shrimp and cook for another 2 minutes.

3. Mix the stock and cornstarch together in a cup until dissolved. Stir into the skillet and continue cooking until the shrimp has cooked through and the sauce has thickened slightly, about 2 minutes.

4. Stir in the tomatoes, then the scallions and hot pepper if using, and heat through. Taste the dish and adjust the seasonings if you like. Serve immediately over the hot rice. This dish is at its best when served right after you make it!

Although the stories about who created Lobster Newburg are conflicting, the most popular tale dates back to a wealthy sea captain, Ben Wenberg, who reportedly prepared the dish in 1876 at Delmonico's in New York City. The rest is history: Lobster Newburg became all the rage, especially with the after-theater crowd, as well as the well-to-do vacationing at the resort hotels on Coney Island. Lobster Newburg is fresh chunks of lobster meat cooked in a rich Cognac or sherry cream sauce at table side in a chafing dish. Though it isn't on the menu at Junior's, it is a dish that's reminiscent of what Junior's stands for: The Very Best!

lobster newburg

MAKES 2 MAIN-COURSE OR 4 FIRST-COURSE SERVINGS

1 recipe Toast Points
(page 158)

1 pound cooked lobster meat
(2 cups)

¼ cup (½ stick) unsalted butter

1⅓ cups heavy whipping cream

Kosher salt and ground white
pepper, to taste

⅓ cup Cognac or light dry sherry

Cayenne pepper or Tabasco,
to taste

4 extra-large egg yolks

1. Make the Toast Points. Cover them with aluminum foil and keep warm.

2. Rinse the lobster meat, discarding any bits of shell, and pat dry with paper towels. Melt the butter in a chafing dish or a large skillet over medium-low heat. When the foaming subsides, immediately add the lobster meat and cook for 2 minutes.

3. Stir in 1 cup of the cream, sprinkle lightly with salt and pepper, and heat gently for another 2 minutes. Do not overcook, as the lobster can become tough. Stir in the Cognac and cayenne to taste.

4. Meanwhile, beat the egg yolks with an electric mixer fitted with the wire whisk attachment on high until light yellow and thick; beat in the remaining ⅓ cup cream. Stir a few tablespoons of the hot lobster cream sauce into the yolks to temper them (this will prevent them from curdling when added to the hot sauce). Then, stirring constantly, add the beaten yolks to the lobster mixture, stirring until smooth. Continue to stir until the mixture thickens and reaches 140°F on an instant-read thermometer. Remove from the heat.

continued

5. Taste and add a little more salt, white pepper, or cayenne, if you wish. Immediately serve hot over the toast points, two toast points for a first-course serving, four for a main-course serving. For the main course, spoon the Newburg over two toast points and garnish with the other two. If you wish, double the recipe for the Toast Points and serve extras.

toast points

MAKES 8 TOAST POINTS (RECIPE MAY BE DOUBLED IF YOU WISH TO SERVE EXTRA)

2 slices white bread, preferably from a sandwich loaf

¼ cup (½ stick) unsalted butter, melted

1. Preheat the oven to 350°F.

2. Using a serrated knife, cut off and discard the bread crusts. Brush both sides of the bread with the melted butter, using a pastry brush. Stack up the slices and cut diagonally in half to make 4 triangles, then make another diagonal slice, to yield 8 buttered triangles.

3. Place the bread on a baking sheet in a single layer. Bake until the toast points are golden brown and crispy, about 20 minutes, turning once or twice.

The Junior's Way

Originally, Lobster Newburg began with steaming a live lobster. But today most fish markets sell lobster meat, usually in half-pound containers. This makes the recipe much faster and easier to cook and serve. You need one-half pound of lobster meat per serving for this recipe.

Sides

Macaroni & Cheese is always on the menu at Junior's — creamy, cheesy, and plenty for a light meal. It's found under Side Orders — right along with their French Fried Onion Rings, always oversized, battered, crispy, and oh-so-good. Now you can make them any time with these recipes — and more too. Start with two of Alan's side-specials: Pan-Braised Vidalias, which are bursting with flavor, and Grilled Corn on the Cob, which he often cooks up for company alongside whatever else he's grilling that day. You'll find other sides, too, made in the Junior's style, though not on their menu. There are Homemade Potato Chips, surprisingly fast and foolproof to make our way, and Mashed Candied Sweets whipped up the old-fashioned way and crowned with melted marshmallows. And every morning at Junior's you can dig into some of their Home Fries, which are twice-cooked potatoes made twice-as-good when tossed with onions. We've even stirred some peppers and bites of bacon into our skillet. These sides are so tempting that folks will want seconds!

There's macaroni and cheese—and then there's Junior's Macaroni & Cheese. Junior's has been serving this dish ever since it opened its doors in 1950. And it hasn't changed. It's still the best, creamiest, cheesiest mac and cheese ever.

junior's macaroni & cheese

MAKES 6 SIDE-DISH OR 4 MAIN-COURSE SERVINGS

½ cup (1 stick) unsalted butter, plus more for buttering dish

3 teaspoons kosher salt, plus more to taste

1 teaspoon ground white pepper, plus more to taste

2 cups (8 ounces) uncooked elbow macaroni

½ cup all-purpose flour

1½ cups whole milk, plus 1 to 2 tablespoons more if needed

1 cup heavy whipping cream

2 teaspoons concentrated chicken soup base or granulated chicken bouillon

10 ounces sharp Cheddar cheese, shredded (2½ cups)

4 ounces American cheese, shredded (1 cup)

¼ cup plain dry breadcrumbs (homemade or store-bought)

1. Preheat the oven to 375°F and butter the bottom and sides of a 2-quart deep-dish baker or casserole.

2. Half-fill a pot with water and add 2 teaspoons of the salt and ½ teaspoon of the white pepper. Bring to a boil over high heat, stir in the macaroni, and cook, uncovered, until al dente, 6 to 7 minutes. Transfer to a colander and rinse with cold water to stop the cooking. Drain well and place in a large bowl.

3. Meanwhile, melt the ½ cup of butter in a large heavy saucepan over medium heat. Whisk in the flour until smooth. Cook until the mixture bubbles, about 2 minutes. Gradually whisk in the milk and cream and continue to cook and stir until the sauce thickens. Blend in the remaining 1 teaspoon salt and ½ teaspoon pepper and the chicken soup base.

4. Using a wooden spoon, stir in both cheeses, about a third at a time, and keep stirring, gently, until the cheeses are incorporated and the sauce is smooth. Add a little extra milk if needed to bring the sauce to a consistency that will coat the pasta. Taste the sauce and sprinkle in a little more salt and pepper, if needed. Pour the sauce over the macaroni and gently mix with a rubber spatula until evenly coated. Spoon the macaroni and all of its sauce into the prepared baking dish. Sprinkle lightly with the breadcrumbs.

continued

5. Bake, uncovered, until bubbly, 25 to 30 minutes. Run under the broiler for a minute or two to brown the breadcrumbs. The mac and cheese is best served when bubbly hot or still warm. Refrigerate any leftovers, tightly covered, and serve within 2 days.

The Junior's Way

The secret to the creaminess of Junior's mac and cheese is the combination of Cheddar and American cheeses; be sure to buy both. The Cheddar adds sharp, cheesy flavor and the American cheese brings its superior melting quality to the table. To avoid "mushy" macaroni, cook the macaroni al dente, which means "to the tooth." The pasta is done when there is a slight resistance to the center when you take a bite.

"Chestnut stuffing is not just for the holidays," explained Chef Adam Marks
in Junior's flagship restaurant in Brooklyn. *"We make it here every day and
serve it with our roast turkey dinners. We use the chestnuts that come in jars,
already shelled and ready to use. The other important ingredient is plain
white bread croutons—be sure to buy the unseasoned ones!"* We tried this
stuffing . . . and really liked it. This is one of those versatile dressings that's
not just for turkey. It goes great with pork chops, pork loin roast, and roasted
chicken too.

chestnut stuffing

MAKES 16 CUPS OF STUFFING (RECIPE CAN BE CUT IN HALF), 8 TO 10 SERVINGS

1 cup (2 sticks) unsalted butter

2 cups diced (¼-inch) celery
(about 4 ribs)

2 cups diced (¼-inch) white onion
(about 2 extra-large)

1 tablespoon minced garlic

1½ cups chopped shelled
precooked chestnuts (from a jar)

1 cup dark raisins

½ cup chopped fresh curly parsley,
plus extra for sprinkling

2 tablespoons chopped fresh
thyme leaves

1 teaspoon dried oregano

2 teaspoons kosher salt, or to taste

½ teaspoon coarsely ground black
pepper, or to taste

3 cups turkey or chicken stock or
broth (homemade or store-bought),
plus more if needed

12 cups unseasoned croutons
(store-bought)

1. Preheat the oven to 375°F and generously butter a 9 x 13 x 2-inch
baking dish.

2. Melt the butter in a large skillet over medium-high heat. Add the celery and
onion and sauté until translucent, about 5 minutes. Add the garlic and sauté for
1 to 2 minutes, just until it softens. Add the chestnuts, raisins, herbs, salt, and
pepper and stir to combine. Pour the stock in all at once, deglazing the pan by
scraping up any browned bits from the bottom of the skillet. Add the croutons
(or as many as your skillet will hold) and stir until all the liquid is absorbed.
Do not overmix or try to break up the croutons. Remove from the heat. If all of
the croutons did not fit in your skillet, transfer to a large bowl and toss with the
remaining croutons to coat. Add a little more broth if needed to pull the mixture together into a stuffing.

3. Transfer the stuffing to the prepared baking dish. Tightly cover with aluminum foil and bake for 40 minutes. Remove the foil, drizzle with a little more
stock if needed to keep it moist, sprinkle with extra parsley and bake 15 minutes more, uncovered. Serve hot or at room temperature. Leftovers? Refrigerate,
tightly covered, and serve the next day. Do not freeze this stuffing.

Junior's has been frying onion rings ever since they opened their doors in 1950. They're big and thick, made from oversized Bermuda onions. Onion rings aren't normally something folks think they can make at home. But if you follow the recipe here, you'll get perfect onion rings every time. Plan to make lots, as these disappear fast.

french fried onion rings

MAKES 6 TO 8 SERVINGS

4 extra-large eggs

1¼ cups milk

2 cups all-purpose flour, plus extra for dusting rings

¼ cup yellow cornmeal

2 tablespoons seasoning salt

1 tablespoon baking powder

1 teaspoon ground white pepper

2 pounds extra-large Bermuda or Spanish onions (buy the biggest ones you can find)

Vegetable oil, for frying

1. In a medium bowl, beat the eggs with an electric mixer fitted with the paddle attachment on medium. With the mixer running, beat in the milk. Turn off the mixer, add the 2 cups of flour, the cornmeal, salt, baking powder, and pepper, and beat on medium until smooth. Let the batter rest at room temperature for 15 minutes (it will thicken slightly as it stands).

2. Meanwhile, peel and trim the onions, then cut them horizontally into ½-inch-thick rounds. Separate into rings, being careful not to tear them (important!). Shake the rings, about one-third at a time, in some flour until lightly coated.

3. Place 4 or 5 onion rings in the batter and gently turn them over with your hands three or four times. Lift out the rings, one at a time, letting any excess batter drip back into the bowl, and place on a tray. When they are all coated, refrigerate the onion rings for 15 minutes to set the coating (important!).

4. Heat 1 inch of oil in a large heavy skillet (cast iron is great) over medium-high heat to 365°F (do not let it smoke). One by one, slide several onion rings into the hot oil without crowding them. Fry a few at a time in a single layer, turning each one once, until light golden and crispy, about 4 minutes total. Make sure the rings do not touch during frying, as that causes steaming and prevents them from frying up crisp. Transfer the fried onion rings to a wire rack to drain. Repeat with the remaining rings. To keep the fried rings hot and crispy while you fry the rest, place the rack with the onions on a baking sheet in a 200°F oven. These are best served hot!

Wherever you shop, and whatever the season, it's easy to find a great selection of apples. Buy two different kinds for this sauce. And take a tip from Alan: "Always serve applesauce cold with potato pancakes . . . never hot, warm, or at room temperature." This also goes great with baked ham!

homemade chunky applesauce

MAKES ABOUT 6 CUPS (8 SERVINGS)

4 pounds apples (use
2 varieties, 2 pounds each;
see The Junior's Way)

2 1/3 cups apple cider, plus more
if needed

1 teaspoon ground cinnamon

1 cinnamon stick (3 inches)

1/3 to 1/2 cup granulated sugar,
depending on the tartness of the
apples

1/4 cup firmly packed light brown
sugar

Pinch of kosher salt

1 tablespoon fresh lemon juice, or
to taste

1. Peel and core the apples, cut into ¾-inch cubes, and place in a large saucepan. Stir in the cider, cinnamon, and cinnamon stick. Bring the mixture to a gentle full boil over medium heat, stirring often. Do not cover.

2. Reduce the heat to medium low and simmer until the apples are tender and saucy, about 30 minutes. Check and stir frequently, adding a little more cider if needed to prevent scorching and keep it saucy.

3. Stir in both sugars, the salt, and lemon juice. Remove from the heat and discard the cinnamon stick. If the mixture is not saucy enough, stir vigorously until the right consistency is reached. Serve warm, cold (if serving with potato pancakes), or at room temperature. Store in an airtight container in the refrigerator for up to 1 week. Do not freeze this sauce.

The Junior's Way

Choose apples that are best for cooking, especially types that are sweet, tender, juicy, and cook up well in a sauce. Some great "saucy" apples: Braeburn, Empire, Fuji, Honeycrisp, Red Rome, and McIntosh. Use equal amounts of two kinds. Some cook up faster than others, giving you a sauce that's saucy and chunky in every bite. Add the sugars at the end. If the sugars are added earlier, the apples will hold their shape and not become saucy.

These potatoes go by several names—home fries, skillet fries, American fries—we like home fries best. This potato side is made the Junior's way—with the best ingredients and that good homemade taste. You can order home fries every morning during breakfast time at Junior's. They make them with potatoes and onions . . . we've stirred in some bites of bacon and peppers, too. Be sure to skillet-fry the potatoes until nicely brown—and just the way you like them. Dish them right out of the skillet, the down-home way.

home fries

MAKES 6 SERVINGS

3 pounds smooth-skinned boiling potatoes (see The Junior's Way)

1 tablespoon kosher salt, plus more to taste

1 teaspoon freshly ground black pepper, plus more to taste

4 ounces bacon, cut into ³/₄-inch pieces

1 cup coarsely chopped yellow or white onion (1 large)

³/₄ cup coarsely chopped red bell pepper (1 extra-large)

³/₄ cup coarsely chopped yellow bell pepper (1 extra-large)

¹/₄ cup (¹/₂ stick) unsalted butter, softened, plus a little more if needed for frying

1. Peel and cut the potatoes into ³/₄-inch cubes (you need 6 cups). Half-fill a large saucepan with water, toss in the potatoes, and stir in the salt and pepper. Bring to a boil over medium-high heat, uncovered, reduce the heat to medium, and boil until the potatoes are crisp-tender and resist slightly when you bite into one, 8 to 10 minutes. Remember, they will be cooked again in the skillet, so don't overcook them. Drain in a colander, rinse under cold running water to stop the cooking, and leave them in the colander to drain well.

2. In a large skillet (use an iron skillet if you have one), cook the bacon over medium heat until it begins to brown, but don't let it crisp up. Using a slotted spatula, transfer to paper towels to drain.

3. Discard all but 3 tablespoons of the bacon fat from the skillet. Add the onion and all of the bell peppers and cook, stirring, over medium heat until tender, about 5 minutes. Add the butter to the skillet. When it has melted, gently fold in the potatoes with a large heatproof spatula, then season with salt and pepper to taste. Reduce the heat to medium low. Using the spatula, turn and press the fries down several times, adding more butter if needed, and cook until they are nicely deep golden with browned edges here and there.

4. Serve hot, right from the skillet. If there are fries left over, tightly cover and refrigerate, then serve the next day. To reheat, melt 2 tablespoons butter in a skillet and warm over medium heat until hot, about 10 minutes, tossing them gently a few times. Do not freeze these potatoes.

The Junior's Way

- Since these potatoes are twice-cooked—boiled, then fried—you need ones that will not fall apart in the skillet. Don't reach for the "bakers" (russets), which are high in starch and tend to lose their shape during cooking to fluff up. Instead, reach for the "waxy" boiling potatoes. They are lower in starch than baking potatoes and will keep their shape when cooked. Look for red-skinned potatoes or Yukon Gold or Yellow Finn potatoes.

- Pop the bacon in the freezer for about 10 minutes (no more) so that it's easy to handle. Use kitchen shears, instead of a knife, to cut the bacon easily into ³/₄-inch pieces.

This easy, foolproof way to make your own potato chips is a must-try recipe. The chips turn out golden, crisp, not greasy, and tasting great. The secrets are several: Start with the right potatoes, slice them very thin, and fry them until they stop bubbling in the pan. This means that most of the water has cooked out and the chips will stay crunchy for a few days, if they last that long!

homemade potato chips

MAKES ABOUT 1 QUART CHIPS (ABOUT 4 SERVINGS); YOU CAN DOUBLE THE RECIPE

2 pounds russet potatoes (see The Junior's Way); do not peel

A good oil for frying (see The Junior's Way)

Kosher or sea salt

1. Cut the potatoes into very thin slices (see The Junior's Way). As you slice, drop them into a large bowl of ice water. When you've finished cutting them all, swish the slices around with your hands, then lay them out on a triple layer of paper towels. Pat them dry.

2. While the potatoes are drying, heat ⅜ to ½ inch of oil in a large heavy skillet (use a cast iron one if you have it) over medium-high heat to between 360° and 365°F.

3. Working in batches of about 10 chips at a time, depending upon the size of your skillet, fry the chips just a minute or two, flipping each one over only once with a spider or large slotted spatula. When the bubbling calms down and the chips are a light golden brown, take them out. If there is still a lot of bubbling, leave them in a few seconds more so the excess water bubbles out. This ensures the chips will be (and stay!) crisp. Remember to let the temperature of the oil come back to 360° before adding the next batch of potatoes. Add a little oil, if necessary, to keep the level of oil at least ⅜ inch high.

4. Transfer the chips from the skillet to a wire rack to drain (see The Junior's Way) while you fry the rest. While the chips are still hot, sprinkle them with salt to your liking. If some chips are not eaten (hard to imagine!), store at room temperature in an airtight container and enjoy the next day.

The Junior's Way

- Pick the perfect potatoes for frying: russets, also called Idahoes, relating to where many are grown.

- Slice the potatoes thin, very thin! Use an ultra-thin (1 mm) or thin (2 mm) slicing disk on your food processor or the slicing side of a hand-held grater. If you're lucky enough to own a mandoline, that's the tool many chefs use. Don't worry if the slices don't come out the same length or shape—they look more homemade that way.

- Don't skip soaking the potatoes in ice water (step 1). Some of the starch soaks out in this step, leaving a potato that fries up crisp, not greasy.

- Use an oil with a high smoking point, which is the temperature at which the oil starts to break down. Try canola, peanut, or safflower oil. And keep the temperature of the oil between 360° and 365°F.

- Slide the chips into the hot oil one by one, so they don't clump together. But do this fast, so the chips will be done at the same time. Fry in small batches so each chip has its own "frying space."

- Watch the bubbles! When the chips first go into the hot oil, the oil will bubble furiously because of the water in the potatoes. When you see very few bubbles left and the chips are turning golden brown, remove them quickly with a slotted spatula or spider. They will continue to brown a little more, as there is still a little oil on the surface that continues to cook and brown the potatoes a little further as they cool. So don't let them cook too long.

- Cool the chips on a wire rack, not on paper towels. They'll stay crispier that way.

Here's a dish to add to your entertaining recipe book. It's an invaluable do-ahead, and tastes like a double helping of pumpkin pie and yummy sweet potatoes in one. The day before your party, peel, cook, mash, and season the potatoes. Swirl them into a pretty baking dish and chill overnight. Bring back to room temperature the next day before popping the dish into the oven. It's a perfect addition to any party menu. Remember to make this for Thanksgiving!

mashed candied sweets

MAKES ABOUT 8 SERVINGS

1/2 cup (1 stick) unsalted butter, melted, plus more for the dish

1 tablespoon kosher salt

1 tablespoon granulated sugar

1/2 teaspoon ground white pepper

3 1/2 pounds yams or bright orange sweet potatoes (see The Junior's Way on page 176)

1 cup firmly packed light brown sugar

1/4 cup maple syrup, plus extra for drizzling

1 tablespoon grated orange rind

1/4 cup fresh orange juice

1 teaspoon ground cinnamon

2 extra-large eggs

One 12-ounce package large marshmallows or one 10 1/2-ounce package miniature marshmallows

Pecan halves, for decoration (optional)

1. Preheat the oven to 350°F. Generously butter a 2-quart baking dish.

2. Half-fill a stock pot with water, add the salt, granulated sugar, and pepper, and bring to a boil over medium-high heat. Meanwhile, peel the potatoes, cut into large chunks, add to the boiling water, and cook until tender but not falling apart, 20 to 25 minutes. Transfer to a colander, hold it under cold running water to stop the potatoes cooking, and then let them drain for a few minutes.

3. Place the potatoes in a large bowl and, using an electric mixer fitted with the paddle attachment, beat on medium speed until light, smooth, and airy. With the mixer running, blend in the brown sugar, butter, maple syrup, orange rind and juice, and cinnamon. Add the eggs, one at a time, and beat until incorporated and smooth. Transfer the sweet potatoes to the prepared baking dish and even out the top with a rubber spatula. If you are making this dish ahead to serve the next day, cover with plastic wrap and refrigerate. Bring back to room temperature the next day before baking.

4. If using large marshmallows, cut as many of them into quarters as you need to cover the top of the potatoes (you'll need about half the bag). Place them, powdered side up, in rings, starting from the outside rim and working toward

continued

the center. (You'll also need about half the bag if using miniatures.) Scatter pecan halves over the marshmallows, if you wish. Drizzle the top with a little maple syrup. Bake until the marshmallows are melted and the potatoes are bubbly and piping hot all the way through, 35 to 45 minutes. Run under the broiler for 1 to 2 minutes to lightly brown the marshmallows. Decorate with a few more pecans if you wish. Serve immediately. Refrigerate any leftovers, tightly covered, and enjoy the next day. Do not freeze.

The Junior's Way

When is a sweet potato a potato—and when is it a yam? They are two different vegetables—and not even related. Sweet potatoes are grown throughout the South and come in two "classes." The pale light yellow ones are thin-skinned, with a dry, white flesh. The reddish, bright orange sweet potatoes are thick-skinned, bright orange and moist on the inside, and mash up great. Yams are easy to spot, as their skins are dark brown—even black—rough, and look a little like the bark on a tree. Inside, they can be off-white, deep red, or even purple. But whatever their color, they have more natural sugar than sweet potatoes and are moister, and thus are the best choice for this recipe, if you can find them in your market.

"I grill a lot of corn on the cob, and my friends love it," states Alan. His way is simple, easy, and great. First he buys the freshest corn he can find—bright green husks with moist kernels. He peels off the husks, smears the ears with softened butter, and wraps each ear individually in foil. He places the corn on his grill, right alongside whatever is being grilled that day. We tried his method, stirring in a variation of the spices used in Junior's Spice mix, this time using fresh garlic—and liked it a lot. If you don't own a grill, or it's not good grilling weather, use this recipe and broil the foil-wrapped ears in the oven.

grilled corn on the cob

MAKES 6 SERVINGS

6 ears corn on the cob

1 cup (2 sticks) unsalted butter, softened, plus more for serving

1 tablespoon kosher salt

1 tablespoon minced garlic (optional)

1 teaspoon paprika (optional)

1 teaspoon freshly ground black pepper (optional)

1. Heat up an outside grill or the broiler: Use medium-hot coals or moderately high heat for a gas grill or high for the broiler. The rack should be about 5 to 6 inches from the heat. If broiling, line a shallow pan with foil.

2. Remove and discard the husks and silks from the corn and rinse under cold running water, leaving some droplets of water on the ears.

3. Place the butter in a small bowl and beat with a wooden spoon until creamy. Smear on the butter as Alan does. If you wish to season the butter, first blend in the salt, garlic, paprika, and pepper. Taste the butter and add more seasoning if you wish. Place each ear of corn diagonally in the center of a 16- to 18-inch square of foil. Roll and crimp the foil around the corn, twisting the ends tightly.

4. Grill or broil the ears, turning occasionally, until the corn is tender and golden, 25 to 30 minutes. Unwrap the corn (be careful of the escaping steam) and serve steaming hot with additional butter.

It's easy (and delicious!) to eat your spinach this way, creamed and flavored with sautéed onions and a hint of nutmeg. To turn this into an easy brunch or light supper dish, top it with a poached egg (see A Different Benedict on page 94 for directions). Although you will not find creamed spinach at Junior's, you will find plenty of perfectly cooked vegetables, all very important for a balanced healthy diet.

creamed spinach

MAKES 4 SERVINGS

1½ pounds fresh baby spinach leaves or 2 pounds fresh spinach leaves

1 teaspoon kosher salt, plus more to taste

¼ cup (½ stick) unsalted butter

1 cup finely chopped onion

2 teaspoons minced garlic, or to taste

3 tablespoons all-purpose flour

2 cups heavy whipping cream, or more if you wish

¼ teaspoon ground nutmeg, or to taste

Cracked black pepper, to taste

1. Wash the spinach well, being sure to remove any sand that might be clinging to the leaves. If using baby spinach, it's not necessary to trim off the stems, as they are very tender. If using regular spinach, trim away the tough stems.

2. Bring 2 inches of water to a boil in a large stockpot over medium heat; add the 1 teaspoon of salt and the spinach. Cover the pan, reduce the heat to low, and let the spinach steam for 5 minutes, until it has wilted and is tender. Drain in a colander, pressing out as much water as possible. Chop finely and keep warm.

3. Meanwhile, melt the butter in a large skillet over medium-high heat. Sauté the onions and garlic until soft, about 2 minutes. Whisk in the flour and cook until the roux bubbles around the edges, about 3 minutes. Whisk in the cream slowly until all is incorporated and the sauce is smooth and thickened. Fold in the well-drained chopped spinach and cook until hot throughout. Stir in the nutmeg to taste and as much salt and pepper as you wish. If you like your spinach extra creamy, blend in a little more cream, 1 tablespoon at a time, until it's as creamy as you like. Serve hot in au gratin dishes.

"When I'm entertaining friends at home," Alan told me, "I often put roasted vegetables on the menu. I use broccoli, cauliflower, and Brussels sprouts, or whichever root vegetables look good in the market. My wife likes to add red and yellow beets for color and flavor, as in this recipe. We often prepare the vegetables the day before, then roast them right before guests are coming." The best part—these vegetables take very little watching during roasting. Let them roast for 15 minutes, then sprinkle with the garlic and walk away until it's time to see if they are done.

roasted vegetables

MAKES 6 TO 8 SERVINGS

1 large bunch broccoli (1 pound)

8 ounces Brussels sprouts

One 1-pound head cauliflower

4 large red beets or 10 miniatures

4 large yellow beets or 10 miniatures

1 extra-large white onion, peeled and ends trimmed

Extra-virgin olive oil

1 tablespoon sea salt, or to taste

1 teaspoon cracked black pepper, or to taste

1 tablespoon minced garlic, or to taste

1. Preheat the oven to 425°F and oil a large shallow roasting pan. Separate and trim the broccoli into bite-sized florets, leaving 1-inch tender stems; you need 4 cups. Trim the stems of the Brussels sprouts and cut each vertically in half; you need 2 cups. Separate the cauliflower into bite-sized florets; you need 2 cups.

2. Peel the beets, trimming away the stems and roots. Cut large beets horizontally into slices ¼ inch thick. If using miniature beets, cut them vertically in half, end to end. Cut the onion horizontally in half, then cut each half into 6 wedges.

3. To coat: Place the beets in one plastic bag and the rest of the vegetables in a second bag. Drizzle with oil and shake gently to coat. Scatter the vegetables in a single layer in the roasting pan. Sprinkle with the salt and pepper. Roast for 15 minutes, sprinkle with the garlic, drizzle with a little more oil, and continue roasting until the vegetables are crispy and tender, about another 20 minutes. Do not stir the vegetables as they roast, as the juices from the red beets can discolor the other veggies. Serve piping hot.

"If you've never pan-braised Vidalias, you must try my way," stated Alan one day. "When I entertain and I'm grilling steaks, I often make a big skillet-full to serve on the side—and never have any left. Cut the onions into slices about ¼ inch thick . . . they'll fall apart into rings during cooking." I had braised these sweet Georgia onions many times, but not like Alan does. The brown sugar and the long caramelizing turn this dish into one of The Best!

alan's pan-braised vidalias

MAKES ABOUT 6 SERVINGS

3 pounds extra-large Vidalia onions

½ cup (1 stick) unsalted butter

¾ cup firmly packed dark brown sugar

2 teaspoons kosher salt, plus more to taste

1 teaspoon ground white pepper, plus more to taste

1 cup beef broth or stock (store-bought or homemade), or more if needed

1. Peel the onions and cut off the tops and bottoms. Cut crosswise into slices ¼ inch thick. You need 6 cups.

2. Melt the butter in a large skillet (use a cast iron one if you have it) over medium heat. Add the onions and sprinkle with the brown sugar, salt, and pepper. Cook, stirring occasionally, until the onions turn deep golden brown in color, about 15 minutes.

3. Drizzle the broth over, reduce the heat to low, taste, and add more salt and pepper if you like. Cover and simmer until the broth has been absorbed and the onions have fallen apart into rings, about 30 minutes. Serve hot!

The Junior's Way

Vidalia onions, golden beauties with a mild, sweet taste, are grown in Toombs County in Georgia. Their season is from late April through mid-November but thanks to advanced storage technology, they are often found on the market through December. Pick firm ones with a light golden brown exterior, round on the bottom, and slightly flat on the top. When you cut them open, they will have a white, almost milky, interior. Store them in a cool, dry spot. Handle Vidalias with care, as they bruise easily!

"You must have our special today," announced Alan. *"Fried green pickles."* In minutes they arrived, alongside one of Junior's pulled pork sandwiches. And what a treat! These pickles have a crunchy coating similar to that of their fried chicken, with a bit of Cajun spice and the snappy "bite" of a homemade fresh pickle, even though it had just come out of the fryer. Serve them hot with Junior's Bar-B-Q Sliders (page 22), ribs, or burgers.

fried green pickles

MAKES 18 TO 24 FRIED GREEN PICKLE STICKS

FOR THE BATTER

1½ cups whole milk

5 extra-large eggs

2 cups all-purpose flour

1 tablespoon kosher salt

1 tablespoon baking powder

1 teaspoon ground white pepper

FOR THE BREADING

2 cups all-purpose flour

2 tablespoons yellow cornmeal

1 tablespoon Old Bay seasoning

1 tablespoon paprika

2 teaspoons kosher salt

1 teaspoon Cajun seasoning, or to taste

6 to 8 large deli dill pickles

Canola or other vegetable oil (but not olive oil)

1. In a large bowl, whisk all the batter ingredients together. Let stand for 15 minutes. Meanwhile, mix the breading ingredients together in a shallow baking dish.

2. To ensure the coating stays on the pickles during frying, dry them well on paper towels. Slice the pickles vertically into thirds, from end to end, about ½ inch thick, or across into 1-inch-thick rounds, whichever you prefer.

3. Working in small batches, dredge the pickles in the breading, shaking off any excess. Then dip them into the batter, turning each one to coat it well. Let any excess batter drip off, then roll the pickles in the breading again. Place on a plate and refrigerate for 15 minutes, until the coating is set (important!).

4. Meanwhile, preheat the oven to 200°F. Line a large shallow pan with paper towels and set a wire rack on top.

5. Heat at least 1 inch of oil in a large frying pan (an iron skillet is great if you have one) over medium heat until hot (360° to 365°F), but not smoking. Gently slide the pickles into the hot oil. It's best to cook only 4 or 5 spears (or about 8 round slices) at a time, depending upon the size of your skillet. Fry until crispy and golden brown, 1 to 2 minutes per side, turning each pickle only once. Using a slotted spatula or spider, transfer the pickles to the rack and keep warm in the oven while frying the rest. Serve hot. Enjoy all when first made; do not store for another day.

The Bread Basket

Sit down to order a meal at Junior's and soon you'll be presented with your very own bread basket, brimming with freshly baked breads. Depending upon what's baking in the bakery that day, the selection can vary, but there are always generous squares of freshly made cornbread and melt-in-your-mouth house-baked rolls. Plus plenty of homemade biscuits . . . over 52,000 come out of Junior's bakery ovens in Brooklyn each year.

Turn the pages of this chapter and find your favorites . . . some are served at Junior's daily, others were created in Junior's delicious homemade style just for this book. You'll find special blueberry muffins with a cheesecake surprise inside, raisin-bran muffins, puffy popovers, and easy cheese biscuits. We've also included Junior's famous Club Rye Onion Loaf and Braided Challah for those days when you have a little extra time to let the dough rise. Whichever you choose, it's guaranteed to be *The Best* bread you've ever baked!

These biscuits are made with heavy cream, sharp Cheddar, and a touch of cayenne. No rolling or cutting is needed . . . just quickly roll them into balls, place them on the baking sheets, and shower them with a little more cheese. Each biscuit takes on its own unique shape as it bakes.

quick cheese biscuits

3/4 cup (1½ sticks) cold unsalted butter, cut into ½-inch cubes, plus extra butter for greasing baking sheets

3 cups all-purpose flour, plus more for flouring your hands

1 cup (4 ounces) finely grated aged sharp Cheddar cheese

2 tablespoons baking powder

1 teaspoon table salt

⅛ teaspoon cayenne pepper, or to taste

¼ cup cold vegetable shortening

3/4 cup heavy whipping cream, plus more as needed

FOR THE TOPPING

1 extra-large egg, slightly beaten

1 teaspoon vegetable oil

About ½ cup (2 ounces) finely grated aged sharp Cheddar cheese

Paprika

MAKES ABOUT TWENTY-FOUR 2-INCH BISCUITS

1. Butter two baking sheets.

2. In a large bowl, combine the flour, cheese, baking powder, salt, and cayenne. Using an electric mixer, mix on low for a few seconds to blend. Add the 3/4 cup butter and the shortening and mix on low until broken down into small pieces the size of peas. Add the cream all at once and continue mixing until a soft dough forms, adding a little more cream, 1 tablespoon at a time, if needed to make a slightly sticky dough.

3. Flour your hands. Using a heaping tablespoonful for each biscuit, roll the dough into 2-inch balls and set on the baking sheets about 1 inch apart. Whisk the egg with the oil and brush on the top of the biscuits. Sprinkle each biscuit with a little cheese and dust with paprika. Let the biscuits rest on the baking sheets for 10 minutes at room temperature.

4. While the biscuits rest, preheat the oven to 400°F. Bake the biscuits just until puffy and golden, about 15 minutes (watch closely and do not let them get too brown!). Serve piping hot with butter and honey. If any are left over, refrigerate and serve the next day. Place in a foil packet and rewarm at 300°F for 10 to 15 minutes to bring them back to room temperature. The baked biscuits also freeze well; use within 2 weeks and defrost at room temperature.

Nothing says "homemade" like freshly baked bread. And these rolls are probably The Best *that will ever come out of your oven! Even if you have never made rolls before, you can mix these up with confidence, knowing they will rise up high and taste heavenly! Shape them into large dinner rolls or small tea rolls and serve hot and plain or with honey or preserves. The tea rolls make perfect mini-sandwiches too.*

junior's pull-aparts

MAKES 20 DINNER ROLLS OR 56 TEA ROLLS

1½ cups whole milk

⅓ cup warm water (105° to 115°F)

Two ¼-ounce packages active dry yeast

⅓ cup plus 1 teaspoon sugar

¾ cup (1½ sticks) unsalted butter, melted, plus extra for brushing rolls

1 tablespoon table salt

2 extra-large eggs plus 1 extra-large egg yolk

6½ to 6¾ cups all-purpose flour, plus extra for flouring

Softened unsalted butter (not melted) for coating bowl and pans

1. Heat the milk in a medium saucepan over medium heat just until bubbles form around the edge; remove from the heat before it comes to a full boil. Transfer to a large bowl of a stand mixer fitted with the paddle attachment and let cool to between 105° to 115°F.

2. Meanwhile, place the warm water in a small bowl. Check the temperature; it should be no cooler than 105°F and no hotter than 115°F. Sprinkle over the yeast and 1 teaspoon sugar; stir until dissolved, then let stand until foamy.

3. Beat the yeast mixture into the cooled milk (see Step 1). Add the melted butter, the remaining ⅓ cup sugar, the salt, and eggs and mix on medium until light.

4. Decrease the speed to low and blend in 6½ cups of the flour in three additions. Stop the mixer and change to a dough hook if you have one. Increase the speed to medium and "knead" the dough for about 8 minutes, adding more flour, 1 tablespoon at a time, if needed to make a smooth dough. Turn out onto a lightly floured work surface and knead just until it comes together into a ball of dough.

5. Coat a large bowl with softened butter. Transfer the dough to the bowl and turn it over once to butter it well, then cover with plastic wrap. Let it rise at room temperature until doubled in size, about 45 minutes.

continued

6. Meanwhile, preheat the oven to 375°F. Set out two 9-inch round baking dishes or pans, about 2 inches high, and generously smear with softened butter. Line the bottoms with parchment and butter well. Turn the dough out onto a lightly floured surface and knead until it is no longer sticky, about 2 minutes.

7. Cut the dough in half. *For Junior's-sized dinner rolls,* divide each half into 10 even pieces. Flour your hands and gently shape the pieces into balls, then place the balls in the prepared pans. Repeat with the remaining dough. (You will have 20 dinner rolls in total.) *For tea rolls,* pinch twenty-eight 1-inch pieces off each dough half and shape into balls. Repeat with the remaining dough. (You will have 56 tea rolls in total.) Place the balls in the pans. Brush the rolls with melted butter and let rise, uncovered, until light and doubled in size, about 30 minutes. Brush with butter again.

8. Bake the rolls until light golden and set, 25 to 30 minutes, brushing with butter the last 10 minutes. Remove from the oven, brush with more melted butter, and let cool in their pans on a wire rack for about 15 minutes. Turn out onto the rack, remove the parchment, and transfer, top side up, to a basket or serving plate. The rolls are best served immediately or when still warm. Baked rolls can be frozen (see The Junior's Way).

The Junior's Way

- When shaping the kneaded dough into balls, use as little flour as possible. Adding flour at this stage can make the rolls tough.

- You can freeze the baked rolls and reheat them to just-baked deliciousness, a real plus for entertaining. Bake the rolls and remove from their pans as directed. Thoroughly cool the rolls, then wrap in foil and freeze; they will keep for up to 1 month. On serving day, open the foil packets and let the rolls stand in their packets at room temperature until defrosted. Brush the rolls generously with melted butter and close the foil packets. Reheat in a preheated 300°F oven for 10 to 15 minutes, or until the rolls are as hot as you like them.

Pull out a pan of these popovers from the oven, right before you're ready to serve dinner…then watch them disappear! They puff up into high, airy golden domes with crispy brown sides, filled with custardy-light goodness inside. Simply melt-in-your-mouth delicious! Even though Junior's doesn't have popovers on their menu, they do specialize in impressing their guests. And these are guaranteed to "Wow"—for they are The Best!

popovers

MAKES 12 POPOVERS

Softened unsalted butter, for the pan

2 cups all-purpose flour

1 tablespoon sugar

1 teaspoon table salt

1/4 teaspoon ground white pepper

6 extra-large eggs

2 cups whole milk

6 tablespoons (3/4 stick) unsalted butter, melted

1. To make the puffiest, moistest popovers ever, start with the perfect popover pan—one with deep tapered cups that stand apart, allowing heat to surround the popovers as they bake. Buy the heaviest-gauge pan you can find, preferably carbon steel. The heavier the metal, the faster the liquid in the batter is turned into steam and the higher the popovers puff.

2. Preheat the oven to 450°F. Butter 12 popover cups. Place in the oven to heat, just until piping hot, but not long enough to burn the butter.

3. In a medium bowl, mix the flour, sugar, salt, and pepper together. In a large bowl, using an electric mixer, beat the eggs on high until thick and lemon colored, about 3 minutes. Beat in the milk. Reduce the speed to low and blend in the flour mixture in one addition, beating just until it disappears. Quickly mix in the melted butter.

4. Spoon the batter into the hot popover cups, filling them three-fourths full (no more!). Bake for 20 minutes, then reduce the oven temperature to 350°F and bake for 10 minutes longer, until golden brown and set (no peeking until the end, please).

5. Remove the popover pan to a wire rack and immediately make a small slit in the side of each popover with a small pointed knife to let the steam escape. Turn off the heat and return the popovers to the warm oven, letting them rest for 10 minutes with the door closed. Serve immediately!

Though these little fried cornbread cakes are not served at Junior's, cornbread is a popular daily offering. They are great with Southern Fried Chicken (page 118) or fried shrimp or fish.

hush puppies

MAKES 36 HUSH PUPPIES

2 cups yellow cornmeal

1 cup all-purpose flour

2 tablespoons sugar

1 teaspoon baking powder

2 teaspoons table salt

½ cup finely chopped onion

1 cup fresh or frozen (thawed and drained) corn kernels

1½ cups whole milk

1 extra-large egg

Oil, for frying (peanut, canola, or a vegetable oil blend)

1. In a large bowl, mix the cornmeal, flour, sugar, baking powder, and salt together. Stir in the onion and corn. Make a well in the center. In a small bowl, whisk the milk and egg together and pour into the well, stirring until blended.

2. Heat 3 inches of oil to 350°F in a deep, heavy Dutch oven. Carefully drop the batter, a heaping tablespoon at a time, into the hot oil. Dip the spoon in a glass of warm water before dropping the next hush puppy, so the batter will slide off the spoon easily. Be sure to check that the temperature of the oil stays at 350°F during frying (no hotter!). To ensure the hush puppies cook and brown evenly, make sure they don't touch each other during frying and don't fry too many at one time. Fry until golden brown, about 3 minutes total, turning the hush puppies as they cook.

3. Using tongs, remove the hush puppies from the oil and drain on a wire rack set over paper towels. Hush puppies are best served hot. Refrigerate any leftovers and serve the next day. To rewarm, place them, uncovered, on a baking sheet in a 300°F oven until hot, 10 to 15 minutes, turning them once.

The Junior's Way

While frying, watch the temperature of the oil closely. If it rises above 350°F, turn down the heat and add a little more oil. Wait a few minutes before adding more spoonsful of batter. If any bits of batter break off, use a slotted spoon or mesh spider tool to remove them from the hot oil so they don't end up burning and give an off-flavor to the remaining batches.

If you have been lucky enough to eat cornbread at Junior's, you already know it's something special. First, it comes out in large squares, at least 2 inches high, warm, and freshly baked. That first bite is bursting with old-fashioned goodness—real corn flavor with a hint of sweetness, so tender that you'll almost think it's cake. In our recipe, we've added corn kernels to give it even more corn flavor. We bake it in a deep skillet; use a cast-iron one if you have it. And for an even more authentic touch, you can "butter" the skillet with bacon grease. Be sure to heat the buttered skillet in the oven before pouring in the batter; this step gives your cornbread a nice crispy, golden brown bottom. If you own a corn-stick pan, use this same batter to make corn sticks.

skillet cornbread

MAKES ONE 12-INCH SKILLET BREAD, ABOUT 2 INCHES HIGH

¾ cup (1½ sticks) unsalted butter, melted, plus more for the pan

2½ cups all-purpose flour

1 cup yellow cornmeal

1½ cups sugar

2½ tablespoons baking powder

1 tablespoon table salt

5 extra-large eggs

2 cups whole milk

⅓ cup water

¼ cup shortening, melted, or vegetable oil

1 tablespoon pure vanilla extract

1 cup fresh or frozen (thawed and drained) corn kernels

1. Preheat the oven to 400°F. Generously butter a 12-inch skillet (use a cast-iron one if you have it) and place in the oven until hot but not smoking. Meanwhile, mix the flour, cornmeal, sugar, baking powder, and salt together in a large bowl.

2. In another large bowl, using an electric mixer, beat the eggs on high until light yellow and frothy, about 3 minutes. Blend in the milk, the ¾ cup of melted butter, the water, melted shortening, and vanilla.

3. Add the flour mixture all at once and mix on low just until the flour disappears, scraping down the bowl once or twice. Do not overmix. Gently stir in the corn kernels until they are well dispersed.

4. Pour the batter into the hot skillet. The batter will come almost to the top and will sizzle when it hits the skillet. This gives the bread a crusty bottom. Bake until the bread is golden brown and a toothpick inserted in the center comes out with moist crumbs (not dry), 55 to 60 minutes. Cut into wedges and serve right from the skillet. Refrigerate any leftovers wrapped in foil and serve

continued

the next day. To rewarm, place the foil packet in a 300°F oven for 10 to 15 minutes. This cornbread freezes great. Wrap in foil and freeze for up to 2 weeks. Defrost at room temperature, then reheat in the foil packet the same way.

CORN STICKS

Generously butter the wells of your corn-stick pan (important!). Fill the wells three-fourths full with the cornbread batter. You will have enough batter to make 18 to 20 sticks, so plan to bake several batches. Or use the extra batter for muffins (see the variation below). Bake at 400°F until set, puffed, and golden, about 20 minutes. Let cool in the pan for 5 to 10 minutes before removing. Great when served piping hot or at room temperature. Makes 18 to 20 corn sticks.

CORN MUFFINS

Line eighteen 2¾-inch muffin cups with cupcake liners (silicone, foil, parchment, or paper) or generously butter. Fill the cups almost to the top with the cornbread batter. Bake at 400°F until golden brown and a toothpick inserted in the center comes out with moist crumbs, about 20 minutes (do not overbake!). Makes 18 muffins.

Any day at Junior's you can order a slice of banana loaf cake—to enjoy right then or wrapped to go. One bite tells all: moist, just sweet enough, full of banana goodness, and melt-in-your mouth delicious. We've made it even better by adding cream cheese (naturally!). This recipe makes two large loaves. Serve one right away, warm! Give the second loaf to a friend or freeze to serve another day.

banana walnut loaf with brown sugar topping

MAKES TWO 9 X 5 X 3-INCH LOAVES

1 cup (2 sticks) unsalted butter, at room temperature, plus more for the pans

3 cups all-purpose flour

$1\frac{1}{2}$ tablespoons baking powder

$1\frac{1}{2}$ teaspoons table salt

1 teaspoon baking soda

$1\frac{1}{2}$ teaspoons ground cinnamon

6 very ripe large bananas

1 teaspoon fresh lemon juice

One 8-ounce package PHILADELPHIA cream cheese (use only full fat), at room temperature, plus extra for spreading on baked loaves, if you wish

2 cups granulated sugar

4 extra-large eggs

$\frac{3}{4}$ cup heavy whipping cream

1 tablespoon pure vanilla extract

$1\frac{1}{2}$ cups coarsely chopped walnuts

FOR THE TOPPING

1 cup firmly packed light brown sugar

1 cup coarsely chopped walnuts

1. Preheat the oven to 350°F. Butter two 9 x 5 x 3-inch loaf pans, line the bottoms with parchment, then butter the parchment.

2. In a small bowl, whisk the flour, baking powder, salt, baking soda, and cinnamon together. In a medium bowl, mash the bananas (you need $2\frac{1}{2}$ cups) with a fork and blend in the lemon juice (important—lemon juice keeps the batter a nice white color).

3. In a large bowl, using an electric mixer, cream the butter, cream cheese, and granulated sugar together on high until light yellow and creamy. Beat in the eggs, one at a time, then the cream and vanilla with the mixer on high. Decrease the speed to low and blend in the flour mixture in three additions, alternating with the mashed bananas in two additions; mix just until the flour disappears. Mix in the walnuts.

4. Divide the batter evenly between the two prepared pans. In a small bowl, toss the topping ingredients together and sprinkle half on top of each loaf. Bake until light golden brown and a toothpick inserted in the center comes out with moist crumbs, about 1 hour. Cool in the pan for 10 minutes, then turn out onto wire racks. This bread is delicious served warm with cream cheese. Wrap and store the bread in the refrigerator for up to 3 days or in the freezer for up to 2 weeks.

The regulars at Junior's know this bread well. It's the one they often request for their sandwiches, especially when ordering corned beef, pastrami, or chopped liver. It's firm enough to slice well, yet still tender and light—not dense. And the taste . . . it's that old-fashioned rye flavor.

club rye onion loaf

MAKES TWO 9 X 5 X 3-INCH LOAVES

1 cup water (105° to 115°F)

Three 1/4-ounce packages active dry yeast

1/2 cup sugar

1 extra-large egg

2 extra-large egg yolks

3/4 cup (1 1/2 sticks) unsalted butter, melted, plus more for the pans and extra for brushing

5 1/2 cups all-purpose flour, plus a little extra if needed

1 cup rye flour (look for it in specialty-food stores or high-end supermarkets or shop online; wrap and freeze extra)

2 tablespoons table salt

2 tablespoons caraway seeds

1 1/2 cups finely chopped onion

FOR THE TOPPING

1 extra-large egg

1 teaspoon vegetable oil

1 small onion, coarsely chopped (1 cup)

1. Make the yeast sponge: Measure out the water into a small bowl and check that the temperature is between 105° and 115°F (no cooler, no hotter!). Stir in the yeast and 1 tablespoon of the sugar and let it stand until foamy and light, about 5 minutes.

2. Meanwhile, in a large bowl, using an electric stand mixer fitted with the paddle attachment, beat the whole egg, 2 yolks, and the butter on high until light yellow. Reduce the speed to low and beat in the yeast mixture. Stop the mixer, add 5 1/2 cups all-purpose flour, the rye flour, the remaining sugar, the salt, and caraway seeds. Mix on low until the flour disappears. Mix in the 1 1/2 cups of onion.

3. Stop the mixer and change to a dough hook, if you have one. Increase the speed to medium and knead the dough until it climbs up the side of the bowl and the mixture becomes a smooth, soft, elastic dough, about 8 minutes. Add a little extra all-purpose flour, 1 tablespoon at a time, during this time if necessary to turn it into a soft dough.

4. Flour your hands, turn the dough onto a lightly floured work surface, and knead by hand for a minute or two, then transfer to a well-buttered bowl and turn over the dough once to coat it well with the butter (don't worry . . . the dough will be sticky). Cover the dough with plastic wrap and let it rise at room temperature until it's doubled in size (this will probably take about 1 1/2 hours).

continued

5. Preheat the oven to 400°F. Generously butter two 9 x 5 x 3-inch loaf pans, line the bottoms with parchment, and butter the parchment. Punch the dough down with your fist to deflate it. Turn the dough onto a lightly floured surface. Flour your hands and lightly knead the dough until it is no longer sticky, about 2 minutes.

6. Divide the dough in half, shape each into a loaf, and transfer to the prepared pans. Pat the loaves, rounding them in the center. Brush with melted butter. Cover the loaves and let them rise until light and doubled in size, 30 to 45 minutes more. For the topping, whisk the egg with the oil and brush the glaze on top of each loaf. Sprinkle each loaf with ½ cup coarsely chopped onion.

7. Bake until the loaves are golden brown on top and sound hollow when lightly thumped, about 50 minutes (do not overbake). Transfer the pans to wire racks and let stand for 10 minutes before turning the loaves out onto the racks to cool on their sides. It is best if you can wait about 30 minutes or more before slicing. Serve warm or at room temperature. To store, cool the loaves completely, then wrap in plastic wrap or foil or place in a zip-top freezer bag. Refrigerate for up to 2 days or freeze for up to 2 weeks. To reheat, wrap in foil, then place in a 300°F oven for 10 to 15 minutes; defrost first if frozen.

The Junior's Way

- If you own a stand mixer with a dough hook, use it for this bread dough. It will save you a whole lot of energy and kneading time. Plus the baked loaf often has a more uniform and finer crumb than one kneaded by hand.

- Junior's often uses this bread to make one of their signature deli "combo" sandwiches. Freshly sliced warm corned beef slices are piled on one slice of bread, the thin slices of warm pastrami are stacked on top. A second slice of bread tops off the sandwich. Dijon mustard is served alongside.

Traditionally, challah is baked for the Jewish Shabbat (Sabbath) or holidays such as Rosh Hashanah and Yom Kippur, oftentimes braided into a fancy loaf using three ropes of dough (some families will use as many as six braids). But at Junior's you can enjoy challah every day. Normally it's baked into a long 18-inch loaf that is sliced and used for their overstuffed sandwiches. This same dough is also often baked into delicious little twin rolls or long, thin baguettes. However it's shaped, Junior's challah is a treat—light, tender, and rich with eggs and a hint of sweetness on the inside, and shiny, glossy, and showered with sesame seeds on the outside. Our recipe makes two loaves— either long 15-inch braids or standard 1½-pound loaves. Enjoy one and freeze the other.

braided challah

MAKES TWO 15-INCH BRAIDED LOAVES OR TWO 9 X 5 X 3-INCH LOAVES

FOR THE DOUGH

Three ¼-ounce packages active dry yeast

½ cup plus 1 tablespoon sugar

¾ cup lukewarm water (105° to 115°F).

7 extra-large egg yolks

5 extra-large eggs

⅓ cup vegetable oil

1 tablespoon table salt

5 cups bleached all-purpose white flour

Unsalted butter, at room temperature, for the bowl and baking sheets

FOR THE GLAZE

2 extra-large eggs

½ teaspoon vegetable oil

2 tablespoons sesame seeds or poppyseeds

1. Dissolve the yeast and 1 tablespoon of the sugar in the water in a small bowl. Let it stand until the mixture is foamy and doubles in size.

2. While the yeast proofs, in a large bowl, using a stand mixer fitted with the paddle attachment, beat the egg yolks and whole eggs on high until light yellow. Add the remaining ½ cup sugar, the oil, and salt and beat until blended. Reduce the speed to low and beat in the yeast mixture, then the flour all at once.

3. Stop the mixer and attach the dough hook, if your mixer has one, and knead on low for 8 minutes. Or knead the dough on a well-floured work surface by hand for 8 minutes. The dough will be sticky.

4. Place the dough in a generously buttered large bowl, turning the dough over a couple of times to coat it well. Cover the bowl with plastic wrap and let the dough rise in a warm place until doubled in size (this will probably take 1½ to 2 hours).

continued

5. Butter two baking sheets well if making 2 long braided loaves or butter two loaf pans (see The Junior's Way). Punch the dough down gently with your fist, then turn it out onto a lightly floured surface. Divide the dough in half. For each braided loaf, cut one piece into thirds and, using the palms of your hands, roll each piece into a rope about 16 inches long and 1½ inches in diameter. Lay the three ropes side by side; pinch them together at the top and tuck under. Braid the three ropes together, all the way down the loaf. Pinch the ends together and tuck under. Repeat with the other piece of dough to shape a second loaf. Transfer each loaf to one of the prepared baking sheets, setting it down on the diagonal.

6. Make the glaze by whisking the eggs and oil together in a small cup. Brush the top and sides of each braid with the glaze, then sprinkle each with 1 table-spoon of sesame seeds. Cover with clean dish towels and let the loaves rise until doubled in size, 30 to 45 minutes.

7. While the loaves rise, preheat the oven to 375°F. Bake the challah until golden, firm to the touch, and hollow sounding when lightly thumped, about 20 minutes. Turn off the oven, leave the door closed, and let the bread rest for 5 minutes. Remove the loaves from the oven and slide onto wire racks to cool for at least 10 minutes more before slicing. The loaves can be left at room temperature, wrapped in foil, overnight but then should be refrigerated and used within 2 days or frozen and used within 2 weeks; defrost at room temperature.

The Junior's Way

To bake the dough as plain loaves, butter two 9 x 5 x 3-inch loaf pans, line the bottoms with parchment, and butter the parchment well. After dividing the dough in half, shape each piece into a loaf about 9 inches long. Place each, seam side down, into a prepared pan. Let rise as directed in the recipe, then glaze and bake at 375°F until golden, firm to the touch, and hollow sounding when lightly thumped, 20 to 25 minutes. Let rest in the oven as directed, then transfer the pans to wire racks and let the bread stand in the pans for 10 minutes before turning out onto the racks to cool. It's best if you can wait for about 15 minutes more before slicing!

Every day you can start your day at Junior's by enjoying a freshly baked bran muffin, filled with lots of bran, fiber, and raisins. They are oversized jumbo ones, so bring your appetite! We've added walnuts in this recipe to give them a little crunch and to decorate the tops. These muffins are especially good when served warm with a generous smear of cream cheese. Our recipe makes a dozen of the home-sized standard muffins; the variation, a half-dozen of Junior's jumbo-sized ones.

bran muffins

MAKES 12 HOME-SIZED OR 6 JUMBO-SIZED MUFFINS

2 cups all-purpose flour

1 tablespoon baking powder

1 teaspoon table salt

1¼ cups all-bran cereal

1¼ cups whole milk

½ cup (1 stick) unsalted butter, at room temperature

¾ cup firmly packed light brown sugar

2 extra-large eggs

¼ cup honey

1 cup dark raisins

1 cup chopped walnuts

1. Preheat the oven to 400°F. Line 12 home-sized (2¾-inch) muffin cups with cupcake liners (silicone, foil, parchment, or paper).

2. In a small bowl, mix the flour, baking powder, and salt together. In another small bowl, soak the bran in the milk until softened, about 2 minutes.

3. While the cereal soaks, in a large bowl, using an electric mixer, cream the butter and brown sugar together on high until light. Beat in the eggs, one at a time, then the honey and bran mixture. Decrease the speed to low and blend in the flour mixture in one addition just until it disappears. Mix in the raisins and ¾ cup of the walnuts.

4. Spoon the batter into the muffin cups almost up to the tops. Sprinkle with the remaining ¼ cup walnuts. Bake the muffins until golden brown and a toothpick inserted in the center comes out with moist crumbs, about 20 minutes. Cool in the pans for 10 minutes, then transfer the individual muffins to wire racks. Remove the cupcake liners if using silicone. The muffins are best served warm. Wrap any leftover muffins in foil, then refrigerate and serve the next day. To rewarm the muffins, place the foil packet in a 300°F oven for 10 to 15 minutes. These muffins may also be frozen up to 2 weeks; defrost before reheating.

continued

JUNIOR'S JUMBO-SIZED BRAN MUFFINS

Using softened butter, generously butter 6 jumbo (4-inch) muffin cups (preferably nonstick ones) or line with paper liners if you have them. Prepare batter and fill as for home-sized muffins, filling the 6 cups almost to the top. Bake the muffins at 375°F until golden brown and a toothpick inserted in the center comes out with moist crumbs, 30 to 35 minutes.

The Junior's Way

- Soaking the bran cereal in milk for a few minutes makes it a lot easier to stir into the batter.

- Before lining the muffin cups with paper or silicone liners, butter the top of the pans around each cup. This prevents the tops of the muffins from sticking to the pan if they rise up and over the sides of the cups.

- To scoop the batter into the cups fast and neatly, use an ice cream scoop.

Although Junior's does not offer gluten-free choices in their restaurants, we know there are many who must follow a diet without gluten for health reasons. With the proliferation of gluten-free products available today, it is now possible, and even easy, to make baked goods that taste very similar to those made with wheat flours. Look for an all-purpose gluten-free baking flour for these muffins in supermarkets, gourmet stores, or online. For that "real apple pie" flavor, we've added two fresh apples (one grated and one chopped), a blend of brown and white sugars, and plenty of apple-pie spice.

gluten-free apple-pie muffins

MAKES SIXTEEN 2³/₄-INCH MUFFINS

2¹/₂ cups gluten-free all-purpose baking flour

1 tablespoon baking powder

2 teaspoons cornstarch

1 teaspoon table salt

1 teaspoon ground cinnamon or apple-pie spice

2 large baking apples (Pink Lady, Granny Smith, or Rome Beauty)

1 cup (2 sticks) unsalted butter, at room temperature

1 cup firmly packed light brown sugar

²/₃ cup granulated sugar

2 extra-large eggs

1 tablespoon pure vanilla extract

³/₄ cup whole milk

1 cup chopped walnuts

1. Preheat the oven to 400°F. Line sixteen 2³/₄-inch muffin cups with cupcake liners (silicone, foil, parchment, or paper). In a small bowl, mix the flour, baking powder, cornstarch, salt, and cinnamon together. Peel and core the apples. Grate 1 apple (you need 1 cup) and coarsely chop the second (you need 1 cup).

2. In a large bowl, using an electric mixer, cream the butter, ²/₃ cup of the brown sugar, and the granulated sugar together on high until smooth and creamy. Beat in the eggs, one at a time, then the vanilla. Decrease the speed to low and blend in the flour mixture in three additions, alternating with the milk in two additions; mix just until the flour disappears. Stir in the grated apple and walnuts by hand.

3. Fill the muffin cups up to the top. Mix the chopped apple with the remaining ¹/₃ cup brown sugar and sprinkle on top of the muffins.

4. Bake the muffins until golden brown and a toothpick inserted in the center comes out with moist crumbs, 20 to 25 minutes. Cool in the pans for 10 minutes, then transfer the individual muffins to wire racks. Remove the cupcake liners if using silicone. These muffins are best served warm. Wrap any leftover muffins in foil, refrigerate, and serve the next day. Rewarm the muffins in the foil packet in a 300°F oven for 10 to 15 minutes. Do not freeze.

Here's what you might expect from Junior's: an oversized, super-delicious, melt-in-your-mouth cake-like muffin that is chock so full of berries that you get one in most every bite. Plus, a surprise of creamy Junior's cheesecake hiding inside of each one. And the taste! Buttery, sweet but not overly so, fresh, and fruity. Although you will not find this particular muffin at Junior's, you will find delicious blueberry muffins and Little Fellas Cheesecakes. We have put these two favorites together to make these over-the-top muffins, which are so good you can even serve them for dessert!

blueberry cheesecake muffins

MAKES EIGHTEEN TO TWENTY 2¾-INCH MUFFINS

3 cups all-purpose flour

1 tablespoon baking powder

1 teaspoon table salt

Three 6-ounce cartons fresh ripe blueberries (about 3 cups)

1 cup (2 sticks) unsalted butter, at room temperature

1 cup granulated sugar

3 extra-large eggs

1 tablespoon pure vanilla extract

1⅓ cups whole milk

FOR THE CHEESECAKE TOPPING

Two 8-ounce packages PHILADELPHIA cream cheese (use only full fat), at room temperature

¼ cup granulated sugar

1 teaspoon cornstarch

1 extra-large egg

1 teaspoon grated lemon zest

1. Preheat the oven to 375°F. Line twenty 2¾-inch muffin cups with cupcake liners (silicone, foil, parchment, or paper). Mix the flour, baking powder, and salt together in a medium bowl. Wash the blueberries, removing any stems, rinse with cold water, drain, and transfer to paper towels.

2. In a large bowl, using an electric mixer, cream the butter and granulated sugar together on high until light. Beat in the eggs, one at a time, then the vanilla until creamy, scraping down the bowl one or two times. Decrease the speed to low and blend in the flour mixture, in three additions, alternating with the milk in two additions, just until the flour disappears. Gently fold in 2 cups of the blueberries by hand, saving the rest for topping the muffins. Scoop the batter into the muffin cups, filling them seven-eighths full, almost to the top.

3. Make the cheesecake topping: Transfer to the paddle attachment. In a medium bowl, using the mixer, beat the cream cheese on high until smooth. Add the remaining topping ingredients, and beat on low just until blended (do not overbeat). Top the muffins with this cheesecake batter, filling them to the

continued

top and spreading the batter to the edges. Finish each off with a few of the remaining blueberries.

4. Bake until the cheesecake topping is set and light golden and a toothpick inserted in the center comes out almost clean, 40 to 45 minutes. Cool in the pans for 15 minutes until the cheesecake firms up, then transfer the individual muffins to wire racks to cool another 15 minutes before serving. Remove the cupcake liners if using silicone. The muffins are best served warm or at room temperature. Refrigerate any leftover muffins and serve chilled. Do not freeze these muffins.

The Junior's Way

Have a little cheesecake topping batter left? Fill muffin liners with the extra batter up to the top and bake in the same muffin tin as the muffins. You'll have mini-cheesecakes, easy-as-pie!

These muffins are a daily offering at Junior's, filled with lots of good things: oats, fresh butter, whole milk, and raisins, with a sprinkling of more oats on top. Here is the recipe two ways—home-sized for the standard muffin tin and a jumbo variation for those Junior's-sized muffins. We have added walnuts for a little crunch and an extra touch of a yummy buttery streusel on top.

oatmeal-raisin-walnut muffins

MAKES 14 TO 16 HOME-SIZED OR 6 JUMBO-SIZED MUFFINS

2 cups all-purpose flour

1 cup old-fashioned Quaker® oats

1 tablespoon baking powder

1$\frac{1}{2}$ teaspoons table salt

$\frac{3}{4}$ cup (1$\frac{1}{2}$ sticks) unsalted butter, at room temperature

$\frac{3}{4}$ cup granulated sugar

$\frac{1}{2}$ cup firmly packed light brown sugar

2 extra-large eggs

1 tablespoon pure vanilla extract

1 cup whole milk

1 cup dark raisins

1 cup coarsely chopped walnuts

FOR THE STREUSEL

$\frac{1}{4}$ cup old-fashioned Quaker oats

3 tablespoons firmly packed light brown sugar

2 tablespoons all-purpose flour

$\frac{1}{2}$ teaspoon ground cinnamon

3 tablespoons cold unsalted butter, cut into small pieces

1. Preheat the oven to 400°F. Line sixteen 2$\frac{3}{4}$-inch muffin cups with cupcake liners (silicone, foil, parchment, or paper).

2. In a medium bowl, mix the flour, oats, baking powder, and salt together.

3. In a large bowl, using an electric mixer, cream the butter and both sugars together on high until light yellow. Beat in the eggs, one at a time, then the vanilla until creamy. Decrease the speed to low and blend in the oat-flour mixture in three additions, alternating with the milk in two additions; mix just until the flour disappears. Stir in the raisins and walnuts by hand. Fill the muffin cups almost to the top. You will have enough batter for 14 to 16; be sure to leave a little space for the streusel.

4. Make the streusel: In a small bowl, combine the oats, brown sugar, flour, and cinnamon. Cut in the butter with a pastry cutter or two forks until crumbs the size of peas appear. Sprinkle over the muffins, using all of the streusel.

5. Bake until the muffins are light golden and a toothpick inserted in the center comes out with moist crumbs, about 20 minutes (do not overbake these muffins!). Cool in the pan for 10 minutes, then carefully slip the individual muffins out onto wire racks, standing them streusel side up to cool. Remove the cupcake liners if using silicone. These muffins are best served warm. Wrap any leftover muffins in foil, then refrigerate and serve the next day. To rewarm,

continued

place the foil packet in a 300°F oven for 10 to 15 minutes. These muffins may also be frozen for up to 2 weeks; defrost at room temperature before reheating.

JUNIOR'S JUMBO-SIZED OATMEAL-RAISIN-WALNUT MUFFINS

Using softened butter, generously butter 6 jumbo (4-inch) muffin cups (preferably nonstick ones) or line with paper liners if you have them. Prepare the batter and fill as for standard-sized muffins, filling the 6 cups almost to the top. Sprinkle the streusel over the muffins. Bake the muffins at 375°F until golden brown and a toothpick inserted in the center comes out with moist crumbs, 30 to 35 minutes.

The Junior's Way

Use a mixer as they do at Junior's to make this muffin batter; it speeds up the mixing process. But avoid overmixing, as that can make the muffins tough and result in an uneven texture with elongated tunnels.

These doughnuts are the old-fashioned kind—thick, cake-like, and melt-in-your-mouth delicious. There's nothing greasy, soggy, or tough about these little cinnamon-y gems. They rise up at least 2 inches tall as they cook into tender rounds, each with their own unique shape and chock-full of homemade goodness. Be sure to fry the doughnut holes; kids like them the best. Shower both doughnuts and the holes with cinnamon-sugar or top them with a creamy vanilla glaze.

doughnuts any time!

5 to 5½ cups all-purpose flour

2 tablespoons baking powder

2 teaspoons table salt

1½ teaspoons ground nutmeg

1 cup whole milk

¼ cup (½ stick) unsalted butter, melted

2 teaspoons pure vanilla extract

2 extra-large eggs

1 extra-large egg yolk

1½ cups sugar

Cooking oil for frying (use corn, peanut, or blended vegetable)

FOR THE CINNAMON-SUGAR COATING

2 cups sugar

1 tablespoon ground cinnamon

¼ teaspoon ground nutmeg

MAKES EIGHTEEN 2½-INCH DOUGHNUTS AND 18 DOUGHNUT HOLES

1. Mix 5 cups of the flour, the baking powder, salt, and nutmeg in a large bowl. Whisk the milk, melted butter, and vanilla together in a medium bowl.

2. In a large bowl, using an electric mixer, beat the whole eggs, egg yolk, and sugar on high until the mixture forms light yellow ribbons. Reduce the speed to low and add the flour mixture in three additions, alternating with the milk mixture in two additions. Blend just until a dough forms, adding a little more flour, if necessary, to make the mixture come together. Cover with plastic wrap and refrigerate the dough for 1 hour.

3. Working with half the dough at a time, roll it out 1 inch thick on a lightly floured work surface. Using a 2½-inch doughnut cutter, cut out the doughnuts, dipping the cutter into a small bowl of flour after each cut. Transfer the cut doughnuts and doughnut holes to a plate or bowl (single layer, please!), loosely cover with plastic wrap or wax paper, and let stand in the refrigerator for 15 minutes.

4. Meanwhile, heat 2 inches of oil to 365°F in a large heavy skillet with high sides. With a slotted spoon, slide the doughnuts, one at a time, into the hot oil (avoid stacking them). Cook until very light golden brown, 3 to 4 minutes total, turning each doughnut once. Transfer to a wire rack (not paper towels) to drain. Add more oil if necessary and let the oil come back to 365°F before frying the next batch.

continued

$5.$ For the cinnamon-sugar, mix all the ingredients together in a pie plate. Let the doughnuts cool for about 10 minutes, just so you can handle them easily, then roll lightly in the sugar, covering them completely. Enjoy! These are best enjoyed the day they are made, preferably still warm!

VANILLA-GLAZED DOUGHNUTS

Set a wire rack on a sheet of parchment or waxed paper. Heat $1/3$ cup heavy cream with 2 teaspoons pure vanilla extract in a medium saucepan over low heat until just warm (do not let it boil!). Remove from the heat and stir in 3 cups sifted confectioners' sugar, adding 1 or 2 teaspoons heavy cream if necessary to reach a "dipping" consistency. Swirl the tops of the doughnuts and doughnut holes in the glaze until coated lightly. Work fast; if the glaze thickens before you have finished, stir in a little more cream. Place on the rack until the glaze has set.

DOUBLE-DIPPED DOUGHNUTS

Prepare the Vanilla Glaze, as for the Vanilla-Glazed Doughnuts, increasing the amounts to $1/2$ cup heavy cream, 1 tablespoon pure vanilla extract, and 4 cups sifted confectioners' sugar. After glazing the doughnuts, let them stand until the glaze no longer feels sticky, about 30 minutes. Then swirl them a second time in the glaze and let stand until set.

The Junior's Way

The secret to the best doughnuts is in the frying. Use fresh vegetable oil. Choose canola, corn, peanut, or safflower oil as they have high smoke points. The best temperature to fry at is around 365°F (if you have a frying thermometer, use it). If the oil starts to smoke, it's too hot. Quickly turn down the heat and add a little fresh oil to cool down the skillet. Otherwise, the oil will break down and give your doughnuts an off taste. Using a slotted metal spatula, gently slide (don't drop or they'll splatter!) the doughnuts a few at a time into the hot oil. Be careful not to add too many or the doughnuts will steam instead of fry, which can make them soggy. Fry the doughnuts until very light golden brown and turn each one only once (it takes only 3 to 4 minutes total). Do not overcook!

Save Room
for Dessert!

Whenever you're dining at Junior's, your waiter stops by your table about halfway through dinner and suggests: "Save room for dessert!" Many simply say: *Cheesecake and coffee, please.* For those in the know, this means a slice of Our Famous No. 1 Original Cheesecake — a whole slice for yourself, one to share, or one to go. It's the same cheesecake that Alan Rosen's Grandpa Harry developed back in the 1950s and was voted Number 1 as "The Best of The Best" by *New York* magazine. The recipe hasn't changed and it's included here for you to bake for friends and family, along with other sweet offerings. Try the Cherry Crumb Pie, topped with buttery crumbs, or the deep, dark, delicious Chocolate Whipped Cream Pie, or Junior's Chocolate Bobka Loaf Cake, a rich sweet yeast cake, swirled with chocolate and walnuts. We've also tucked in two new cheesecake creations, Whoopie Pie Cheesecake and Crème Brûlée cheesecake, as well as two gluten-free dessert choices. It's time to celebrate The Junior's Way, by baking one of their famous desserts today!

As the name implies, the recipe for Junior's famous original cheesecake has been baked the very same way since the 1950s. And for good reason. It's simply The Best cheesecake you can find. "There will never be a better cheesecake than the cheesecake they serve at Junior's on Flatbush Avenue . . . it's the best cheesecake in New York," wrote Ron Rosenblum (Village Voice, July 26, 1973). The next year, a jury of six cool-headed cheesecake lovers for New York magazine named Junior's the Champion Cheesecake. I asked Alan Rosen what makes it so special: "It's light but not crumbly, oh-so-creamy but not dense, and with that heavenly cream cheese flavor that makes Junior's New York cheesecake famous the world over."

Surprisingly, this is one of the easiest cakes to make. Just follow this recipe that we have specially adapted for your home kitchen. You'll soon proudly be slicing up the best cheesecake you've every tasted!

original new york cheesecake

MAKES ONE 9- OR 8-INCH CHEESECAKE, ABOUT 2½ INCHES HIGH

FOR ONE 9-INCH CHEESECAKE

1 recipe 9-inch Junior's Sponge Cake Crust (page 217)

Four 8-ounce packages PHILADELPHIA cream cheese (use only full fat), at room temperature

1²/₃ cups sugar

¼ cup cornstarch

1 tablespoon pure vanilla extract

2 extra-large eggs

³/₄ cup heavy whipping cream

continued

The day before you plan to serve the cheesecake:

1. Preheat the oven to 350°F. Make and bake the cake crust as directed and leave it in the pan. Keep the oven on.

2. In a large bowl, using an electric mixer fitted with the paddle attachment if your mixer has one, beat 1 package of the cream cheese, ⅓ cup of the sugar, and the cornstarch together on low until creamy, about 3 minutes, scraping down the bowl several times. Blend in the remaining cream cheese, one package at a time, beating well and scraping down the bowl after each.

3. Increase the mixer speed to medium and beat in the remaining sugar, then the vanilla. Blend in the eggs, one at a time, beating well after each. Beat in the cream just until completely blended. The filling will look light, creamy, airy,

continued

1 recipe 8-inch Junior's Sponge Cake Crust (recipe follows)

Three 8-ounce packages PHILADELPHIA cream cheese (use only full fat), at room temperature

1⅓ cups sugar

3 tablespoons cornstarch

1 tablespoon pure vanilla extract

2 extra-large eggs

⅔ cup heavy whipping cream

and almost like billowy clouds. Be careful not to overmix! Gently spoon the batter over the crust.

4. Place the cake pan in a large shallow pan containing hot water that comes halfway (about 1 inch) up the side of the springform. Bake until the edge is light golden brown, the top is light gold, and the center barely jiggles, about 1¼ hours. If the cake still feels soft around the edge, let it bake for 10 minutes more (the cooking time will be about the same for both the 8- and 9-inch cheesecakes). Remove the cheesecake from the water bath, transfer to a wire rack, and let cool for 2 hours (just walk away—don't move it). Then, leave the cake in the pan, cover loosely with plastic wrap, and refrigerate until completely cold before serving, preferably overnight or for at least 6 hours.

On serving day:

5. Release and remove the side of the springform, leaving the cake on the bottom of the pan. Place on a cake plate. Refrigerate until ready to serve. Slice with a sharp straight-edge knife, not a serrated one, rinsing the knife with warm water between slices. Refrigerate any leftover cake, tightly covered, and enjoy within 2 days, or wrap and freeze for up to 1 month.

The Junior's Way

Always bake the cheesecake in a water bath as they do at Junior's. It keeps the heat in the oven moist and helps the cake bake slowly, gently, and evenly. It also helps to ensure that your cake will have a smooth top, with no large cracks.

junior's sponge cake crust

No one really knows just whose idea it was to use a sponge cake crust for Junior's cheesecake. It worked, and that same recipe continues to work today.

FOR ONE 9-INCH CAKE CRUST

Softened unsalted butter, for buttering the pan

$1/3$ cup sifted cake flour

$3/4$ teaspoon baking powder

Pinch of table salt

2 extra-large eggs, separated

$1/3$ cup sugar

1 teaspoon pure vanilla extract

2 drops pure lemon extract

2 tablespoons unsalted butter, melted

$1/4$ teaspoon cream of tartar

FOR ONE 8-INCH CAKE CRUST

Softened unsalted butter, for buttering the pan

$1/4$ cup sifted cake flour

$1/2$ teaspoon baking powder

Pinch of table salt

2 extra-large eggs, separated

$1/4$ cup sugar

$3/4$ teaspoon pure vanilla extract

2 drops pure lemon extract

2 tablespoons unsalted butter, melted

$1/4$ teaspoon cream of tartar

1. Preheat the oven to 350°F and generously butter the bottom and side of a 9- or 8-inch springform pan (preferably a nonstick one). Wrap the outside with aluminum foil, covering the bottom and extending it all the way up the side.

2. In a small bowl, sift the flour, baking powder, and salt together.

3. In a large bowl, using an electric mixer, beat the egg yolks on high for 3 minutes. With the mixer running, slowly add 2 tablespoons of the sugar and continue beating until thick light yellow ribbons form in the bowl, about 5 minutes more. Beat in the extracts.

4. Sift the flour mixture over the batter and stir it in by hand, just until there are no remaining white flecks. Blend in the melted butter.

5. In another clean bowl, using clean, dry beaters, beat the egg whites and cream of tartar together on high until frothy. Gradually add the remaining sugar and continue beating until stiff peaks form (the whites will stand up and look glossy, not dry). Fold about one-third of the whites into the batter, then the remaining whites. Don't worry if you still see a few white specks, as they'll disappear during baking.

6. Gently spread the batter over the bottom of the prepared pan and bake just until set and golden (not wet or sticky), about 10 minutes. Touch the cake gently in the center. If it springs back, it's done. Watch carefully and don't let the top brown. Leave the crust in the pan and place on a wire rack to cool. Leave the oven on while you prepare the batter for the cheesecake.

Bake a Junior's cheesecake for your friends and family, and they will know you think they're special. This cheesecake is even more of a celebration because of the raspberry whipped cream mousse that is swirled on top. Make it a day ahead of when you want to serve it and pop it into the freezer overnight. The next day, move it to the refrigerator a couple of hours before serving. This makes it easier to slice.

raspberry mousse cheesecake

MAKES ONE 9-INCH CHEESECAKE, ABOUT 2³/₄ INCHES HIGH

Softened unsalted butter, for buttering the pan

1 recipe 9-inch Vanilla Wafer Crumb Crust (page 220)

FOR THE CHEESECAKE

Three 8-ounce packages PHILADELPHIA cream cheese (use only full fat), at room temperature

1¹/₃ cups sugar

¹/₄ cup cornstarch

1 tablespoon pure vanilla extract

2 extra-large eggs

²/₃ cup heavy whipping cream

The day before you plan to serve the cheesecake:

1. Preheat the oven to 350°F and generously butter the bottom and side of a 9-inch springform pan. Wrap the outside with aluminum foil, covering the bottom and extending all the way up the side. Make the Vanilla Wafer Crumb Crust, patting the crumbs three-fourths of the way up the side of the pan, and place in the freezer for 15 minutes to set. Bake the crust for 8 minutes and transfer to a wire rack to cool. Keep the oven on.

2. Meanwhile, make the cheesecake: In a large bowl, using an electric mixer fitted with the paddle attachment if your mixer has one, beat 1 package of the cream cheese, ¹/₃ cup of the sugar, and the cornstarch on low until creamy, about 3 minutes, scraping down the bowl several times. Blend in the remaining cream cheese, one package at a time, beating well and scraping down the bowl after each. Increase the mixer speed to medium and beat in the remaining 1 cup sugar, then the vanilla. Blend in the eggs, one at a time, beating well after each. Beat in the cream just until completely blended. Be careful not to over-mix! Gently spoon the batter into the crust.

3. Place the cake pan in a large shallow pan containing hot water that comes halfway (about 1 inch) up the side of the springform pan. Bake until the edge is golden brown and the center is light golden tan, about 1¹/₄ hours. Transfer to a wire rack and let cool for 2 hours (just walk away—don't move it). Leave the cake in the pan, cover loosely with plastic wrap, and refrigerate until completely cold, preferably at least 4 hours.

FOR THE RASPBERRY MOUSSE AND GARNISH

10 ounces frozen dry-pack whole raspberries (see The Junior's Way), thawed and drained well

3 cups heavy whipping cream

⅓ cup sugar

1 tablespoon pure vanilla extract

12 vanilla wafers, such as NABISCO® Nilla® Wafers (to make ½ cup coarse crumbs)

One 6-ounce carton fresh raspberries, washed and dried

4. Meanwhile, make the raspberry mousse. Purée the well-drained raspberries by pulsing on high in a food processor. In a large bowl, using an electric mixer, whip the cream on high just until it thickens and peaks begin to form. With the mixer running, blend in the sugar and vanilla. Fold in the raspberry purée by hand. Spread the mousse on top of the cake (still in the pan). Smooth it out evenly with a metal spatula (an offset icing spatula works well for this), pushing it all the way out to the side of the pan. Wash and dry the bowl of the food processor, then pulse the vanilla wafers into crumbs. Sprinkle evenly over the top of the cake. Cover with plastic wrap and place the cake in the freezer overnight, until the mousse is firm and set.

On serving day:

5. About 2 hours before serving (no sooner), let the cake stand at room temperature for about 15 minutes, then release and remove the side of the springform. Transfer to a cake plate, leaving the cake on the bottom of the pan. Refrigerate the cake until it's time to serve (it'll take about 2 hours to defrost in the refrigerator so you can slice it easily). This mousse slices best if it's very cold and still slightly frozen, so do not take it out of the freezer too far ahead. Right before serving, cluster the fresh raspberries in the center of the cake. Slice the cake with a sharp straight-edge knife, not a serrated one. Top each slice with a few fresh raspberries. Freeze any leftover cake, tightly wrapped, and enjoy within 2 weeks.

continued

The Junior's Way

- Look for frozen unsweetened dry-pack raspberries for this cake; they're so much easier to use than starting with fresh berries. We've saved the fresh raspberries for garnishing.

- To thaw the berries, place them in a strainer over a plate and let stand until almost thawed and still cold. Before puréeing for this recipe, press them lightly to extract any excess juice. Discard the juice.

vanilla wafer crumb crust

This bakes into a crust that tastes like a delicious soft buttery cookie. It's the perfect crust for cheesecakes made with fruit, Junior's Cheesecake Tart (page 251), and ice cream pies.

MAKES ONE 9-INCH CHEESECAKE CRUST, ONE 11- OR 12-INCH TART CRUST, OR ONE 8- OR 9-INCH PIE CRUST

50 vanilla wafers, such as NABISCO Nilla Wafers

1/3 cup sugar

1 teaspoon baking powder

1/2 cup (1 stick) unsalted butter, melted

1. Pulse the wafers in a food processor until you have fine, even crumbs, about 30 seconds. Add the sugar and baking powder and process for a few seconds more. Avoid processing too much. The crumbs should be slightly coarse, not very fine or powdery. You need 2 cups of crumbs, lightly packed.

2. With the processor running, slowly add 6 tablespoons of the melted butter and process until the crumbs are moist and come together. Add a little more butter if needed to make the crust easy to form. Shape the crust as the recipe directs and freeze for 15 minutes before baking as directed in the recipe.

Imagine baking up the "best of both possible desserts" all in one. Here it is: a slice of Junior's famous cheesecake with the taste and spice of the best pumpkin pie you've ever eaten. At Junior's, cheesecakes are always coming out of the ovens, but pumpkin ones are only served around the holidays. Now you can have them both, any day you like—and enjoy creaminess, richness, and subtle spice in every bite.

pumpkin cheesecake

MAKES ONE 9-INCH CHEESECAKE, ABOUT 3 INCHES HIGH

Softened unsalted butter, for buttering the pan

1 recipe 9-inch Junior's Graham Cracker Crumb Crust (page 226)

Three 8-ounce packages PHILADELPHIA cream cheese (use only full fat), at room temperature

1^1/$_3$ cups granulated sugar

^{1}/$_3$ cup cornstarch

^{1}/$_2$ cup firmly packed light brown sugar

1 tablespoon pure vanilla extract

2 teaspoons pumpkin pie spice, plus more for sprinkling

3 extra-large eggs

1^1/$_4$ cups 100% pure canned pumpkin, not pumpkin pie mix

^{1}/$_2$ cup heavy whipping cream

5 to 6 large graham crackers for decorating (optional)

The day before you plan to serve the cheesecake:

1. Preheat the oven to 350°F. Generously butter the bottom and side of a 9-inch springform pan. Wrap the outside with aluminum foil, covering the bottom and extending all of the way up the side. Shape the graham cracker crust, pressing the mixture into the bottom and three-fourths of the way up the side. Freeze for 15 minutes, then bake for 8 minutes. Let cool on a wire rack. Keep the oven on.

2. In a large bowl, using an electric mixer fitted with the paddle attachment if your mixer has one, beat 1 package of the cream cheese, ^{1}/$_3$ cup of the granulated sugar, and the cornstarch together on low until creamy, about 3 minutes, scraping the bowl down several times. Blend in the remaining cream cheese, one package at a time, beating well and scraping down the bowl after each.

3. Increase the mixer speed to medium and beat in the remaining 1 cup granulated sugar, the brown sugar, vanilla, and pumpkin pie spice. Blend in the eggs, one at a time, beating well after each. Blend in the pumpkin, then the cream, just until completely mixed. Be careful not to overmix! Gently spoon the pumpkin batter into the crust.

continued

4. Place the cake pan in a large pan containing hot water that comes halfway (about 1 inch) up the side of the springform. Bake until the edge is light golden brown and the top is light beige-golden orange, about 1¼ hours. Remove the cheesecake from the water bath, transfer to a wire rack, and let cool for 2 hours (just walk away—don't move it). Leave the cake in the pan, cover loosely with plastic wrap, and refrigerate until completely cold, preferably overnight or at least 4 hours.

On serving day:

5. If you wish to decorate the cake, break or cut the graham crackers into ½-inch pieces or crumble into coarse crumbs by hand. Release and remove the side of the springform, leaving the cake on the bottom of the pan. Place on a cake plate. Make a ring of the graham cracker pieces around the outside edge of the cheesecake. Refrigerate until ready to serve. Slice with a sharp straight-edge knife, not a serrated one. Refrigerate any leftover cake, tightly covered, and serve within a few days, or wrap and freeze for up to 1 month.

The Junior's Way

- For this cake, the bakers use canned pumpkin, the kind that's 100% pure pumpkin purée, not pumpkin pie mix. Pumpkin from the can works better in baking than cooked fresh pumpkin because the moisture and flavor are consistent, cake after cake.

- Look for pumpkin pie spice in the spice section of the supermarket. It's all the spice this cake needs. It varies by manufacturer, but typically it's a blend of warm spices such as cinnamon, ginger, nutmeg, allspice, cloves, and mace.

Junior's has created yet another cheesecake phenomenon, this time marrying crème brûlée with their famous cheesecake. Decadent, yes! Out of this world delicious, yes! Impossible to take a small piece, yes! A graham cracker crust starts it off, baked with a layer of Junior's Original Cheesecake. Next it's crowned with a layer of a heavenly custard crème. Then it gets the final crème brûlée treatment—a burnt caramel mirror on top! This cake deserves your very best cake plate!

crème brûlée cheesecake

MAKES ONE 9-INCH CHEESECAKE, ABOUT 3 INCHES HIGH

Softened unsalted butter, for buttering the pan

One 9-inch Graham Cracker Crumb Crust (page 226)

FOR THE CHEESECAKE LAYER

Three 8-ounce packages PHILADELPHIA cream cheese (use only full fat), at room temperature

1⅓ cups granulated sugar

3 tablespoons cornstarch

1 tablespoon pure vanilla extract

2 extra-large eggs

⅔ cup heavy whipping cream

FOR THE CRÈME BRÛLÉE LAYER

4 cups heavy whipping cream

1 large vanilla bean or 1 tablespoon pure vanilla extract

8 extra-large egg yolks

⅓ cup granulated sugar

⅛ teaspoon table salt

The day before you plan to serve the cheesecake:

1. Preheat the oven to 350°F and generously butter the bottom and side of a 9-inch springform pan. Wrap the outside with aluminum foil, covering the bottom and extending all the way up the side.

2. Make and shape the graham cracker crust, pressing the mixture into the bottom and three-fourths of the way up the side. Freeze for 15 minutes, then bake for 8 minutes. Cool on a wire rack. Keep the oven on.

3. Make the cheesecake layer: In a large bowl, using an electric mixer fitted with the paddle attachment if your mixer has one, beat 1 package of the cream cheese, ⅓ cup of the granulated sugar, and the cornstarch on low until creamy, about 3 minutes, scraping down the bowl several times. Blend in the remaining cream cheese, one package at a time, scraping down the bowl after each. Increase the mixer speed to medium and beat in the remaining 1 cup granulated sugar, then the vanilla. Blend in the eggs, one at a time, beating well after each. Beat in the cream just until completely blended. Be careful not to overmix! Spoon the batter into the baked crust.

4. Place the cake pan in a large shallow pan containing hot water that comes halfway (about 1 inch) up the side of the pan. Bake until the edges are light golden brown and the center is light gold, about 1¼ hours. Remove the cheesecake from the water bath, remove the foil from the pan, and transfer to a wire

FOR THE CARAMEL BRÛLÉE
MIRROR

¹/₄ cup firmly packed light
brown sugar

¹/₄ cup granulated sugar

Fresh raspberries, for garnish
(optional)

rack. Let the cake cool for 2 hours (just walk away—don't move it). Leave the cake in the pan, cover loosely with plastic wrap, and refrigerate until completely cold, at least 4 hours.

5. While the cheesecake chills, make the crème brûlée layer: Pour the cream into a heavy medium saucepan. If you're using the vanilla bean, slit the bean and scrape out the seeds into the cream, then add the bean to the cream. Heat the cream over medium heat until bubbles begin to form around the edge, then remove from the heat immediately (do not let it boil or it might curdle).

6. Meanwhile, in a large bowl, using an electric mixer fitted with the whisk attachment, beat the egg yolks until frothy, then slowly add the granulated sugar, then the salt, and continue beating until light yellow, thick, and creamy. Slowly beat in about 1 cup of the hot cream, to temper the yolks, then whisk this mixture back into the hot cream in the saucepan. Cook over medium heat until thickened, about 5 minutes, being careful not to let it boil and stirring almost constantly. Remove from the heat and discard the vanilla bean. If using vanilla extract instead of a vanilla bean, stir it in now. Transfer to a heatproof dish, press a piece of plastic wrap directly against the surface (this will keep a skin from forming), and refrigerate until thoroughly chilled and slightly set, about 2 hours. Gently spoon the custard on top of the cold cheesecake still in its pan, covering the cake. Spread it out evenly. Cover loosely with plastic wrap and place in the freezer overnight.

On serving day:

7. Make the caramel brûlée mirror: About 2 hours before you plan to serve the cheesecake, remove it from the freezer. Preheat the broiler until hot. In a small bowl, mix the two sugars together and sprinkle over the top of the cold cake (still in its pan), covering it completely. Place the cake on the top rack of the oven and broil about 3 inches from the heat until the sugar melts and caramelizes, 3 minutes. Watch carefully so it does not burn! Transfer the cake to the refrigerator, still in the pan, and chill for at least an hour, until the caramel hardens and you are ready to serve. Remove the side of the springform, leaving the cake on the bottom of the pan, and place the cake on your prettiest serving plate. It's now ready to WOW your guests! Serve as is or with a few fresh raspberries if you like.

continued

graham cracker crumb crust

MAKES ONE 8- OR 9-INCH GRAHAM CRACKER CRUMB CRUST WITH 2-INCH SIDES

15 large cinnamon graham crackers

½ cup sugar

1 teaspoon ground cinnamon (optional)

½ cup (1 stick) unsalted butter, melted, plus more if needed

1. Pulse the crackers in a food processor for about 30 seconds, until you have fine, even crumbs. Add the sugar and cinnamon if you wish, and then process for 1 minute more. You will have about 2 cups of crumbs.

2. With the processor running, slowly add the melted butter through the feed tube. Continue processing until the crumbs are moist and come together, adding a little more butter if needed. The crumbs should be moist but not soaked with butter. Shape the crust as the recipe directs and freeze for 15 minutes before baking as directed in the recipe.

Leave it to Junior's to take a traditional Amish pie and turn it into a cheesecake phenomenon! A whoopie pie is a big chocolate cake-like sandwich filled with yummy marshmallow crème. Junior's adds a layer of their delicious cheesecake to the equation, creating a show-stopping dessert that simply looks and tastes The Best. Be sure to make and freeze the cheesecake layer the day before you intend to make the Whoopie Pie Cheesecake.

whoopie pie cheesecake

MAKES ONE 9-INCH CHEESECAKE-FILLED LAYER CAKE

1 recipe Cheesecake Layer for the Whoopie Pie (page 228)

FOR THE WHOOPIE PIE CAKE LAYERS

Softened unsalted butter, for buttering the pan

1³/₄ cups all-purpose flour

¹/₂ cup natural unsweetened cocoa powder

1 tablespoon baking powder

1 teaspoon table salt

¹/₂ teaspoon baking soda

1 cup (2 sticks) unsalted butter, at room temperature

1¹/₄ cups granulated sugar

3 extra-large eggs

4 ounces semisweet chocolate, melted and cooled (see The Junior's Way on page 259)

1 tablespoon pure vanilla extract

¹/₂ cup whole milk

¹/₂ cup boiling water

continued

The day before you plan to serve the cheesecake:

1. Make and bake the cheesecake layer. Freeze overnight.

2. Prepare the cake layers. Butter two 9-inch round cake pans and line with parchment; butter the parchment. In a small bowl, sift the flour, cocoa, baking powder, salt, and baking soda together.

3. In a large bowl, using an electric mixer, cream the butter and sugar together on medium high until light yellow and creamy, about 3 minutes. Add the eggs, one at a time, beating for a few seconds after each. Beat in the melted chocolate and vanilla. Reduce the mixer to the lowest speed and add the flour mixture in three additions, alternating with two additions of the milk, until all have been incorporated (the batter will be thick). Stir in the boiling water with a wooden spoon (the batter will loosen a little). Fill one prepared cake pan with two-thirds of the batter for the top layer, the other pan with the remaining batter for the bottom layer.

4. Bake the cakes just until set around the sides, about 25 minutes for the thinner layer and 30 to 35 minutes for the thicker one. The cakes are done when a toothpick inserted in the center comes out with moist crumbs (not clean). Let the cakes cool on a wire rack for 15 minutes, then remove from pans and cool completely. Wrap in plastic wrap and refrigerate until ready to assemble the cake the next day.

continued

**FOR THE MARSHMALLOW FILLING
AND DECORATION**

1 recipe Marshmallow Crème Filling
(page 248)

1 to 2 tablespoons sanding (or
granulated) sugar for sprinkling

On serving day:

5. Make the Marshmallow Crème Filling. Refrigerate until ready to use.

6. Remove the frozen cheesecake from the pan (see The Junior's Way on page 230).

7. Assemble the Whoopie Pie Cheesecake: Place the thinner chocolate cake layer on a cake plate, top side down. Spread with one-third of the Marshmallow Crème Filling (about 1 cup) and top with the cheesecake layer. Spread with the rest of the filling, then set the other cake layer, top side up, on top. Sprinkle lightly with the sugar, just enough to make the top glisten. Refrigerate until ready to serve. Refrigerate any leftover cake, tightly covered, and enjoy within 3 days. Do not freeze this cake.

cheesecake layer for the whoopie pie

Make and freeze this cheesecake layer at least a day before you're planning to make the Whoopie Pie Cheesecake.

MAKES ONE 9-INCH LAYER

Two 8-ounce packages
PHILADELPHIA cream cheese (use
only full fat), at room temperature

²/₃ cup sugar

¼ cup cornstarch

1 tablespoon pure vanilla extract

2 extra-large eggs

½ cup heavy whipping cream

1. Preheat the oven to 350°F. Generously butter a 9-inch springform pan and cover the outside almost up to the top with aluminum foil, covering the bottom and extending all the way up the side.

2. In a large bowl, using an electric mixer fitted with the paddle attachment if your mixer has one, beat 1 package of the cream cheese, ⅓ cup of the sugar, and the cornstarch together on low for about 3 minutes to make a stable starter batter. Blend in the remaining cream cheese on low for 3 minutes, beating well and scraping down the bowl several times.

3. Increase the mixer speed to medium (no faster!) and beat in the remaining ⅓ cup sugar, then the vanilla. Blend in the eggs, one at a time, beating well after each. Beat in the cream just until completely blended. The batter will look light, creamy, airy, and almost like billowy clouds. *Be careful not to overmix!* Gently spoon into the prepared pan.

continued

4. Place the springform in a large shallow pan containing hot water that comes halfway (about 1 inch) up the side of the springform. Bake the cheesecake until the edge is light golden brown and the center barely jiggles when you shake the pan, 1 to 1¼ hours. If the cake still feels soft around the edge, let it bake for 10 minutes more.

5. Transfer the cake from the water bath to a wire rack and let sit for 2 hours (just walk away—don't move it). Leave the cake in the pan, cover loosely with plastic wrap, and freeze at least overnight or until you're ready to assemble the Whoopie Pie Cheesecake.

6. Remove the cheesecake layer from the pan as directed in The Junior's Way.

The Junior's Way

To easily remove the cheesecake layer from the pan, freeze it overnight in its pan. Take the cake from the freezer and let it stand for 15 minutes at room temperature. To remove the cake, warm the bottom of the pan either by setting it on a hot wet towel or on a burner over very low heat for 10 to 15 seconds. This is just long enough to let the butter used to grease the pan melt, but not long enough to make the pan too hot to hold. Using potholders, release the latch on the side of the pan. Next, very gently insert a long, narrow metal spatula between the bottom of the cake and the pan, moving it slowly in a circle. Then gently lift up the edge of the cake with the spatula, just enough to release the vacuum between the bottom of the cake and the pan. Use the spatula and your hands to gently lift the cake up slightly and place it onto the frosted bottom layer of the Whoopie Pie.

At Junior's, we want those of you who are on a sugar-free, gluten-free diet — or are baking for friends and family who are — to be able to enjoy Junior's cheesecake. We've left the cane sugar out of this recipe, substituting it with a no-calorie natural sugar alternative. And we've made a shortbread crust from almond flour instead of wheat flour. Now you can have Junior's cheesecake at home, the sugar-free and gluten-free way.

junior's sugar-free, gluten-free strawberry swirl cheesecake

MAKES ONE 9-INCH CHEESECAKE, ABOUT 2 INCHES HIGH

FOR THE SHORTBREAD CRUST

Softened unsalted butter, for buttering the pan

1 cup almond meal/flour (see The Junior's Way on page 232)

1 tablespoon Splenda® Granulated No-Calorie Sweetener (see The Junior's Way on page 232)

½ teaspoon table salt

3 tablespoons unsalted butter, melted

FOR THE CHEESECAKE

1 cup Splenda Granulated No-Calorie Sweetener

¼ cup cornstarch (see The Junior's Way on page 232)

Four 8-ounce packages PHILADELPHIA cream cheese (use only full fat), at room temperature

2 tablespoons pure vanilla extract

2 extra-large eggs

¾ cup heavy whipping cream

continued

The day before you plan to serve the cheesecake:

1. Preheat the oven to 350°F. Generously butter the bottom and side of a 9-inch springform pan (preferably nonstick). Wrap the outside with aluminum foil, covering the bottom and extending all the way up the side, so the water will not leak into the cake as it bakes.

2. Make the crust: In a medium bowl, combine the almond meal, Splenda, and salt. Stir in the melted butter until moistened. Using your fingertips, spread the soft dough evenly over the bottom of the pan. Bake the crust just until it no longer looks moist on the top and feels almost set when you touch it, 8 to 9 minutes. Transfer to a wire rack. Leave the oven on.

3. Make the cheesecake: In a large bowl, using an electric mixer fitted with the paddle attachment if your mixer has one, mix ½ cup of the Splenda and the cornstarch on medium until the cornstarch is distributed. Add 1 package of the cream cheese and beat for about 3 minutes to make a stable starter batter. Blend in the remaining cream cheese, one package at a time, beating well and scraping down the bowl after each. This will take about another 3 minutes.

4. Increase the mixer speed to medium (no faster!) and beat in the remaining ½ cup Splenda, then the vanilla. Blend in the eggs, one at a time, beating well

continued

One 10-ounce package frozen unsweetened dry-pack strawberries, thawed and well drained
1 tablespoon cornstarch

after each. Beat in the cream just until completely blended. The batter will look light, creamy, airy, and almost like billowy clouds. *Be careful not to overmix!* Spoon the batter over the baked almond shortbread crust in the pan.

5. Make the strawberry swirl: Purée the well-drained strawberries in a food processor. Stir in the 1 tablespoon of cornstarch. Top the batter with about 6 heaping teaspoonsful of purée, pushing it down about three-fourths of the way into the batter. Using a table knife or a thin spatula, cut through the batter, swirling the knife as you go to make a strawberry marbled design on the top of the batter. Place the pan in the center of a large shallow pan containing hot water that comes about 1 inch up the side of the springform. Bake until the edge is light golden brown and the top is light golden tan, about 1 hour. Watch carefully, as cakes made with Splenda tend to brown faster than those made with sugar. If the center is still very jiggly, let the cake bake for 5 to 10 minutes more.

6. Remove the cake from the water bath, transfer to a wire rack, remove the foil, and leave it on the rack (don't move it) for 2 hours. The less you move the cake, the less likely it will crack. Once it has cooled, cover the pan loosely with plastic wrap and refrigerate overnight, until the cake is completely cold. On serving day, remove the springform ring and serve this cake from the bottom of the pan (do not try to transfer it to a serving platter). Refrigerate any leftover cake, tightly covered, and serve within 2 days. Do not freeze this cake.

The Junior's Way

- Almond meal/flour, made from finely ground blanched almonds, is a great gluten-free alternative for our shortbread crust, giving it a rich, moist texture.

- Splenda Granulated No-Calorie Sweetener, the brand name for sucralose, is a good sugar-free substitute to use when baking this Junior's cheesecake. If you're on a sugar-free diet, it's fine. Buy the granulated form of Splenda sold in the larger plastic bag. We have found you'll need less Splenda than sugar to deliver the same amount of sweetness in a recipe.

- Cornstarch, made from corn kernels, such as Argo® and Bob's Red Mill® cornstarch, is gluten-free; it adds stability to the cheesecake during baking.

Whenever I pass the "to go" counter at Junior's, their Little Fella cheesecakes are displayed front and center. Someone always seems to be buying one, even two or three, for snacking "on the run." The "regulars" have also discovered that a boxful of these Little Fellas is the perfect house gift. Although you won't find these Chocolate Chip Little Fellas at Junior's, we've created them using the mini-chips you can buy in supermarkets. Folks love them, as they get at least one or two chocolate chips and some of Junior's delicious cheesecake in every bite.

chocolate chip little fellas

MAKES 16 LITTLE FELLAS

Three 8-ounce packages PHILADELPHIA cream cheese (use only full fat), at room temperature

1⅓ cups sugar

¼ cup cornstarch

1 tablespoon pure vanilla extract

2 extra-large eggs

¾ cup heavy whipping cream

1 cup mini-chocolate chips (not regular size), plus extra for decorating

1 recipe Little Fellas Cream Cheese Buttercream (page 235)

Early in the day, or the day before you plan to serve the Little Fellas:

1. Preheat the oven to 350°F. Line sixteen 2¾-inch muffin cups with cupcake liners (silicone, foil, parchment, or paper).

2. In a large bowl, using an electric mixer fitted with the paddle attachment if your mixer has one, beat 1 package of the cream cheese, ⅓ cup of the sugar, and the cornstarch together on low until creamy, about 3 minutes, scraping down the bowl a few times. Blend in the remaining cream cheese.

3. Increase the mixer speed to medium and beat in the remaining 1 cup sugar, then the vanilla. Add the eggs, one at a time, beating well after each. Beat in the cream just until it's completely blended. *Be careful not to overmix!* Fold in the chips using a wooden spoon.

4. Divide the batter among the muffin cups (fill each one up to the top). Place the muffin tin in a large baking or roasting pan, then add hot water so it comes about 1 inch up the sides of the tin. Bake until set and the centers are slightly puffy and golden, 30 to 35 minutes. Remove the muffin tin from the water bath to a wire rack and let cool for 2 hours. Cover the cakes with plastic wrap (do not remove from the tin) and refrigerate until cold, at least 2 hours.

continued

Fill the cupcake liners up to the top with batter. The cakes will rise a little in the center as they bake, but then settle to a nice flat top as they cool. Be sure the Little Fellas are very cold before frosting them. If you're in a hurry, skip piping the frosting step. Instead, quickly swirl the frosting into peaks with a pointed knife as you go.

4 cups (1 pound) sifted confectioners' sugar

¼ teaspoon table salt

1 cup (2 sticks) unsalted butter, at room temperature (important!)

1 tablespoon light corn syrup

1 tablespoon pure vanilla extract

12 ounces (1½ packages PHILADELPHIA cream cheese (use only full-fat), at room temperature

Heavy whipping cream, if needed

On serving day:

5. To frost, make the buttercream and pipe or swirl the frosting onto the top of each cake while the cakes are still in the tin. Decorate each with a few extra chips, then place them in the refrigerator. When ready to serve, using a small spatula or knife, gently lift each Little Fella from the muffin tin and place on a serving platter. If using silicone liners, remove them. Refrigerate any leftover Little Fellas, covered, and enjoy for up to 3 days. These are best eaten fresh; do not freeze.

little fellas cream cheese buttercream

Junior's loves cream cheese—a lot! So when they have cupcakes, cheesecakes, Little Fellas, or any cake to frost, they often whip up this delicious cream cheese buttercream. In true Junior's fashion, it has three-quarters of a pound of cream cheese. It's one of those frostings you'll use time and again, because it swirls, it pipes, and it holds its shape perfectly every time.

MAKES 5 CUPS ICING, ENOUGH TO DECORATE THE TOPS OF 16 LITTLE FELLA CHEESECAKES OR THE TOP AND SIDES OF A 2-LAYER 8- OR 9-INCH CAKE; RECIPE MAY BE DOUBLED

1. In a medium bowl, sift the confectioners' sugar and salt together in a medium bowl.

2. In a large bowl, using an electric mixer fitted with the whisk attachment if you have one, beat the butter on high until creamy, about 3 minutes, scraping the bowl down once or twice. With the mixer running, beat in the corn syrup and vanilla.

3. Reduce the speed to low and add the confectioners' sugar in two additions. Return the mixer speed to high and blend in the cream cheese, 1 package first and then the remaining ½ package, scraping the bowl down several times. Beat until the icing looks light, airy, and almost fluffy, about 3 minutes more. Add a little cream, 1 tablespoon at a time, if needed, to bring the icing to spreading consistency.

Back in the 1950s, when Junior's opened its door in Brooklyn, marble cake, a phenomenon since Victorian days, became a popular celebration cake. Although marble cake is not baked at Junior's, it is kin to many of the triple-layer "skyscraper" cakes they sell in their bakeshops and restaurants. To "marble" the cake layers, we used the same swirling technique that the bakers at Junior's use for many fruit- or chocolate-swirled cheesecakes. Our cake is three layers of yellow cake with dark chocolate swirls marbled throughout, then frosted and decorated with Junior's buttery, rich fudge frosting.

chocolate marble cake with fudge frosting

MAKES ONE 3-LAYER 9-INCH CAKE, ABOUT 5 INCHES TALL

Softened unsalted butter, for buttering the pans

3 cups sifted cake flour

1 tablespoon baking powder

1 teaspoon table salt

1²/₃ cups whole milk

1 cup heavy whipping cream

1 tablespoon pure vanilla extract

1 cup (2 sticks) unsalted butter, at room temperature

2¹/₄ cups sugar

6 extra-large eggs, separated

¹/₂ teaspoon cream of tartar

6 ounces bittersweet chocolate (at least 60% cacao), melted (see The Junior's Way on page 259)

¹/₄ cup boiling water

¹/₄ teaspoon baking soda

1 recipe Junior's Fudge Frosting (page 238)

1. Preheat the oven to 350°F. Butter three 9-inch layer cake pans, line the bottoms with parchment, and butter the parchment. In a medium bowl, sift the flour, baking powder, and salt together. Combine the milk, cream, and vanilla and let stand at room temperature until ready to add to the batter (Step 3).

2. In a large bowl, using an electric mixer, cream the butter on high until light yellow, then add the sugar gradually and continue to beat until light and fluffy. Add the egg yolks, one at a time, beating well after each addition.

3. Decrease the speed to low and add the flour mixture in three additions, alternating with two additions of the milk mixture, beginning and ending with flour. In another large bowl, with clean, dry beaters, beat the egg whites and cream of tartar on high until stiff peaks form. Fold into the cake batter (don't worry if a few white specks remain, as they will disappear during baking).

4. In a small bowl, combine the melted chocolate, boiling water, and baking soda and let stand until it starts to thicken slightly, 2 to 3 minutes. Measure 1 cup of the white batter into a medium bowl and stir in the chocolate mixture until it's blended well.

5. Divide the remaining white batter among the three prepared cake pans. Top each layer with about 6 heaping tablespoonsful of chocolate batter, pushing the batter about two-thirds of the way down into the white batter. Using a table knife or a thin spatula, cut through the layers, swirling the knife as you go. Stop when you've swirled the batter all over once (more swirling at this stage might result in a chocolate cake instead of the nice marbled black and white one you want).

6. Bake the cake layers until a toothpick inserted in the center comes out with moist crumbs, 30 to 35 minutes. Transfer the pans to a wire rack and let cool for 10 minutes. Turn the layers out on the racks and cool completely.

7. When you're ready to frost the cake, make the Fudge Frosting (see page 238). Place one layer top side down on your prettiest cake plate. Spread about 1¼ cups of frosting on top. Place the second layer top side down and spread another 1¼ cups frosting on the top. Cover with the third layer, bottom side down. Brush the crumbs away from the top and side of the cake. Frost the side and top, smoothing it flat (an offset icing spatula works great for this). If you wish, use a pastry bag fitted with a medium open-star tip to pipe some of the frosting into a shell border all around the bottom of the cake and/or fleurs-de-lis or rosettes around the top edge and in the center. Refrigerate until an hour before serving. Refrigerate any leftovers, tightly covered, and serve within 2 days. Or slice, wrap the slices individually in plastic wrap, and freeze for up to 2 weeks.

continued

The Junior's Way

- When baking cakes, especially towering ones like this beauty, it's important to start with ingredients that are at room temperature, such as butter, milk, cream, or eggs. Take butter out of the refrigerator about 2 hours before you plan to use it, and cream, milk, and eggs, about half an hour.

- Be sure to use cake flour, not all-purpose flour, in this cake. Since cake flour has less gluten (protein), it results in a more tender, finer grain. This means your cake will have even more of that melt-in-your-mouth "yummy" factor!

junior's fudge frosting

This creamy chocolate buttercream is the perfect frosting for marble cake.

MAKES 6 CUPS FROSTING (ENOUGH TO FILL, FROST, AND DECORATE THE TOP AND SIDE OF AN 8- OR 9-INCH 3-LAYER CAKE)

6 cups sifted confectioners' sugar (1½ pounds)

½ teaspoon table salt

1½ cups (3 sticks) unsalted butter, at room temperature (important!)

6 tablespoons (¾ stick) margarine (see The Junior's Way)

2 tablespoons dark corn syrup

2 tablespoons unsweetened dark cocoa powder

1½ tablespoons pure vanilla extract

1 pound bittersweet chocolate (at least 60% cacao), melted (see The Junior's Way on page 259) and cooled

4 to 5 tablespoons cold heavy whipping cream

1. In a medium bowl, sift the confectioners' sugar and salt together.

2. In a large bowl, using an electric mixer, beat the butter and margarine together until creamy, about 3 minutes, scraping the bowl down once or twice. While the mixer is running, beat in the corn syrup, cocoa, and vanilla. Blend in the melted chocolate.

3. Reduce the speed to low and add the confectioners' sugar in two additions. Add 2 tablespoons of the cream and beat on high for 3 minutes, adding more cream, 1 tablespoon at a time, as needed to reach spreading consistency. The icing should be airy, almost fluffy, with a rich chocolate color. To keep the frosting fresh while you work, place a damp paper towel over the top and refrigerate. The frosting is best used within 30 minutes of mixing. Frost and decorate as directed in the cake recipe.

The Junior's Way

- This buttercream is not all butter; there's a little margarine in it also. This gives the frosting a velvety smooth texture and adds a little lightness. The dark corn syrup keeps it smooth and glossy.

- Use a long, narrow metal spatula (about 12 inches long including the handle and 1 inch wide) to frost and decorate a cake. Use a shorter one (about 8 inches long and ¾ inch wide) for frosting cupcakes and cookies. The offset-handled spatulas are best for these frosting jobs.

- Before you begin icing a cake, brush away any crumbs from the side and top. This gives a smooth professional look, without any unsightly bubbles or bumps.

Bobka is a cherished Jewish tradition, and Junior's Chocolate Bobka Loaf Cake is a signature dessert item that's made the same way today, using the same recipe, that Alan's Grandpa made it in the 1950s. The bakers mix up a rich, sweet yeast dough, then roll it out, smear it with almond paste, and top it with a chopped chocolate dough, mini-chocolate chips, and walnuts. They roll it up jellyroll style, twist it into a rope, shower it with a cinnamon-y streusel, let it rise, and then bake it to perfection. After baking, the loaves get a sprinkle of confectioners' sugar and a drizzle of melted chocolate. This recipe makes two large loaves. Give the second one to a friend or freeze (it will keep for up to 2 weeks) and serve another day.

junior's chocolate bobka loaf cake

MAKES THREE LOAVES (9 X 5 X 3 INCHES)

The day before you plan to make the bobka:

1. Heat the milk in a medium saucepan over medium heat just until bubbles form around the edge; remove from the heat before it comes to a full boil. Transfer to a large bowl of a stand mixer fitted with the paddle attachment, and let the milk cool to between 105° and 115°F.

2. Meanwhile, place the warm water in a small bowl. Check the temperature; it should be no cooler than 105°F and no hotter than 115°F. Sprinkle over the yeast and 1 teaspoon sugar; stir until dissolved, then let stand until foamy.

3. Beat the yeast mixture into the cooled milk. Add the 1 cup of melted butter, the remaining 1¼ cups sugar, the vanilla, salt, eggs, and egg yolks and mix on medium until light, about 3 minutes.

1 cup whole milk

⅓ cup warm water (105° to 115°F)

Two ¼-ounce packages active dry yeast

1¼ cups plus 1 teaspoon granulated sugar

1 cup (2 sticks) unsalted butter, melted, plus more for brushing the loaves

1 tablespoon plus 1 teaspoon pure vanilla extract

1 tablespoon plus 1 teaspoon table salt

2 extra-large eggs plus 2 extra-large egg yolks, whisked

6½ to 7 cups all-purpose flour

Softened unsalted butter, for buttering bowl and pans

continued

continued

1 recipe Almond Smear
(page 242)

1 recipe Chopped Chocolate Dough
(page 243)

About 25 NABISCO® FAMOUS®
Chocolate Wafers

1 cup finely chopped walnuts

3/4 cup mini-chocolate chips

1 recipe Cinnamon-y Streusel
(page 243)

Sifted confectioners' sugar

4 ounces chocolate, melted (see
The Junior's Way on page 259)

4. Decrease the speed to low and blend in the 6½ cups of the flour in three additions. Stop the mixer and change to a dough hook if you have one. Increase the speed to medium to "knead" for about 8 minutes, adding a little more flour if needed to achieve a smooth dough (it should be light and smooth). Turn out onto a lightly floured work surface and knead just until it comes together in a soft ball of dough.

5. Coat a large bowl with softened butter. Transfer the dough to the bowl and turn it over once to butter all sides well. Cover with plastic wrap and let the dough rise at room temperature until doubled in size, about 2 hours. Divide the dough into three equal balls and wrap each individually in plastic wrap. Place in zip-top plastic bags and refrigerate overnight.

On baking day:

6. Generously smear three 9 x 5 x 3-inch loaf pans with softened butter. Line the bottoms and up the sides with parchment and butter well. Remove one ball of dough from the refrigerator, keeping the other two refrigerated. Make the Almond Smear and Chopped Chocolate Dough and process the wafers in a food processor to make 1 cup fine crumbs.

7. On a lightly floured surface, roll out the first ball of dough into a 16 x 12-inch rectangle that is ⅛ inch thick. Spread the rectangle with ½ cup of the Almond Smear, covering it up to ¼ inch from all edges. Scatter ⅓ cup of the Chopped Chocolate Dough over all. Sprinkle each loaf with ⅓ cup of the walnuts and ¼ cup of the chocolate chips, then cover with ⅓ cup of the chocolate wafer crumbs. Starting at one of the narrow ends, roll the rectangle up, jellyroll style. Gently twist the roll of dough about 12 times, or until you have a loaf 9 inches wide. Fold the ends under and seal the seam and the ends with some melted butter, then place seam side down in one of the prepared loaf pans. Repeat with the remaining two balls of dough, Almond Smear, Chopped Chocolate Dough, chocolate chips, walnuts, and chocolate wafer crumbs, making three loaves of Bobka. Brush the top of all three loaves with the melted butter.

continued

The Junior's Way

To ensure there is filling in every bite, make sure each of the fillings cover the dough up to ¼ inch from all the edges.

8. Make the Cinnamon-y Streusel and sprinkle half over each loaf. Let the loaves rise, uncovered, at room temperature until light and doubled in size, about 45 minutes.

9. Meanwhile, preheat the oven to 350°F. Bake the loaves until golden, about 1 hour, or until the loaves feel firm. Turn off the oven and let the loaves remain for 10 minutes. Transfer the loaves to a wire rack, brush the tops with melted butter, and let cool in the pans for 30 minutes. Gently turn out the loaves, remove the parchment, and let the loaves cool on their sides for 30 minutes; turn them right side up. To decorate the loaves you plan to serve now, sprinkle the tops with confectioners' sugar. Using a small pointed spoon (a grapefruit spoon works well), drizzle the loaves with the melted chocolate. Let the loaves cool for at least another hour before slicing. Wrap any leftovers in plastic wrap, refrigerate, and enjoy within 3 days. To freeze the extra loaves, cool completely, but do not decorate. Wrap in plastic wrap and then in aluminum foil or freezer paper. To defrost, let the loaf stand at room temperature (do not defrost in a microwave or an oven). After the bobka has defrosted, decorate with the confectioners' sugar and the chocolate drizzle as directed above.

almond smear

MAKES 1½ CUPS, ENOUGH FOR 3 LOAVES

7 to 8 ounces almond paste
(1 tube or can)

1 cup confectioners' sugar

¼ cup (½ stick) unsalted butter, softened

¼ cup heavy whipping cream

In a medium bowl, using an electric mixer fitted with the whisk attachment, beat all the ingredients together on medium-high until creamy and a spreading consistency. Use on three loaves of Junior's Chocolate Bobka Loaf Cake (½ cup each) or smear onto your favorite coffeecake dough.

chopped chocolate dough

MAKES 1½ CUPS, ENOUGH FOR 3 LOAVES

6 ounces semisweet chocolate

¼ cup sugar

6 tablespoons (¾ stick) unsalted butter, at room temperature

Chop the chocolate into large chunks, then transfer to a food processor and pulse for about 30 seconds until you have fine, even crumbs (no finer!). Add the sugar and process for 15 seconds to mix. Add the butter and pulse until a ball of dough forms.

cinnamon-y streusel

MAKES 1 CUP, ENOUGH FOR 3 LOAVES

⅔ cup all-purpose flour

¼ cup firmly packed light brown sugar

3 tablespoons granulated sugar

2 teaspoons ground cinnamon

6 tablespoons (¾ stick) unsalted butter, softened

In a medium bowl, stir the flour, both sugars, and cinnamon until mixed. With a pastry cutter or two forks, cut in the butter until ¾-inch clumps form.

Here's that same carrot cake that Junior's customers love—moist, tender, and melt-in-your-mouth delicious with plenty of fine shreds of fresh carrots, dark raisins, and walnut pieces in every bite. But instead of the three-layer carrot cake the bakers make every day, we've baked this one in a sheet pan to yield 20 big-sized servings. Double the recipe and you have plenty for a crowd of hungry folks. Frost with the best cream cheese frosting ever, swirling it fast to give your creation a professional touch.

carrot sheet cake with junior's cream cheese frosting

MAKES ONE 15 X 10-INCH SHEET CAKE OR TWO 9-INCH SQUARE CAKES; 18 TO 20 SERVINGS

Softened unsalted butter, for buttering the pan(s)

3 cups all-purpose flour

1 tablespoon ground cinnamon

1 tablespoon baking powder

1 teaspoon baking soda

1 teaspoon table salt

6 extra-large eggs

2 1/2 cups sugar

1 1/3 cups vegetable oil

1 tablespoon pure vanilla extract

1 pound carrots, peeled and finely grated (about 2 1/2 cups; see The Junior's Way on page 245)

1 1/3 cups dark raisins

1 1/3 cups coarsely chopped walnuts

1 recipe Junior's Cream Cheese Frosting (page 245)

1. Preheat the oven to 350°F and butter one 15 x 10 x 2-inch sheet cake pan or two 9-inch square cake pans. Line the bottom with parchment (don't worry if it comes up the sides), then butter the parchment. In a medium bowl, stir the flour, cinnamon, baking powder, baking soda, and salt together.

2. In a large bowl, using an electric mixer, beat the eggs on high about 3 minutes. Gradually add the sugar, beating constantly until light yellow ribbons form, about 3 minutes. With the mixer running, slowly drizzle in the oil, then the vanilla. Reduce the mixer speed to low and blend in the flour mixture, then mix in the carrots, raisins, and walnuts.

3. Spread out the batter evenly in the prepared sheet pan. Bake the cake until a toothpick inserted in the center comes out with moist crumbs (not clean), 50 to 55 minutes for the sheet cake and 40 to 45 minutes for the 9-inch-square cake. Let cool completely on a wire rack.

4. When the cake has cooled, remove it from the pan and transfer to a serving tray. Make the frosting and spread evenly over the top. For a fancier finish, swirl into a decorative design (see The Junior's Way). Refrigerate any leftovers, tightly covered, and enjoy within 2 days, or tightly wrap individual pieces, place in zip-top freezer bags, and freeze for up to 2 weeks.

junior's cream cheese frosting

Junior's loves cream cheese, especially when it's whipped into this delicious cream cheese frosting. It acts like a buttercream frosting, meaning it's easy to work with and gives you plenty of swirling time before it sets.

MAKES 7 CUPS FROSTING (ENOUGH TO FROST AND DECORATE THE TOP AND SIDES OF A 15 X 10-INCH SHEET CAKE OR TWO 9-INCH SQUARE CAKES, 16 TO 18 CUPCAKES, OR TO FILL AND FROST AN 8- OR 9-INCH 2-LAYER CAKE)

4 cups sifted confectioners' sugar (1 pound)

¼ teaspoon table salt

1 cup (2 sticks) unsalted butter, at room temperature (important!)

¼ cup (½ stick) vegetable shortening

1 tablespoon light corn syrup

1 tablespoon pure vanilla extract

Two 8-ounces packages PHILADELPHIA cream cheese (use only full fat), at room temperature (important!)

Heavy whipping cream, if needed

1. In a medium bowl, sift the confectioners' sugar and salt together.

2. In a large bowl, using an electric mixer fitted with the whisk attachment if you have one, beat the butter and vegetable shortening together until creamy, about 3 minutes, scraping down the bowl once or twice. With the mixer running, beat in the corn syrup and vanilla.

3. Reduce the speed to low and add the confectioners' sugar in two additions. With the mixer on high, blend in the cream cheese, one package at a time, beating well after each addition, then beat for 3 minutes more. If needed, add cream, 1 tablespoon at a time, to bring the icing to spreading consistency. The frosting should look light, airy, almost fluffy. This is best used within an hour of mixing.

The Junior's Way

- Time-saving tip: Shredded fresh carrots are available in most supermarket produce sections, usually sold in 10-ounce bags; one bag gives you exactly the 2½ cups needed for this cake. They are coarsely shredded, though, so process them in an electric food processor for a few seconds to break the shreds into smaller, finer ones, which bake up best in this cake.

- To frost the cake, use a small spatula (about ¾ inch wide) and start at the top narrow left-hand corner. Swirl the frosting on the diagonal, across the cake, to the opposite right-hand bottom corner. Repeat, starting from the top right-hand corner and working to the bottom left-hand corner.

Junior's pastry chefs created these deep, dark devil's food S'more cupcakes using a combination of semisweet chocolate and cocoa for a rich chocolate flavor. They are moist, tender, and airy and come with a surprise inside. Take a bite and you'll discover a pocket of white crème filling, which tastes very much like melted marshmallows. It's also used to ice the tops, which are then embellished with a sprinkle of graham cracker crumbs and a swirl of ganache.

s'more cupcakes

MAKES TWENTY 2¾-INCH FILLED CUPCAKES

FOR THE CUPCAKES

1¾ cups all-purpose flour

½ cup natural unsweetened dark cocoa powder

1 tablespoon baking powder

1 teaspoon table salt

½ teaspoon baking soda

1 cup (2 sticks) unsalted butter, at room temperature

1¼ cups sugar

3 extra-large eggs

4 ounces semisweet chocolate, melted and cooled (see The Junior's Way on page 259)

1 tablespoon pure vanilla extract

½ cup whole milk

½ cup boiling water

FOR FILLING, FROSTING, AND DECORATION

1 recipe Marshmallow Crème Filling (page 248)

9 large graham crackers

1 cup Junior's Chocolate Ganache (page 263) or 4 ounces semisweet chocolate melted (see The Junior's Way on page 259)

1. Preheat the oven to 350°F. Butter the complete top of twenty 2¾-inch muffin cups (see The Junior's Way on page 248); line with cupcake liners (silicone, paper, foil, or parchment). In a small bowl, sift the flour, cocoa, baking powder, salt, and baking soda together.

2. In a large bowl, using an electric mixer, cream the butter and sugar together on medium until light yellow and creamy and ribbons begin to form, about 3 minutes. Add the eggs, one at a time, beating a few seconds after each. Beat in the chocolate and vanilla. Reduce the mixer speed to low and mix in some of the flour mixture, then some of the milk. Repeat until all have been incorporated. Blend in the boiling water.

3. Fill the muffin cups to the top. Bake until set and a toothpick inserted in the center comes out with moist crumbs (not clean), about 25 minutes. Cool in the tin on a wire rack for 15 minutes, then turn out the cupcakes onto the rack to cool completely before filling and frosting. If using silicone liners, remove them. While the cupcakes cool, make the Marshmallow Crème Filling. Refrigerate until ready to use.

4. To fill and frost, gently press your thumb about three-fourths of the way down into the center of each cupcake (not to the bottom!). Use a small demitasse spoon to stuff the hole with filling. Ice the tops, spreading the marsh-

continued

mallow crème out evenly, instead of in peaks, and all the way to the edge. This gives the best "canvas" for decorating with the ganache.

5. To finish the edges, break the graham crackers into crumbs with your hands and make a ½-inch-wide border around the edge of each cupcake.

6. Make the ganache or melt the chocolate: Use a plastic squeeze bottle or a pastry bag fitted with a small round tip to decorate the cakes with zigzag swirls. Refrigerate the cupcakes, without wrapping, until the icing has set. They are best if allowed to return to room temperature before serving. Wrap any leftover cupcakes, refrigerate, and enjoy within a few days. Do not freeze these cupcakes.

marshmallow crème filling

½ cup (1 stick) unsalted butter, at room temperature

One 7-ounce jar Marshmallow fluff®

2 teaspoons pure vanilla extract

4 cups (1 pound) confectioners' sugar

6 tablespoons heavy whipping cream

MAKES 3 CUPS, ENOUGH TO FILL ONE 9-INCH WHOOPIE PIE CHEESECAKE OR FROST 20 S'MORE CUPCAKES

1. In a large bowl, using an electric mixer, cream the butter, fluff, and vanilla together on medium high until light yellow. Turn off the mixer.

2. Add the confectioners' sugar and beat on medium high until it's no longer visible. With the mixer running, add the cream and continue beating until the frosting is a spreading consistency.

The Junior's Way

During baking, these cupcakes might rise and spread out onto the edge of the muffin cups. This is a good thing, as it gives wider tops to frost. To ensure the cupcakes are easy to remove, even if they have this extra "cake collar," butter the complete top of the muffin tin well, especially around the edge of the muffin cups. After the cakes have baked, let them cool in their tin on a wire rack for about 15 minutes (but no longer!). If the cupcakes have spread onto the rims, gently run a small spatula around the edge to release them. Then turn out the cupcakes onto the rack (they should fall out on their own when the tin is carefully turned upside down). If some cupcakes are still in the pan, gently lift out each one, being careful not to break off their edges.

Here at Junior's, we believe that everyone should be able to enjoy great food and great desserts…even if you, or someone in your family, are on a gluten-free diet. Now, thanks to the gluten-free baking mixes available in supermarkets, you can bake good-tasting breads and desserts at home, like these cupcakes with a creamy, delicious peanut butter frosting.

gluten-free
peanut butter cupcakes

MAKES ABOUT TWENTY 2¾-INCH CUPCAKES

2 cups gluten-free all-purpose baking flour, such as Bob's Red Mill or King Arthur®

1 tablespoon baking powder

2 teaspoons cornstarch

1 teaspoon table salt

³/₄ cup (1½ sticks) unsalted butter, at room temperature

³/₄ cup smooth gluten-free peanut butter (we used Skippy® Honey-Roast, see The Junior's Way on page 250)

1¼ cups granulated sugar

¹/₃ cup firmly packed light brown sugar

3 extra-large eggs

1 tablespoon pure vanilla extract

³/₄ cup whole milk

1 recipe Peanut Buttercream Frosting (page 250)

One 8-ounce sweet or semisweet chocolate bar, grated (see The Junior's Way on page 250)

1. Preheat the oven to 350°F. Line twenty 2¾-inch muffin cups with cupcake liners (silicone, paper, foil, or parchment).

2. In a small bowl, stir the flour, baking powder, cornstarch, and salt together. In a large bowl, using an electric mixer, cream the butter, peanut butter, and both sugars together on medium until the mixture is light brown and creamy, about 2 minutes. Add the eggs, one at a time, beating a few seconds after each. Beat in the vanilla. At the lowest speed possible, mix in the flour mixture in three additions, alternating with the milk.

3. Fill the muffin cups almost to the top of the liners (about seven-eighths full) with the batter. There is enough batter for about 20 cupcakes. Bake until set and a toothpick inserted in the center of each comes out clean, 20 to 25 minutes (do not overbake!). Cool in the tins on a wire rack for 15 minutes, then remove from the tins and transfer to a wire rack to cool completely before frosting. If using silicone muffin liners, remove them.

4. When you are ready to frost the cupcakes, prepare the frosting, then swirl or pipe it on top of each cupcake (use a medium open-star tip). Sprinkle each cupcake with some grated chocolate. Refrigerate, uncovered, until the frosting sets, about an hour, then loosely cover with foil if you like. These are best enjoyed within 2 days. Do not freeze.

continued

peanut buttercream frosting

This frosting is light, creamy, and so easy to swirl onto cupcakes.

MAKES ABOUT 4½ TO 5 CUPS PEANUT BUTTERCREAM, ENOUGH TO FROST ABOUT 20 CUPCAKES

4 cups sifted confectioners' sugar (1 pound)

¼ teaspoon table salt

1 cup (2 sticks) unsalted butter, at room temperature (important!)

1 cup smooth gluten-free peanut butter (see The Junior's Way)

1 tablespoon light corn syrup

1 tablespoon pure vanilla extract

½ cup cold heavy whipping cream, plus more if needed

1. In a medium bowl, stir the confectioners' sugar and salt together.

2. In a large bowl, using an electric mixer fitted with the whisk attachment if you have one, beat the butter and peanut butter on high until creamy, about 3 minutes, scraping the bowl down once or twice. With the mixer running, beat in the cornsyrup and vanilla. Reduce the speed to low and add the confectioners' sugar in two additions, alternately with half the cream, and beat on high for 3 minutes. Add the rest of the cream and beat until the icing looks light, airy, and almost fluffy. If it's not spreadable, add a little more cream, 1 tablespoon at a time, until it's easy to spread and swirl. To keep the frosting fresh, place a damp paper towel over the top and refrigerate. Use within 30 minutes of mixing.

The Junior's Way

- Gluten-free baking flours can be found in supermarkets, gourmet food markets, and online. The baking flours are a blend of various flours, all from nonwheat sources, such as tapioca flour, potato starch, sorghum, and bean flours like fava and garbanzo.

- Generally, peanut butter is gluten-free—whether natural or hydrogenated—but if you want to be absolutely certain, check the company's Web site or call the product line phone number on the label.

- The cornstarch stabilizes the batter and keeps the cupcakes from crumbling.

- For nicely grated chocolate for decorating, buy a thick 8-ounce bar of sweet or semisweet chocolate and use at room temperature (not straight from the refrigerator). Hold the bar vertically, with the long side on a chopping board. Using a serrated knife, scrape down the end of the bar, allowing the curls to fall away into a pile. The larger the pieces, the prettier the curls.

Junior's likes to WOW its customers, especially when it comes to desserts. Though you won't find this tart on their menu, it has the same cheesecake filling they're famous for, this time in a vanilla wafer crumb crust topped with hand-glazed raspberries. It's guaranteed to make a million-dollar impression, every time!

junior's cheesecake tart

MAKES ONE 11- OR 12-INCH TART

Softened unsalted butter, for buttering the pan

1 recipe Vanilla Wafer Crumb Crust (page 220)

Two 8-ounce packages PHILADELPHIA cream cheese (use only full fat), at room temperature

¾ cup sugar

3 tablespoons cornstarch

1 tablespoon pure vanilla extract

2 extra-large eggs

⅔ cup heavy whipping cream

Two 6-ounce cartons fresh raspberries (choose firm ones, not overly ripe, and similar in size)

One 12-ounce jar currant jelly

The day before you plan to serve the tart:

1. Preheat the oven to 350°F and generously butter the bottom and side of an 11- or 12-inch tart pan (preferably a nonstick one with a removable bottom and 1-inch side). Wrap the outside with aluminum foil, covering the bottom and extending all the way up the side. Shape the tart shell (see The Junior's Way on page 253) and freeze for 15 minutes, then bake just until set and light golden, about 8 minutes. Leave the oven on.

2. In a large bowl, using an electric mixer fitted with the paddle attachment if you have one, beat 1 package of the cream cheese, ¼ cup of the sugar, and the cornstarch on low until creamy, about 3 minutes, scraping down the bowl a few times. Beat in the remaining package of cream cheese.

3. Increase the mixer speed to medium and beat in the remaining ½ cup sugar and the vanilla. Beat in the eggs, then the cream. At this point, mix the filling only until completely blended. *Be careful not to overmix!*

4. Gently spoon the cheese filling into the prebaked tart shell. Place the pan in a large, shallow pan and add hot water so it comes only about halfway up the side of the tart pan (important!).

5. Bake the tart until the edge is set and the center barely jiggles, 35 to 40 minutes. Transfer the pan to a wire rack and let cool for 1 hour. Cover the cake loosely with plastic wrap and refrigerate until it's completely cold, preferably overnight or for at least 4 hours.

continued

On serving day:

6. While the tart chills, glaze the raspberries. Wash the berries and drain on paper towels (very important!). Place a wire rack over a few paper towels (to catch the drips). Melt the jelly in a microwave or a small pan over low heat. Hold each raspberry with small tweezers or a long pick such as a cake tester and dip the berry completely into the jelly, then quickly pull it out before the warm jelly "wilts" the berry. Place on the rack and let stand to dry for about an hour. Refrigerate the berries on the rack until ready to decorate the tart. These raspberries are at their best when glazed about an hour (no more!) before decorating the tart.

7. To serve, remove the side of the tart pan. Slide the tart off the bottom of the pan onto a cake plate (or leave the tart on the bottom of the pan and place right on the serving plate). Decorate with a double ring of glazed raspberries, pointed ends up, carefully arranged around the outside rim of the tart. Chill until serving time. Cover and refrigerate any leftover tart and enjoy the next day. Do not freeze this tart.

The Junior's Way

Here's a tip for shaping the crust. Spread out the crumb mixture in the tart pan, working it from the center up the side. To shape, use a 1/3-cup metal measuring cup (with a handle) to flatten the crumbs evenly on the bottom and to press the crumbs up the side.

Take a look at Junior's bakery case and you'll see rows of pies, including their mile-high meringue pies. This key lime version isn't offered in their restaurants, but it's the perfect pie for impressing guests; easy to make, it's a sweetly refreshing ending to a hearty meal. Pat out a quick graham cracker crust, whip up the filling with Key lime juice and sweetened condensed milk, then swirl on a meringue and bake until light golden brown. This pie is best served chilled, so make it a day ahead of when you plan to serve it.

key lime meringue pie

MAKES ONE 9-INCH DEEP-DISH PIE; SERVES 6 TO 8

Softened unsalted butter, for buttering the pie plate

1 recipe 9-inch Graham Cracker Crumb Crust (page 226)

FOR THE KEY LIME FILLING

5 extra-large egg yolks

3 cups sweetened condensed milk (see The Junior's Way)

1 cup Key lime juice (bottled or fresh)

FOR THE MERINGUE

5 extra-large egg whites

1/2 teaspoon cream of tartar

1 cup sugar

The morning of the day you plan to serve the pie:

1. Preheat the oven to 350°F. Generously butter a 9- to 9 1/2-inch deep-dish pie plate, with 2-inch sides. Shape the crust, pressing the crumbs flat on the bottom and working them all the way up the side to about 1/8 inch above the edge of the pie plate. Finish the edge by pinching the crust between your thumb and second finger all around. Freeze for 15 minutes, then bake until set, about 8 minutes. Set on a wire rack to cool.

2. Make the Key lime filling: In a large bowl, using a mixer, beat the egg yolks on high until thick and light lemon in color, about 3 minutes. Reduce the speed to medium and beat in the condensed milk, then the lime juice. Beat only until the mixture thickens (avoid overbeating, as this can cause the custard to separate). Spoon the filling into the cooled crust and bake the pie until it looks slightly set on top, about 15 minutes. Transfer to a wire rack. Leave the oven on.

3. Make the meringue: In a large bowl with clean, dry beaters, beat the egg whites and cream of tartar on high until soft peaks form. With the mixer running, gradually add the sugar in four additions and continue to beat until stiff, glossy peaks form. Do not beat past the stiff peak stage, or the meringue might fall or "weep" during baking. To help the meringue attach to the filling, lightly score the filling by running the prongs of a fork across it in vertical lines. Spoon on the meringue and swirl into peaks (see The Junior's Way). Make sure to get a good seal with the crust.

4. Bake the pie just until the meringue turns golden and some of the peaks turn light brown, about 10 minutes. Transfer to the rack and let cool completely at room temperature, then refrigerate, uncovered, for a couple of hours more or overnight. Refrigerate any leftover pie and enjoy in the next day or two. Do not freeze this pie.

The Junior's Way

- Take a tip from the pastry chefs: beat the meringue until stiff, glossy peaks form. To top the pie with the meringue, start at the outside edge, spooning the meringue all around and making sure to have a complete seal to the pie crust (otherwise the filling will weep when baked). Pile the remaining meringue in the center and use a small spatula or a thin-bladed knife to swirl it into impressive peaks.

- You need 3 cups of sweetened condensed milk for this pie, which means you'll need to buy three 14-ounce cans (they each contain about 1¼ cups). We used Eagle Brand®, but any sweetened condensed milk will work fine in this recipe. Evaporated milk, found on the same supermaket shelf, will not.

Alan's Grandpa Harry and his brother Mike were partners in the Enduro luncheonettes that operated in New York City in the 1930s. Customers knew they could always get a slice of one of their legendary just-baked pies. Cherry pie was on the menu often. This pie is similar to the one on Junior's menu, except it has a topping of buttery crumbs instead of a top pastry crust.

cherry crumb pie

MAKES ONE 9- OR 9½ INCH DEEP-DISH CHERRY PIE

Softened unsalted butter, for buttering the pie plate

½ recipe (1 disk) All-Butter Pie Pastry (page 101)

FOR THE CHERRY FILLING

⅔ cup granulated sugar

⅓ cup firmly packed light brown sugar

2 tablespoons all-purpose flour

2 tablespoons quick-cooking tapioca

1 teaspoon ground cinnamon

½ teaspoon table salt

6 cups pitted sour pie cherries, jarred or canned (about 2¼ pounds)

1 tablespoon fresh lemon juice

½ teaspoon pure almond extract

2 tablespoons unsalted butter, cut into pieces

FOR THE BUTTERY CRUMB CRUST

¾ cup all-purpose flour

¾ cup granulated sugar

1 teaspoon baking powder

½ teaspoon table salt

½ teaspoon ground nutmeg

½ cup (1 stick) cold unsalted butter, cut into small pieces

1. Preheat the oven to 375°F and generously butter a deep-dish 9- or 9½-inch pie plate with 2-inch sides. Make the pastry. Roll out one disk ⅛ inch thick on a lightly floured work surface and trim to a 17-inch circle. Transfer to the pie dish, leaving a 2-inch overhang all around. Fold the edge of the pastry toward the outside, making a 1-inch stand-up edge, and flute it. Place the crust in the freezer to firm up while you make the filling and crumb topping.

2. In a medium bowl, mix together both sugars, the flour, tapioca, cinnamon, and salt. In a large bowl, gently work through the well-drained cherries and discard any pits. With a rubber spatula, gently stir in the lemon juice and almond extract. Pour the sugar mixture over the cherries and gently stir to mix. Spoon the cherry filling into the pie shell and top with the butter. Bake for 15 minutes, then remove from the oven. Lower the temperature to 350°F.

3. In a medium bowl, mix together all the ingredients for the Buttery Crumb Crust, except the butter. Using a pastry cutter, work the butter into the mixture until crumbs the size of peas appear. Spread the crumbs evenly over the cherry filling, pushing them out to the edge to cover the top completely.

4. Bake the pie until the crust is golden and the filling is bubbling, 35 to 40 minutes. Lay a piece of foil on top if it's browning too fast. Cool on a wire rack for 4 to 6 hours to allow the filling to set before serving. Cover and refrigerate any leftover pie, and enjoy within the week. Do not freeze.

When Alan's Grandpa Rosen opened Junior's in 1950, he knew he needed an excellent bake shop. He hired Eigel Peterson, a Danish-born baker. Together, he and Eigel created a line of desserts that helped make Junior's famous, including their whipped cream pies. Here is Junior's Chocolate Whipped Cream Pie, with its deep dark chocolate-y filling, crowned with a mini-mountain of sweetened whipped cream and chocolate curls.

chocolate whipped cream pie

MAKES ONE 9- TO 9½-INCH DEEP-DISH PIE, ABOUT 5 INCHES TALL

FOR THE CRUST

½ recipe (1 disk) All-Butter Pie Pastry (page 101)

Softened unsalted butter, for buttering the pie plate

FOR THE CHOCOLATE CREAM FILLING

1½ cups sugar

¼ cup all-purpose flour

¼ cup cornstarch

2 tablespoons unsweetened dark cocoa powder

½ teaspoon table salt

2 cups whole milk

1 cup heavy whipping cream

4 extra-large egg yolks

8 ounces bittersweet chocolate (at least 60% cacao), melted

2 tablespoons unsalted butter

1 tablespoon pure vanilla extract

1. Prepare and chill the pastry. Preheat the oven to 400°F and generously butter a 9- to 9½-inch deep-dish pie plate with 2-inch sides. On a lightly floured surface, roll out the pastry ⅛ inch thick and trim to a 17-inch circle. Transfer to the pie plate, leaving a 2-inch overhang. Fold the edge of the pastry toward the outside, making a 1-inch stand-up edge, and flute. Prick all over with a fork and freeze for 15 minutes to firm up the edge.

2. Blind-bake the crust: Line the chilled crust with aluminum foil all the way up the sides, pressing it so it helps to hold up the fluted edge. Fill with pie weights, uncooked rice, or dried beans. Bake for 10 to 15 minutes until set. Remove the foil and the weights. Return the crust to the oven and bake until the bottom is dry, set, and light golden all over, 5 minutes more. Transfer to a wire rack and cool completely (very important!). Turn off the oven.

3. Make the chocolate cream filling: In a large, heavy saucepan, mix the sugar, flour, cornstarch, cocoa, and salt together. Whisk in the milk and cream until dissolved. Cook over medium heat, whisking occasionally, just until bubbles form around the edge of the pan, about 8 minutes. Remove from the heat.

4. Meanwhile, in a large bowl, using an electric mixer, beat the egg yolks on high until light yellow and thick. Reduce the speed to low and beat in about 2 cups of the hot cream mixture. Pour this into the hot cream in the saucepan. Cook over medium heat, whisking constantly, until the custard thickens,

FOR THE WHIPPED CREAM TOP

3 cups heavy whipping cream

½ cup sugar

2 tablespoons pure vanilla extract

1 thick king-sized (about 7 ounces) dark chocolate candy bar (without nuts), such as Hershey's Special Dark® Chocolate, at room temperature

about 2 minutes. Watch carefully and do not let the custard boil or stick to the pan. Remove from the heat, whisk in the melted chocolate, then the butter and vanilla. Pour into a heatproof bowl, lay a piece of plastic wrap directly on the surface of the custard (this will keep a skin from forming), and refrigerate until thickened but not set, about 1 hour.

5. Spoon the custard into the cooled pie shell, lay a piece of plastic wrap directly on the surface again, and refrigerate until completely set, at least 2 hours more or overnight if you are serving the pie the next day.

6. Make the whipped cream top: In a large bowl, using an electric mixer fitted with the whisk attachment, whip the cream until frothy. Continue whipping while you add the sugar and vanilla. Whip until the cream holds stiff peaks when you pull the beaters up (no further!). Swirl or pipe the cream (using a pastry bag fitted with a large open-star tip) on top of the pie and refrigerate.

7. Decorate the top: Make the chocolate curls from the chocolate candy bar (see The Junior's Way). Arrange the curls on top of the pie, covering it almost completely but letting a little of the white cream show through. Refrigerate until chilled, about 2 hours. This is best served the day it is made. Refrigerate any leftovers and serve the next day. Do not freeze.

The Junior's Way

- The microwave is great for melting chocolate. Chop it into uniform pieces and place in a microwave-safe, heat-safe container. Make sure the dish is dry, as even one or two drops of water can cause the chocolate to "seize" and clump. Microwave at 50% to 70% power in 30- to 60-second intervals, stirring in between. It will take about 1 minute to melt an ounce of chocolate.

- To make chocolate curls, buy the thickest, darkest chocolate bar you can find. Keep it at room temperature. Stand the chocolate bar up at a slight angle on a cutting board. Slowly scrape all the way down the bar with a vegetable peeler. The chocolate will fall away in a pile of soft curls.

Even if you've never made candy, you can make these truffles! They are simple and foolproof. And even though truffles are not on Junior's menu, we wanted you to have the recipe. We've created two different kinds: one with chocolate centers made from crushed Oreos and cream cheese, the other with delicious centers made from Junior's frozen cheesecake. Coat them with Junior's Chocolate Ganache and decorate however you like—crushed pecans, flaked coconut—or just leave them plain. The best part: You can make them a couple of days ahead, so they're great for a party.

junior's chocolate
no-bake truffles

MAKES ABOUT 4 DOZEN TRUFFLES

One 16.6-ounce package OREO® Chocolate Sandwich cookies (regular-size 2-inch cookies)

One 8-ounce package PHILADELPHIA cream cheese (use only full fat), at room temperature

Softened unsalted butter, as needed

4 cups Junior's Chocolate Ganache (recipe page 263)

Finely chopped pecans

Angel flake coconut, toasted if you wish

1. Line three cake pans that can go into the freezer with parchment or waxed paper, securing it with a dab of butter.

2. Place the cookies in a food processor and pulse for about 30 seconds until reduced to fine, even crumbs, but not powdery. Avoid overprocessing, as the cookies can turn into a fine chocolate meal. Add the cream cheese and continue to pulse until the mixture turns into a chocolate dough and white specks of cheese are no longer visible.

3. Grease your hands with soft butter and roll the cookie dough into ¾-inch truffle balls (you will have 40 to 50 balls), placing them in the prepared cake pans. Be sure the truffles do not touch each other. Place in the freezer until firm, at least 30 minutes.

4. Meanwhile, make the ganache and place it in the freezer for about 10 minutes to thicken to dipping consistency.

continued

• Here's a tip from Alan: After rolling the cookie or cheesecake dough into balls, freeze them until they are firm before coating them with ganache. The ganache will coat more evenly and set up faster.

• Don't have a food processor for crushing the Oreos? Place about one-third of the Oreos in a zip-top plastic bag and seal, leaving a small opening for the air to escape. Roll a rolling pin over the bag, crushing the cookies into fine crumbs, and place in a large bowl. Continue until all the cookies have been crushed. Add the cream cheese and mix until a chocolate dough forms.

5. Remove the truffles and ganache from the freezer. Using your hands, dip each truffle into the ganache, swirling to coat evenly, then return to the cake pans. Continue until all the truffles are coated; again, don't let the truffles touch each other.

6. Spread out the pecans on one plate and the coconut on another. Roll about one-third of the truffles, one by one, in the pecans, returning each one to a pan. Then roll another third in the coconut; leave the last third "plain" chocolate-coated. You will now have three different kinds of truffles (this makes a great dessert presentation).

7. Refrigerate until the truffles are firm and the ganache is set, about 1 hour. Store in the refrigerator in airtight containers, separating the layers with waxed paper and enjoy within the week. Let the truffles stand at room temperature about 15 minutes before serving. Do not freeze.

CHEESECAKE TRUFFLES

Instead of making the chocolate Oreo dough, make and bake a layer of cheesecake as for the Whoopie Pie (page 228). Let cool as directed, then freeze. When ready to shape the truffles, let the cheesecake stand at room temperature for a few minutes, just until it is pliable enough to roll into balls, no longer. Shape, coat, and dip in chocolate as directed for the Chocolate No-Bake Truffles. If the cheesecake softens too much to roll into balls, simply place it back in the freezer a few minutes until it's cold enough to roll again easily. These are so rich and delicious that they are best left plain, with only their chocolate coating showing (forget the nuts or coconut for these!).

junior's chocolate ganache

Junior's loves ganache! You'll find it popping up as a topping for their cheesecakes, as a filling for cakes, the coating for truffles, and even used in swizzles and swirls of icing to give a dessert that professional "finished" look. Buy the best bittersweet chocolate you can afford, preferably at least 60% or higher cacao.

MAKES ABOUT 4 CUPS GANACHE, ENOUGH TO COAT 48 TRUFFLES OR FILL, FROST, AND DECORATE THE TOP AND SIDE OF A 3-LAYER CAKE

3 cups heavy whipping cream

1½ pounds bittersweet chocolate (at least 60% higher cacao), coarsely chopped

1 tablespoons pure vanilla extract

1 tablespoon light corn syrup

1. Combine the cream and chocolate in a heavy medium saucepan and stir over medium-low heat until the chocolate melts and the mixture begins to bubble a little around the side. Quickly whisk the mixture until it comes together into a smooth chocolate sauce. Remove from the heat and whisk in the vanilla and corn syrup.

2. Pour the ganache into a heatproof bowl that can go into the freezer. Chill in the freezer just until it thickens, 10 to 15 minutes. Remove and use immediately to coat truffles or glaze and ice a cake fast, before the ganache has the chance to thicken too much to spread easily.

The Junior's Way

The corn syrup in this recipe is important, even though it's only 1 tablespoon. That's all that's needed to keep the ganache nice and shiny, even when you place your chocolate dessert or candies in the refrigerator.

Menus for Entertaining at Home Like Junior's

The Best parties begin with great menus. To help make planning get-togethers for your friends and family even easier, we have created a few menus featuring some of our most favorite recipes in this book. *Happy entertaining!*

ALAN'S BACKYARD BARBECUE
Baked Stuffed Clams (page 11)
Salmon for Friends (page 151)
Charcoal Broiled Prime Filet Mignon Steaks (page 129)
Grilled Corn on the Cob (page 177)
Alan's Pan-braised Vidalias (page 182)
Greek Salad (page 31)
Original New York Cheesecake (page 214)
Long-Stem Fresh Strawberries

HANUKKAH–FESTIVAL OF LIGHTS DINNER
Junior's Chopped Chicken Liver (page 18), with Party Rye,
    Cucumber Slices, and Cherry Tomatoes
Junior's Brisket with Roasted Vegetables in
    Delicious Country Gravy (page 127)
Potato Pancakes (page 111) with Homemade Chunky
    Applesauce (page 168) and sour cream sprinkled with
    chopped scallion greens
Cinnamon-Sugar Doughnuts (Doughnuts Any Time, page 209)
Sweet Blintzes with Hot Chocolate Sauce (page 107)

The Best THANKSGIVING FEAST
Deviled Eggs with Smoked Salmon and Red Caviar (page 8)
Smoked Salmon Canapés (page 9)
Roast Turkey with Cornbread Stuffing and Giblet Gravy
    (page 121)
Mashed Candied Sweets (page 174)
Iceberg Wedge with Junior's Blue Cheese Dressing (page 45)
    and topped with toasted walnuts
Cranberry Sauce
Pumpkin Cheesecake (page 221)

BETH'S EASTER SUNDAY BRUNCH
Quiche à la Junior's (page 100)
Iron Skillet Ham Steak with Red-Eye Gravy (page 150)
Fresh Fruit Salad on Romaine (page 35)
    with Poppyseed Dressing (page 49)
Praline French Toast Bread Pudding (page 103)

STAR-SPANGLED PICNIC ON THE PATIO
BAR-B-Q Baby Back Ribs (page 145)
Grown-up Tuna Mac (page 41)
Junior's Red Skin Potato Salad (page 33)
Pickled Beets and Onions (page 30)
Fried Green Pickles (page 183)
Corn Sticks (page 194)
Carrot Sheet Cake with Junior's Cream Cheese Frosting
    (page 244)

RING-IN-THE-NEW-YEAR BUFFET
Alan's Salmon Platter (page 10)
Hot & Spicy Deviled Eggs (page 8)
Honey-glazed Ham on the Bone (page 147)
Junior's Macaroni & Cheese (page 162)
Roasted Vegetables (page 181)
Wedges of cantaloupe and honeydew melon drizzled
    with Junior's Balsamic Dressing (page 51)
Junior's Pull-Aparts (page 187) served with whipped butter
    and strawberry jam
Junior's Cheesecake Tart (page 251)

BLOW OUT THE CANDLES (KIDS BIRTHDAY PARTY)
Mini Pigs in the Blanket (page 15)
Southern Fried Chicken (page 118)
Homemade Potato Chips (page 172)
S'more Cupcakes (page 246)
Watermelon Wedges

Metric Equivalents

LIQUID/DRY MEASURES	
U.S.	METRIC
1/4 teaspoon	1.25 milliliters
1/2 teaspoon	2.5 milliliters
1 teaspoon	5 milliliters
1 tablespoon (3 teaspoons)	15 milliliters
1 fluid ounce (2 tablespoons)	30 milliliters
1/4 cup (4 tablespoons)	60 milliliters
1/3 cup (5 1/3 tablespoons)	80 milliliters
1/2 cup (8 tablespoons)	120 milliliters
1 cup (16 tablespoons)	240 milliliters
1 pint (2 cups)	480 milliliters
1 quart (4 cups; 32 ounces)	960 milliliters
1 gallon (4 quarts)	3.84 liters
1 ounce (by weight)	28 grams
1 pound	454 grams
2.2 pounds	1 kilogram

OVEN TEMPERATURES		
°F	GAS MARK	°C
250	1/2	120
275	1	140
300	2	150
325	3	165
350	4	180
375	5	190
400	6	200
425	7	220
450	8	230
475	9	240
500	10	260
550	Broil	290

Index

Numbers in **bold** indicate pages with photos